1990

Constructions of reason

Constructions of reason

Explorations of Kant's practical philosophy

ONORA O'NEILL
University of Essex

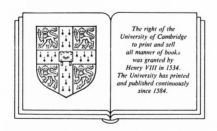

*The right of the
University of Cambridge
to print and sell
all manner of books
was granted by
Henry VIII in 1534.
The University has printed
and published continuously
since 1584.*

CAMBRIDGE UNIVERSITY PRESS

CAMBRIDGE

NEW YORK   PORT CHESTER   MELBOURNE   SYDNEY

Published by the Press Syndicate of the University of Cambridge
The Pitt Building, Trumpington Street, Cambridge CB2 1RP
40 West 20th Street, New York, NY 10011, USA
10 Stamford Road, Oakleigh, Melbourne 3166, Australia

First published 1989

Printed in the United States of America

Library of Congress Cataloging-in-Publication Data

O'Neill, Onora, 1941–

Constructions of reason : explorations of Kant's practical philosophy /
Onora O'Neill.

p.   cm.

ISBN 0-521-38121-5. – ISBN 0-521-38816-3 (pbk.)
1. Kant, Immanuel, 1724–1804 – Contributions in ethics.
2. Ethics, Modern – 18th century.   3. Reason – History – 18th century.
4. Act (Philosophy) – History – 18th century.   I. Title.
B2799.E8054   1990
170'.92 – dc20   89–10040

British Library Cataloguing-in-Publication Data

O'Neill, Onora

Constructions of reason: explorations of Kant's practical philosophy.

1. Ethics. Theories of Kant, Immanuel, 1724–1804
I. Title
170'.92'4

ISBN 0-521-38121-5 hard covers
ISBN 0-521-38816-3 paperback

Con O'Neill
1912–1988
In Memory

Contents

Preface

Kant is revered for his unswerving defense of human freedom and respect for persons, and for his insistence that reason can guide action. He is also reviled for giving a metaphysically preposterous account of the basis of freedom and an intermittently repellent and simultaneously vapid account of human obligations. Many contemporary proponents of "Kantian" ethics want the nicer bits of his ethical conclusions without the metaphysical troubles. They hope to base a "Kantian" account of justice and of rights on broadly empiricist conceptions of self, freedom and action. In these essays I have taken a different tack. I have tried to set Kant's ethics in the context of his own accounts of reason, action and freedom, to argue that these should not be read as a metaphysical extravaganza and to show that his ethical theory is neither pointlessly empty nor relentlessly nasty.

The governing idea behind this reading of the Kantian enterprise is that we must take seriously the idea of a critique of reason. From this almost everything else follows. The very standards of reason will have to be vindicated: If these are neither given nor self-evident, they can have a recursive but not a foundationalist vindication. Philosophy must begin with the task of showing why any standards or procedures for orienting our thinking should have authority for us and count as standards of reason. This initial task is practical: The theoretical enterprise cannot get going unless standards of reason are established. Accordingly the principle that Kant calls "the supreme principle of practical reason" – the Categorical Imperative – must be central not just to his ethics but to his whole philosophy.

If the Categorical Imperative is central to Kant's thinking, we must question not only attempts to place "Kantian" ethics in an empiricist setting, but also the equally popular strategy of separating Kant's practical from his theoretical philosophy. Many of Kant's readers, from Heine to Putnam, have suspected that he kept double books. They admire his splendid critique of the metaphysical tradition but think that he regrettably lost his nerve and relegated agency and freedom to the very transcendent realm whose reality he had denied. Kant's moral philosophy then looks, as it did to Nietzsche, like an anemic and hypocritical Platonism: It is "pale, Northern, Königsbergian". Seen in this light it is a cultural albatross that should be jettisoned. Our thinking will be clearer and better if we reject Kant's accounts of freedom, agency and morality, and build on his sound attack on Platonism. I believe that the stakes are higher. If the practical use of reason is more fundamental, we cannot bracket ethics while still helping ourselves to Kant's critique of metaphysics or to his understanding of the enterprise of science. Without practical reason, which Kant thinks brings justice and virtue in its wake, theoretical inquiry is simply disoriented. Our choice is between standards of reason that can govern both practice and theory, and disoriented consciousness. Merely theoretical uses of reason appear to provide an instrumental purchase on the world; but they cannot ground value-neutral knowledge and science because they are themselves grounded on principles for guiding action.

This critique of value-neutrality would have little impact if practical reason did not bring justice and virtue in its wake. If the supreme principle of practical reason had only a formal or ceremonial role in the conduct of life, we could appropriate Kant's critique of metaphysics, accept that it rests on an account of practical reason, but still view ethics as distant terra incognita. Here too Kant's critics have been vociferous. They charge that the Categorical Imperative leads no further than empty formalism. Kant failed (grotesquely, according to Mill) to derive any principles of duty from it. If the critics are right, we can accept whatever standards of reason are needed for theoretical inquiry without commitment to significant constraints on action. Kant, however, thought that the supreme principle of practical reason played a central and substantive part in the construction of justice and of virtue. I have tried to show that the Categorical Imperative, although it never provides a practical algorithm, sets significant constraints on action. We cannot emerge from disoriented consciousness without committing ourselves to ethics.

The essays divide quite naturally into three groups. Those in Part I, "Reason and critique", are the most textual but also the most speculative and exploratory. They offer an antifoundationalist, constructivist account of the Kantian enterprise. Taken together they set the Categorical Imperative in a somewhat unusual light. The Categorical Imperative is often presented as a bare, formal demand on action that remains when we abstract from desires and inclinations. This is, of course, a route Kant sometimes takes in arguing to the Categorical Imperative. It is an approach that hides why he thinks that this is the supreme principle of practical reason. The alternative route that I explore reveals why he links his vindication of reason to autonomy and morality.

The essays in Part II, "Maxims and obligations", try to show that the Categorical Imperative is basic not only to reason, but to action and to ethics as well. These chapters move onto the familiar terrain of Kant's ethical theory. I offer an account of Kant's theory of action, in particular of the pivotal notion of a maxim, that enables one to consider how and how far Kant's ethics can guide action. Kant, I argue, derives principles of obligation by way of a strict, modal reading of the Categorical Imperative, which does not refer to agents' desires and preferences, nor even to the refined preferences of idealized agents. This rather austere reading of some of the most familiar Kantian texts both bypasses much of the communitarian critique of abstraction in ethics and affords glimpses of neglected, and I believe fertile, domains of practical reasoning. I argue that the traditional (and incompatible) allegations of empty formalism and rigid prescriptivism are both misplaced. Kant offers an ethic of principles rather than of rules; he stresses obligations rather than rights; despite the cultural myopia of his notorious example, his reasoning requires rather than rejects sensitivity to context.

The essays in Part III, "Kant's ethics and Kantian ethics", explore differences between Kant's ethics and some recent, would-be Kantian ethical positions. These discussions take up the importance of imperfect obligations, the nature of deliberation and judgment and some of the contrasts between Kant's constructivism and recent "Kantian" accounts of justice. I believe that the discussions in Parts II and III suggest that contemporary divisions between defenders of "abstract" rights and justice who are "agnostic about the good for man" and advocates of "communitarian" (or feminist) accounts of traditions of virtue are misleading. A convincing theory of justice for finite rational beings is completed rather than challenged by a doctrine of virtue.

The essays have been written over a five-year period. Although some of the earlier ones have been slightly revised to correct what now seem to me mistakes, there are no doubt still discrepancies. The level of scholarly responsibility also varies. The chapters in Part I are the most textual but also the most adventurous. Those in Part II till well-ploughed fields, and the relative absence of controversy masks considerable dependence on recent debates. The essays in Part III are informed by, but do not explicitly contribute to, the task of interpreting Kant's enterprise.

Many friends and colleagues have helped me in many discussions of these topics over recent years. A mere list of names would trivialize what I owe. They will see the philosophical weight and inevitability of this debt acknowledged and articulated in the first two chapters. I add my thanks.

Abbreviations

References to and citations of Kant's writings are given parenthetically in the text, using the following abbreviations:

A *Anthropology from a Pragmatic Point of View*
CF *The Conflict of the Faculties*
CJ *Critique of Judgment*
CPR *Critique of Pure Reason*
CPrR *Critique of Practical Reason*
DV *The Doctrine of Virtue* (Pt. II, *Metaphysics of Morals*)
FI *First Introduction to the Critique of Judgment*
G *Groundwork of the Metaphysic of Morals*
IUH *Idea of a Universal History from a Cosmopolitan Point of View*
L *Logic*
MEJ *The Metaphysical Elements of Justice* (Pt. I, *Metaphysics of Morals*)
MM *The Metaphysics of Morals* (for citations of the introduction only; see *MEJ, DV,* for other citations)
PP *Perpetual Peace*
R *Religion within the Limits of Reason Alone*
SRL *On a Supposed Right to Lie out of Benevolent Motives*
TP *On the Common Saying: This May Be True in Theory, but It Does Not Apply in Practice*
WE *An Answer to the Question: "What Is Enlightenment?"*
WOT *What Is Orientation in Thinking?*

Citations for the *Critique of Pure Reason* use the standard "A" and "B" pages of the First and Second editions. Those for other works give the volume and page number for the Prussian Academy edition (e.g., [*G*, IV, 424]). Where the English translation referred to lacks these page numbers in the margins, a further page number referring to the translation listed in the references is included (e.g., [*IUH*, VIII, 19–20; 43–4]). For full bibliographical details see the References.

PART I

Reason and critique

I

Reason and politics in the Kantian enterprise

I start with two puzzles about Kant's account of reason. The first is well known. It is that the very idea of a critique of reason seems incoherent. How can critique be undertaken without presupposing some conception of reason? Yet if a conception of reason is presupposed, won't the aim of a critique of reason be vitiated by presupposing what is to be criticized?

The second puzzle is about the status of the Categorical Imperative. It can be put in this way. Kant claims both of the following:

1. The practical use of reason is more fundamental than its theoretical or speculative use.[1]
2. The Categorical Imperative is the supreme principle of practical reason.

Hence he must surely also be committed to a claim that will startle many of his readers:

3. The Categorical Imperative is the supreme principle of reason.

The two puzzles are linked: If Kant is committed to (3), any vindication of reason must vindicate the Categorical Imperative.

Yet the claim that the Categorical Imperative is the supreme principle of reason is likely to meet skepticism, if not scorn. Surely, it will be said, the supreme principle or principles of reason must be certain abstract rules of inference or practical algorithms; and surely the Categorical Imperative (if it has any standing) is the supreme principle only of morality. To see whether such skepticism and scorn are well directed I shall try to trace Kant's inquiry into the authority of reason.

I shall approach this topic by asking the rather obvious question, "Where does

1   See, for example, *CPrR*, V, 120–2, esp. "Thus in the combination of pure speculative with pure practical reason in one cognition, the latter has the primacy, provided that this combination is not contingent and arbitrary but a priori, based on reason itself and thus necessary. Without this subordination, a conflict of reason with itself would arise, since if the speculative and the practical reason were arranged merely side by side (co-ordinated), the first would close its borders and admit into its domain nothing from the latter, while the latter would extend its boundaries over everything and, when its needs required, would seek to comprehend the former within them. Nor could we reverse the order and expect practical reason to submit to speculative reason, because every interest is ultimately practical, even that of speculative reason being only conditional and reaching perfection only in practical use."

the *Critique of Pure Reason* begin?" In answering this question and coming to see what can and what cannot be done to vindicate reason we are, I believe, led to a reading of the first *Critique,* and indeed of the very idea of critique, that reveals why the Categorical Imperative is the supreme principle of all reasoning.

On the reading that I shall propose the first *Critique* is not only deeply antirationalist but profoundly political. Kant's rejection of rationalist views is well known, deep and systematic. It is fundamental to his account of metaphysics and religion. Yet his rejection of rationalism is also suspect. Many of his readers have thought that he eventually endorses the substantial view of the self that he ostensibly repudiates, and that his ethical writings return to the transcendent theology and metaphysics that he so convincingly put into question in earlier works. I shall argue that his antirationalism can and should be taken seriously and systematically. The deep structure of the *Critique of Pure Reason* and the view of philosophical method that it exemplifies are both antirationalist and antifoundationalist.

The claim that the first *Critique* is a political work is also likely to meet skepticism and scorn, although it is not a new claim.[2] On standard views of the matter, Kant's political writings are at most a corollary of his ethical theory, whose critical grounding is suspect. I hope to unsettle this view by showing that a series of connected political and juridical metaphors constitute the deep structure of the *Critique of Pure Reason.*

I shall approach Kant's views on philosophical method, critique of reason and politics by way of an account of the macrostructure of the first *Critique* and of the claims of its two prefaces. I shall say almost nothing about the five hundred pages of the "Transcendental Doctrine of Elements", but will discuss the account of reason and method that we find in the "Transcendental Doctrine of Method", in parts of the *Critique of Judgment* and in some of Kant's overtly political essays. To provide a contrasting background for this line of inquiry I shall first rehearse Descartes's views on method. These provide a benchmark for judging how far Kant's antirationalism marks not only his metaphysical conclusions but also his view of how philosophy can be done.

Philosophical method in Descartes

At the beginning of his *Discourse on the Method* Descartes tells us that "reason or sense . . . exists whole and complete in each of us" (p. 112): He can look into *himself* to discover what reason is. The project of introspection was begun when Descartes was "completely free to converse with myself about my own thoughts" (p. 116), and was rewarded with the discovery of a method of rightly conducting the mind that moves from methodic doubt, through analysis of problems

---

2   See, for example, Hans Saner, *Kant's Political Thought: Its Origins and Development;* and Hannah Arendt, *Lectures on Kant's Political Philosophy.*

into their most elementary constituents, to the systematic reconstruction of human knowledge on the secure foundations of indubitable constituents. Descartes claims that he has "reaped such fruits from this method that I cannot but feel extremely satisfied with the progress I have made in the search for truth" (p. 112). The conception of reason as innate in each of us vindicates the sequence of topics in the *Discourse on the Method* and in the *Meditations:* Secure biographical continuity permits introspective meditation, which is the context for systematic doubt and for discovering the method of reason; method is the basis for metaphysics and metaphysics for science. It is wholly appropriate to this vision of the relation of self, method and metaphysics that the literary form of both works frames science in metaphysics, metaphysics in method and method either in autobiography or in equally first-personal meditation.[3]

The coherent structure has a cost. Descartes's method is discovered in the course of introspection. Introspection and meditation require the meditator's continuing life. Descartes exempts his own life and continuity from radical doubt: He assumes that practical and theoretical uses of reason can be kept entirely distinct. If he did not assume this, the radical doubt his method prescribes would undermine the conduct of his own life and so the context of his meditation, the disclosure of method and the basis for metaphysics and science. If practical and theoretical uses of reason cannot be kept separate, the unvindicated categories of the autobiographical context in which reason is disclosed may be projected onto and perhaps color the supposed methods of reason. Method will then fail to provide a presuppositionless foundation for all knowledge, and so reason will not be vindicated. On the other hand, if thought and action can be held separate, as Descartes supposes,[4] meditation and autobiography may permit the disclosure of methods of (theoretical) reasoning, which will provide foundations for metaphysics and science. The separation of thought and action is not itself grounded, but is indispensable to Descartes's work. It preserves a vantage point from which to discern the methods of (theoretical) reason and to use them to probe beliefs; it preserves life and politics from the corrosive, perhaps revolutionary, effects of radical doubt; it mediates (although it does not vindicate) the transition from the perhaps fleeting certainty of "cogito ergo sum" to the continuing mental life that warrants "sum res cogitans". In Descartes's work the grounding of reason is closely linked to its political impotence. Only the repudiation of politics, and more generally of criticism of action, allows him a meditative perspective from which to discern and deploy the methods of reason without self-stultification.

---

3 Amelie Oksenberg Rorty, "The Structure of Descartes' *Meditations*"; L. Aryeh Kosman, "The Naive Narrator: Meditation in Descartes' *Meditations*"; Jonathan Rée, *Philosophical Tales,* Chap. 1.

4 For evidence, consider Descartes's adoption of provisional maxims to secure an ordered life during the project of pure inquiry (*Discourse* 3) and his repudiation of political revolution at the moment he affirms the project of theoretical revolution (*Discourse* 2), as well as the references in footnote 3 above.

Kant's philosophical enterprise evidently follows quite a different route. I shall take as my starting point a striking *textual* difference. In the *Critique of Pure Reason* the discussion of method is not preliminary, as foundations have to be. It takes place only *after* the main work has been completed, in the "Transcendental Doctrine of Method". How can we make sense of this traditional but anti-foundationalist textual strategy? What is Kant's actual starting point? His prefatory claims offer certain clues that are picked up retrospectively in his discussions of method and of the authority of reason at the end of the first *Critique*. I shall consider these in turn.

The motto and prefaces of the first *Critique*

The *Critique of Pure Reason* begins with a motto that Kant added to the Second Edition. The motto is taken from the last paragraph of Bacon's preface to his *Instauratio Magna*.[5] Bacon's preface contains many thoughts that are paralleled or extended (and some that are repudiated) in Kant's work. It seems to be a reasonable guess that Kant chose this passage, in which Bacon makes certain requests of his readers, as a motto because it encapsulates what is basic to his own work, and possibly because it conveys something that could not readily be communicated in the body of the work, and that perhaps had not been fully expressed in the First Edition. The passage runs as follows (Kant quotes the parts italicized):

Postulata autem nostra quae afferimus talia sunt. *De nobis ipsis silemus: de re autem quae agitur petimus, ut homines eam non opinionem sed opus esse cogitent: ac pro certo habeant non sectae nos alicujus, aut placiti, sed utilitatis et amplitudinis humanae fundamenta moliri. Deinde ut suis commodis aequi,* exutis opinionem zelis et praejudiciis, *in commune consultant;* ac ab erroribus viarum atque impedimentis, nostris praesidiis et auxiliis, liberati et muniti, laborum qui restant *et ipsi in partem veniant. Praeterea, ut bene sperent; neque Instaurationem nostram, ut quiddam infinitum et ultra mortale, fingant et animo concipiant: quum revera sit infiniti erroris finis et terminus legitimus . . .* (quum) nos omnem istam rationem humanam praematuram, anticipantem, et a rebus temere et citius quam oportuit abstractam, (quatenus ad inquisitionem naturae) ut rem variam et perturbatam et male extructam rejiciamus. Neque postulandum est ut ejus judicio stetur, quae ipsa in judicium vocatur.

This may be rendered, again with Kant's selections italicized:

However, I make the following requests. *Of myself I shall say nothing: but on the matter at issue I ask that men should think it not an opinion but a task; and that they should be confident that I seek to support not some sect or doctrine but the basis of human greatness and well-being. Next [I ask] that they should deal fairly with their affairs* and set aside their staunchly held views and presuppositions and *discuss together;* and being freed and secured from the errors and obstacles of these ways [of thought] by the supports and assistance that I offer, *they should involve themselves in the tasks that remain. Moreover [I ask] that they should be of good hope, and that they should not*

---

5 Francis Bacon, *Instauratio Magna*, pp. 132–3.

imagine that my Instauration is something unlimited and beyond mortal powers when in truth it is the end and rightful stopping point of infinite error . . . I reject all that premature, anticipating human reasoning that abstracts from things rashly and faster than it should (so far as the inquisition of nature is concerned) as something that is unreliable, distorted and ill built. It cannot be demanded that I should be placed under the judgment of that which is itself on trial.

Nothing, it seems to me, could provide a more explicit contrast with the starting point of the Cartesian enterprise. Bacon refuses to speak of himself. His undertaking is not solitary: He invites his readers to join in a common task. The first step is to discuss and plan together. The task is not superhuman. It promises practical rather than theoretical benefits. It should not be judged by unvindicated standards. Kant embraces and extends these Baconian themes.

Kant too says nothing about himself. Autobiography provides no framework for the discovery of method. However, repudiating a Cartesian approach is a delicate matter. To reject an autobiographical starting point explicitly in the text would backfire, since it would emphasize, and so tacitly endorse, that starting point. Explaining why one is not going to talk about oneself is self-defeating. Kant resolves this problem deftly by quoting Bacon's requests to his readers. He says nothing of himself; even what he says about speaking of oneself is said by another and said outside the text. Mottoes are hors d'oeuvres. This is a first step in setting Cartesian beginnings at a distance.

In the First Edition Kant does not, I think, fully repudiate a Cartesian starting point. There he claims that

I have to deal with nothing save reason itself and its pure thinking; and to obtain complete knowledge of these, there is no need to go far afield, since I come upon them in my own self. (*CPR*, Axiv)

This perspective has vanished in the preface of the Second Edition, where the first paragraph makes it clear that the problem of vindicating reason is a shared one, which arises

if the various participants are unable to agree in any common plan of procedure. (*CPR*, Bvii)

Reason may be (in whole or in part) "in" each participant, but it cannot be discovered by introspection: Kant insists that we are opaque, not transparent, to ourselves (*G*, IV, Chap. 1; *R*, VI, Pt. I; *DV*, VI, 446). The motto fits this un-Cartesian starting point. Kant will tell us nothing about himself; he will talk about the task. Autobiography is not the starting point. This is not just authorial modesty or self-effacement: Kant tells us about problems that he, Immanuel Kant, has had in writing, as well as hopes that he has for his project. Sometimes he is quite boastful about the advances he has made. Yet if he rejects an autobiographical starting point, the vindication of reason cannot be achieved by its disclosure in introspection and meditation. The starting point has to be somewhere else.

Where does Kant start? If he can't begin by vindicating philosophical method, where can he begin? The motto offers the clue that we must see the enterprise as practical: It is a task, not a body of opinions, and moreover a task that has to be shared. The first move must then presumably be to recruit those others who will form the task force.[6]

Accordingly, both prefaces begin with a discursive, indeed time-honored and attention-compelling, conversational gambit. In the First Preface we are told some scurrilous (and, unsurprisingly, sexist) gossip. There is a scandal! And in high places too! The Queen of the Sciences, Metaphysics, is not all that she is supposed to be. In the Second Preface even stronger aspersions are cast on the would-be queen. She prevaricates, and so "ever and again we have to retrace our steps, as not leading us in the direction in which we desire to go" (*CPR*, Bxiv). The frustration is palpable: "The procedure of metaphysics has hitherto been a merely random groping, and, what is worst of all, a groping among mere concepts" (*CPR*, Bxv). Here reason "not merely fails us, but lures us on by deceitful promises, and in the end betrays us!" (*CPR*, Bxv). Our speculative passion is frustrated: "it embraces not Juno, but a cloud" (*CPrR*, V, translator's introduction, xv).

This popular, gossipy starting point introduces a deeper theme. Reason's betrayal constitutes a crisis in the foundations of the European sciences – in the rationalist enterprise – that threatens our thinking with complete disorientation: "it precipitates itself into darkness and contradiction" (*CPR*, Aviii); "ever and again we have to retrace our steps" (*CPR*, Bxiv). Amid this disorientation Kant has to reach for some audience. Who is supposed to listen? Who is invited to become a fellow worker on the shared task?

Kant's intended initial audience is not hard to discern. He locates the frustrations of metaphysics historically. Reason's betrayal is a crisis for those who have some idea of the history of European metaphysics and science. The points of reference are the ancient philosophers, rationalists and empiricists, logic, geometry and modern science. (The history of European philosophy, seen now in a sharper critical light, is also where the first *Critique* ends.) No definition of audience is explicitly argued: Starting points cannot be explicitly argued. Rather, a series of gestures and allusions to shared points of reference is used to constitute and welcome an audience, and in the Second Preface to invite new readers to join in an enterprise that has already drawn to it various critics and fellow workers.[7]

---

6 From a Cartesian or other foundationalist perspective the strategy will appear perverse; but for nonfoundationalists it need not. Plenty of Kant's predecessors did not place method at the beginning of their enterprise. See the discussion of Bacon's method in James Stephens, *Francis Bacon and the Style of Science*.

7 Since autobiography is irrelevant, Kant does not name, but only thanks, these critics (*CPR*, Bxliii), and expresses his appreciation of "these worthy men, who so happily combine thorough-

The approach is perhaps comparable to Aristotle's way of adducing what the many, the wise and others say. We are not to take it that the starting point of the prefaces is the foundation of Kant's argument. It is simply a matter of assembling some modes of discourse as material from which to begin. The task of recruiting new fellow workers to the task is central to both prefaces, its success more confidently anticipated in the second.

What is missing in the prefaces of the first *Critique?*

This discursive starting point and its strategies for forming an audience, indeed a task force, of critics who will become fellow workers omits a great deal. It does not show how a critique of reason could avoid begging questions, although Kant seems confident that it can do so. It certainly does not vindicate the Categorical Imperative. All that we get initially is a gesture toward the thought that a critique of reason must be a *reflexive* and *political* task:

It is a call to reason to undertake anew the most difficult of all its tasks, namely, that of self-knowledge, and to institute a tribunal which will assure to reason its lawful claims, . . . but in accordance with its own eternal and unalterable laws. This tribunal is no other than the *critique of pure reason*. (*CPR*, Axi–xii)

I shall return to the juridical and political metaphors in which reason's task is here described. For the present I merely note that describing a critique of reason as a reflexive and (quasi-) juridical or political task shows very little about whether or how the task is to be done. It does, however, offer a clue to the absence of an account of method in the prefaces. If the task of critique of reason is in some way analogous to a tribunal's reflexive review of its own procedures, the vindication of reason cannot come first. Tribunals can pass judgment only when they have been constituted. The task of constituting a "tribunal" must come earlier on the agenda. But if we lack indubitable foundations, we will not initially have any way of judging what reason is. We will remain unsure whether there are any principles that should have authority in orienting our thinking and would deserve to be thought of as principles of reason.

We should not then be surprised at the silence about method in the prefaces; but we might expect a promissory note. In the First Preface we are merely warned that the task of a critique of reason is difficult and not yet complete. The Second Preface is a little more revealing; it suggests that a plan is needed, but that it cannot be borrowed from anywhere else. Kant surveys the successes of logic,

ness of insight with a talent for lucid exposition – which I cannot regard myself as possessing – ". At the end of the First Preface he had written, defensively, that "this work can never be made suitable for popular consumption" (*CPR*, Axviii); at the end of the Second Preface his (perhaps misplaced) hopes for the now-shared task have risen: "if men of impartiality, insight, and true popularity devote themselves to its exposition, it may also, in a short time, secure for itself the necessary elegance of statement" (*CPR*, Bxliv).

mathematics and science and claims that in each case the source of success lay in having a *plan* of inquiry: "reason has insight only into that which it produces after a plan of its own" (*CPR*, Bxiii). The first stage of our task is not introspection but *planning*.

This seems no more than a way of displacing the problem; for how are we to know *which* plan counts as reason's own? In the prefaces Kant does not claim that we can recognize reason's plan. We can only make a proposal, rather than judge its success. The plan proposed for the reform of metaphysics is the famous "Copernican" hypothesis: We are to conduct a *trial*.

We must therefore make trial [*Versuch*] whether we may not have more success in the tasks of metaphysics, if we suppose that objects must conform to our knowledge. (*CPR*, Bxvi)

Kant does not prove; he *proposes*. The proposal must be tested. It is tempting to jump to the conclusion that since he proposes that we should "make trial," he assumes at this stage that a certain sort of trial, with analogues to political institutions such as courts, tribunals and laws, is to be conducted. However, at this point he does not rely on political and juridical metaphors. I think the reason is plain enough. Laws and tribunals are only one way of "making trial"; even if they turn out to be the appropriate way, they must be instituted before legal proceedings can begin; so we cannot yet judge reason. All that can be done at an early stage of an enterprise is to suggest or propose a plan. Kant's proposal for the critique of reason does not assume or assert that we must adopt a modification of rationalist methods; rather it is "put forward in this preface as an hypothesis only" (*CPR*, Bxxii,n).

We can respond in various ways. We could complain: The omission of a method and its vindication is glaring and vitiates Kant's enterprise. Without reason even the assumptions about audience are unjustifiable, indeed incommunicable. We need to know right away what a critique of reason would be. We can denounce Kant's still-unvindicated faith in "criticism" and deny that it will banish bad and bogus metaphysics (*CPR*, Bxxxiv) or show that "the labours of reason can be established on a firm basis" (*CPR*, Bxxxv). We can get impatient when we are told that critique does not oppose the dogmatic procedure of reason, but only *dogmatism*, which is "the dogmatic procedure of reason, *without previous criticism of its own powers*" (*CPR*, Bxxxv), and that what went wrong with Wolff's work was lack of "critique of the organ, that is, of pure reason itself" (*CPR*, Bxxxvii). We can be unsatisfied because understanding of reason's self-criticism is just what seems illusory.

Or we can wait. Kant makes us wait for a long time. He does not return to these topics until far on in the first *Critique*, when he has completed both the constructive account of transcendental idealism and his criticism of metaphysical illusions. What can be the point and purpose of discussing method when the task is near complete? If a method has been needed, shouldn't it have been presented beforehand? If it has not, why should it be presented now?

Should we complain or wait? Perhaps it depends on what we think would be the better plan. I shall make trial of the thought that it is worth waiting, at least until we have examined the moves Kant makes in the "Transcendental Doctrine of Method".

The cottage of Immanuel Kant

The "Transcendental Doctrine of Method" follows the completion of many of the philosophical tasks Kant sets himself. Many of the implications of the Copernican hypothesis are worked out in the "Transcendental Doctrine of Elements". However, the account of method is no mere appendix; for nothing has been said about the vindication of reason. Kant's central arguments, and the entire account of transcendental idealism, will be radically incomplete unless he can say something about the postponed vindication of reason. In the "Doctrine of Method" Kant briefly summarizes what he has done, reminds us why the task is not completed and proceeds to an account of what it would be for certain ways of conducting thinking to have authority and to count as principles of reason.

He turns immediately to queries about starting points and procedures. Once more a contrast with the Cartesian picture is his point of departure:

> If we look upon the sum of all knowledge of pure speculative reason as a building for which we have at least the idea within ourselves, it can be said that in the "Transcendental Doctrine of Elements" we have made an estimate of the materials, and have determined for what sort, height and strength of building they will suffice. Indeed, it turned out that although we had in mind a tower that would reach the heavens, yet the stock of materials was only enough for a dwelling house – just roomy enough for our tasks on the plain of experience and just high enough for us to look across the plain. The bold undertaking had come to nothing for lack of materials, quite apart from the babel of tongues that unavoidably set workers against one another about the plan and scattered them across the earth, each to build separately following his own design. Our problem is not just to do with materials, but even more to do with the plan. Since we have been warned not to risk everything on a favorite but senseless project, which could perhaps exceed our whole means, yet cannot well refrain from building a secure home, we have to plan our building with the supplies we have been given and also to suit our needs. (*CPR*, A707/B735, trans. O. O'N.; cf. A319/B376)

Here we find more explicit comments on topics on which the prefaces said little. Like Descartes, Kant uses metaphors of construction to explain his view of philosophical method; but he starts with a more down-to-earth view of building projects. The result is a quite different vision of philosophical procedures. We are to look on what has been done in the "Transcendental Doctrine of Elements" as an *estimate* or *inventory* of our building materials, which has instructed us about some constraints on what we can build. The result is in some ways disappointing, especially when matched against the rationalist ambition to build "a tower that would reach the heavens". However, rationalism failed because it took no account either of the paucity of materials or of the disagreements about the plan among the fellow workers. It relied on the fiction of a unitary and authoritative architect, whose innate ideas correspond to their real archetypes, to construct the edifice of human knowledge. All that could be built by relying on such a fiction was disagreement, strife and mutual noncomprehension. Like the Tower of Babel, the edifice of rationalism was doomed to collapse. The disputes of metaphysics are ample evidence that the lofty structures of our metaphysical dreams cannot be built.

On the other hand, Kant acknowledges that we cannot turn our backs on the task of construction: "we cannot well refrain from building a secure home". Skepticism would condemn us to a "nomadic" existence that does not meet our deepest needs, including the needs of reason. We were told in the very first sentence of the First Preface that the insatiable needs of human reason are at the heart of our predicament:

Human reason has this peculiar fate that in one species of its knowledge it is burdened by questions which, as prescribed by the very nature of reason itself, it is not able to ignore, but which, as transcending all its powers, it is also not able to answer. (*CPR*, Avii)

Even if we do not need a lofty tower, we need shelter. Even on "the plain of experience" we have tasks, and we need to be able to form a view of our immediate surroundings. We may not need a lofty tower that reaches the heavens, but we do need at least a modest cottage. Instinct provides an inadequate basis for human life (*G*, IV, 395–7), and we must guide our actions by adopting certain practical principles as our maxims. To approach this task responsibly we must begin by recognizing that "Our problem is not just to do with materials, but even more to do with the plan." The plan must be one that can be followed by a plurality of "fellow workers" whose coordination is guaranteed neither by instinct nor by preestablished harmony. The materials assembled in the "Transcendental Doctrine of Elements" are constraints on the building that can be built; but they do not determine what the plan should be. The "Transcendental Doctrine of Method" aims to explain what sort of plan for using these materials can have authority. I shall comment selectively on the first few sections of this rich and diverse text; my aim is to show how and why the account of reason's authority that Kant develops is articulated in political metaphors and how this determines the form of his vindication of reason.

Discipline, critique and negative instruction

The titles of the sections of the first chapter of the "Transcendental Doctrine of Method" each contain the term *discipline*, which Kant uses to refer to a form of "negative instruction". It is

> the compulsion, by which the constant tendency to disobey certain rules is restrained and finally extirpated. (*CPR*, A709/B737)

Although a discipline may yield no determinate knowledge, it can be valuable:

> where the limits of our possible knowledge are very narrow, where the temptation to judge is great, where the illusion that besets us is very deceptive, . . . there the *negative* instruction, which serves solely to guard us from errors, has even more importance than many a piece of positive information by which our knowledge is increased. (*CPR*, A709/B737)

If a critique of reason is to be possible, then, our thinking too must be disciplined. Usually discipline is *external* to an activity, but here there is and can be no external source of discipline. It is a constant theme of Kant's writing that thinking that submits to any "external" authority is (at best) a deficient, "private" approximation to reason.[8] Yet Kant acknowledges:

> that reason, whose proper duty it is to prescribe a discipline for all other endeavours, should itself stand in need of such discipline may indeed seem strange. (*CPR*, A710/B738)

We may fancy that a critique of reason is dispensable because specific (e.g., empirical or mathematical) uses of reason actually dispense with critique without coming to grief. Not so, says Kant, when we are concerned to ground the very procedures of reason:

> where neither empirical nor pure intuition keeps reason to a visible track . . . it stands so greatly in need of a discipline, to restrain its tendency towards extension beyond the narrow limits of possible experience and to guard it against extravagance and error, that the whole philosophy of pure reason has no other than this strictly negative utility. (*CPR*, A711/B740)

Since reason needs discipline, which cannot be external, it must rely on self-discipline, "a system of precautions and self examination" (*CPR*, A711/B739). One purpose of the "Transcendental Doctrine of Method" is to explain this reflexive character of a critique of reason. This is why the discussion of philosophical method *must* come at the end of a critique of reason. At the beginning we had no "material" to discipline; now a hypothesis about how we might embark on the tasks of reason has supplied some material, but has not shown how this material is

---

8 For further discussion of the account of Kant's use of the public/private distinction see Chapter 2 in this volume.

to be combined into the edifice of knowledge. It has, however, provided a vantage point for a reflexive task, which could not be undertaken initially, but only retrospectively, reflectively, toward the end. (This point, I think, itself reflects Kant's view of temporality as the form of human experience: For us reflection is never instantaneous mirroring; it is iteration.) To undertake the self-critique of reason at the beginning would be to submit to some tribunal that lacks authority. Like Bacon, Kant rejects the jurisdiction of such tribunals.

Weighing anchor: the last skirmish with rationalism

After this preliminary explanation of the strategy of postponing the vindication of reason, Kant rehearses and deepens his rejection of the rationalists' paradigm of reason by attacking their favored analogy between mathematical and philosophical method. He offers two objections: Philosophy cannot be done *more geometrico,* and in any case mathematics cannot be done *more analytico.*

Although mathematics provides a contagious example of success in pure reasoning (*CPR,* A712–13/B740–1), its methods not only are useless but lead to illusion and fantasy in philosophy. It is important then to

cut away the last anchor of these fantastic hopes, that is, to show that the pursuit of the mathematical method cannot be of the least advantage in this kind of knowledge. (*CPR,* A726/B754)

The analytic and axiomatic method cannot anchor mathematics, which works not by analyzing well-defined concepts but by constructing concepts in intuition; still less can mathematics anchor philosophy, which has neither definitions nor axioms.

The distinction between analytic and synthetic judgments has been used throughout the first *Critique.* Already in the introduction Kant comments on the meager role that analytic judgments can have in mathematics (*CPR,* B14–18), and insists that in mathematics, as in science and metaphysics, the important thing is to understand how synthetic a priori judgments are possible. Only in the "Transcendental Doctrine of Method" do we see clearly why (unlike his rationalist predecessors) Kant is so unimpressed by the knowledge purportedly offered by analysis. His reflections on analyticity are as stringent as Quine's: Only stipulative definitions can ground knowledge of analytic truths, which are therefore limited to domains where we are free to stipulate. We are free to stipulate neither in mathematics nor in metaphysics. Philosophy simply lacks definitions from which analytic judgments could be derived. It lacks axioms. Even in mathematics, which has axioms, these are synthetic a priori truths grounded in the forms of human intuition, and can ground neither analytic mathematical truths nor knowledge of a transcendent reality. Philosophy also lacks demonstrations. The edifice of human knowledge that can be reached *more geometrico* is not lofty and stable, but ludicrously flimsy:

In philosophy the geometrician can by his method build only so many houses of cards. (*CPR*, A727/B755)

Since such a structure is quite inadequate for our "tasks on the plain of experience", we will realize that

The definition . . . ought, in philosophy, to come rather at the end than at the beginning of our enquiries. (*CPR*, A731/B759)

Correspondingly, the account and vindication of reason must come at the end and not at the beginning of a critique of reason.

The politics of reason: the rejection of force

Discipline is a matter only of "negative instruction". Kant's first negative claim is that mathematics can offer no generalizable model for the use of reason. His critique of rationalist conceptions of method is valuable, but since it reaches only this negative conclusion it does not show how philosophy is to be done, or reason vindicated. The discussion simply moves on to further negative claims about reason. The most fundamental of these rejects the thought that reason could be understood or vindicated by analogy with force or power.

In "The Discipline of Pure Reason in Its Polemical Employment" Kant argues that reason can only lose authority by appeal to power or force:

Reason must in all its undertakings subject itself to criticism; should it limit freedom of criticism by any prohibitions, it must harm itself, drawing upon itself a damaging suspicion. Nothing is so important through its usefulness, nothing so sacred, that it may be exempted from this searching examination, which knows no respect for persons. Reason depends on this freedom for its very existence. For reason has no dictatorial authority; its verdict is always simply the agreement of free citizens, of whom each one must be permitted to express, without let or hindrance, his objection or even his veto. (*CPR*, A738/B766)

Here the discipline of reason is contrasted with a familiar mode of political discipline. It is not like the discipline imposed by dictators or conquerors who coerce obedience, but like the discipline of those who must interact without relying either on imposed or on preestablished harmony. Reason's authority — if it has any — would be undermined by appeal to any "alien" authority, which would itself stand in need of vindication.[9]

Negative instruction, of course, leaves matters indeterminate. Might there not be countless ways of interacting with others where nothing is imposed? For all we

9   Relativist and historicist thinkers disagree. On a certain (perhaps unconvincing) reading of Wittgenstein the claim that "in the end there must be agreement in judgment" suggests that nothing more than bare facts of agreement grounds reason. Kant holds that mere agreement, whether enforced or adventitious, could have no authority.

can initially see, the rejection of the image of reason as force or polemic fails to show why any specific ways of thinking should count as reasoned ways and others as unreasoned.

Kant, however, thinks that negative instruction can show us more about the discipline of reason. The problem of seeing which modes of thinking – if any – are authoritative presupposes not only the lack of a "dictator", but the presence of a *plurality* of noncoordinated (potential) actors or thinkers. Kant uses the imagery of "citizens" or "fellow workers" to contrast the situation with that facing the subjects of a dictator who imposes common standards. He does not suggest that reason's authority is based on a constitutional convention, but reminds us that there is a *plurality* of potential reasoners. If we assume no "dictator", we deny that reason could have *either* a transcendent or a historicist "vindication".

What other possibility is there? Are we not left with the thought that there is no authority for thinking, and that the images of "nomadic" restlessness to which Kant gestures are all that remain once we dispel metaphysical illusion? Before drawing this conclusion we must see why Kant's account of the authority of reason uses not only the images of plurality but specifically those of constitutionality and political order.

The reason why Kant is drawn to explicate the authority of reason in political metaphors is surely that he sees the problems of cognitive and political order as arising in one and the same context. In either case we have a plurality of agents or voices (perhaps potential agents or voices) and no transcendent or preestablished authority. Authority has in either case to be constructed. The problem is to discover whether there are any contraints on the mode of order (cognitive or political) that can be constituted. Such constraints (if they can be discovered) constitute respectively the principles of reason and of justice. Reason and justice are two aspects to the solution of the problems that arise when an uncoordinated plurality of agents is to share a possible world. Hence political imagery can illuminate the nature of cognitive order and disorientation, just as the vocabulary of reason can be used to characterize social and political order and disorientation. Kant frequently characterizes skepticism as a failure of discursive order, hence as anarchy; just as he characterizes dogmatism (rationalism) as a form of despotism, a triumph of unjust discursive order.

The claim, however, remains merely negative. Reason is not a dictator. Hence the defense or vindication of reason is always a frustrating task. As soon as we seek to buttress the authority of reason by appeal to other, "alien" authorities we undermine the only authority it can have:

it would be absurd to look to reason for enlightenment, and yet to prescribe beforehand which side she must necessarily favour. Besides, reason is already of itself so confined and held within limits by reason, that we have no need to call out the guard, with a view to bringing the civil power to bear upon that party whose alarming superiority may seem to

16

us to be dangerous. In this dialectic no victory is gained that need give us cause for anxiety. (*CPR*, A747/B775)

This explains why Kant (surprisingly to the modern ear) often speaks of reasoning that is premised on power or force as a "private" use of reason. The speech of officers to troops, of ministers to their congregations, of officials to taxpayers – all are said to be "private" uses of reason (see *WE*). The point is that they are deprived (*privatus*), incomplete uses of reason. In all such communication there is a tacit, uncriticized and unjustified premise of submission to the "authority" that power of office establishes. The antithesis to private, partial exercises of reason must be a (more fully) public use of reason that steadfastly renounces reliance on powerful but ungrounded "authorities" in favor of self-discipline. (We need not think that this renunciation can be total: Actual reasoning occurs in and must to some extent be premised on institutions that may depend on unvindicated power relations. This is just to say that the principles of reason constrain but do not provide algorithms for thought or action.) Reason is unique in that criticism that relies on force damages and fails to secure it; yet contests in which no force is brought to bear may establish it. Hence we are recommended to adopt a form of self-restraint that would be out of place in power contests. We are told

[to] allow . . . your opponent to speak in the name of reason, and combat him only with the weapons of reason. (*CPR*, A744/B772)

Reason, Kant suggests, *cannot* be simply a mode of war or polemic. The only legitimate use of polemic in reasoning is in self-defense, when it may be used to rebut arguments for propositions whose contraries we cannot prove. Such polemic aims only to indicate failures in others' reasoning (*CPR*, A740–1/B767–8) by invoking whatever limited conception of reason the "private" reasoning criticized deploys: It is internal critique. Polemic uses weapons that are not those of reason, but only in self-defense. Beyond contexts of self-defense, reasoning is simply weakened by depending on any sort of force; hence

there can, properly speaking, be no polemic of pure reason. (*CPR*, A750/B778)

The politics of reason: tribunals and algorithms

The negative instruction has been extended. Neither mathematics nor force offers an adequate model of cognitive authority. Kant uses a wider range of political metaphors to extend his account of the authority of reason. I shall look at three of these to outline the additional contribution that each makes to his negative instruction on the authority of reason. The three political metaphors on which he rests most are those of *tribunal, debate* and *community*.

The image of reason as a tribunal links the authority of reason and the rule of law in rather specific ways:

The critique . . . arriving at all its decisions in the light of fundamental principles of its own institution, the authority of which no one can question, secures to us the peace of a legal order, in which our disputes have to be conducted solely by the recognised methods of *legal action* . . . [and] are . . . ended by a *judicial sentence* which, as it strikes at the very root of the conflicts, effectively secures an eternal peace. (*CPR*, A751–2/B779–80)

This image has a certain difficulty and a certain merit. The difficulty is that the authority of political tribunals is itself grounded in power, and ultimately in force. Perhaps it is ominous that Kant compares the constitution of reason with the Hobbesian social contract, where

the state of nature is a state of injustice and violence, and we have no option save to abandon it and submit ourselves to the constraint of law . . . (*CPR*, A752/B780)

Do we have no option but to accept the authority of reason? If so, isn't reason's authority also ultimately based on coercion or polemic, contrary to the suggestions Kant makes?

The images of a contract or tribunal of reason need not, however, be taken literally, or as referring to historical events. The central point that Kant makes with these analogies is that reason's authority must (since it receives no antecedent or transcendent vindication) be seen as a *practical and collective task,* like that of constituting political authority. Those who face the task find no antecedent coordination; that is why Babel remains a constant threat. Critique of reason is possible only if we can find a strategy by which a plurality of potential reasoners could interact without relying on force, or on the fiction of preestablished harmony. (Actual pluralities may of course use such capacities to fight and dispute: There is no assumption that reasoners are always in peaceful relations or harmony, or that human societies can be maintained without force.) If there are any such modes of coordination, they could, as it were *retrospectively,* be said to be principles of reasoning, and even spoken of as the terms of a "contract of reason" or as a "tribunal of reason". If the political analogies are not taken too literally, Kant may yet vindicate his claim that reason is no dictator.

The image of reason's authority as analogous to that of a tribunal also has a certain merit in that it suggests immediately that reason is not algorithmic. To have a tribunal is not to have an algorithm that the tribunal follows. If that were what tribunals did, they would be redundant. Tribunals deliberate and reach verdicts; there are moves that they may not and had better not make as they move toward a verdict, but their charters and procedures do not fully determine every move. Theirs is the genuinely practical task of judging; hence the tribunal provides an appropriate image for a critique or judging of reason. If Kant depicts the authority of reason as a tribunal that judges and deliberates, then presumably he thinks that reason too does not consist of algorithms for thinking or acting, which can be formulated as abstract rules.

The claim that reason is nonalgorithmic sheds some light on Kant's anti-

foundationalist textual strategy that postpones the discussion of reason until after
the elaborate inventory of materials in the "Transcendental Doctrine of Elements".
The "Doctrine of Elements" depicts cognitive capacities none of which can be
deployed in abstraction from the others; yet it does not reach a determinate
account of their integrated deployment. The story is familiar to all of Kant's
readers: Human beings can receive a manifold of intuition, subject to the struc-
tural constraints of the forms of intuition. They can synthesize this manifold
using empirical concepts in accordance with the categories of the understanding.
However, they can deploy the categories in complete acts of judgment only if they
adopt and follow certain Ideas of reason or maxims of judgment (*CJ*, V, 182) to
organize this judging. In the end a *practical* principle must guide all complete acts
of judgment. This is why at the end of the "Doctrine of Elements" we have only
an "inventory" of disconnected "materials" and not a "construction". In making
trial of the Copernican hypothesis we discovered that the complex capacities that
we call sensibility and understanding are not usable without "Ideas of reason",
that is, without the adoption of maxims to regulate the use of these capacities in
thinking and acting. An account of human knowledge will be systematically
indeterminate unless these maxims are identified and vindicated. Here we begin
to see why Kant thinks that *practical* reason is fundamental to all reasoning, why
there can be no complete rules for judging and why human reasoning is, as we
might say, nonalgorithmic, down to the bottom. But we are still far from seeing
which maxims for the integrated use of our more specific cognitive capacities have
an authority that justifies us calling them Ideas (or principles) of reason.

The metaphor of the tribunal is used to make the point that we cannot expect the
principles of reason to dominate and control all reasoned thought and action.
Thought and action can at most be constrained, not fully determined by principles
of reason. This does not mean that abstracted aspects of human reasoning are all
nonalgorithmic; it is, after all, from certain abstracted modes of reasoning that we
gain our understanding of what algorithms are. It follows only that any thinking or
decision making that actually follows algorithms, whether or not it works within
the limits of the supreme principle of reason, depends on some specific and perhaps
groundless premises that permit a decisive selection of well-formed formulae and
valid inferences. Algorithmic procedures taken in the abstract are incomplete,
"private" uses of reason; formal calculi and models of rational choice presuppose
rather than articulate what is most crucial for reasoning.

Going back to the metaphors of construction, we might put it this way: The
elements of human knowledge are not self-constructing; they must always be put
together according to some plan or other. No master plan is inscribed in each one
of us; rather we must devise a plan that assembles the various elements. This plan
must not presuppose unavailable capacities to coordinate, such as a preestablished
harmony between reasoners or between each reasoner and a transcendent reality.
The most basic requirement for construction by any plurality of agents must then

be negative. It can be no more than the requirement that any fundamental principles of thought and action we deploy be ones that it is not impossible for all to follow. There may be many differing detailed plans that fall within this constraint. We have been shown only a negative constraint on reason; any principle of thinking and acting that can have authority cannot enjoin principles on which some members of a plurality cannot (not "would not"!) act. Yet this is already a great deal, for it might equally be stated as the requirement that in thought as well as in action we must, if we are to evade the threat of Babel, act only on that maxim through which we can at the same time will that it be a universal law. Here we begin to understand why Kant held that the Categorical Imperative was the supreme principle not just of practical but of all reasoning.

The politics of reason: debate and recursion

Kant's account of the politics of reason does not lay everything on the metaphor of a tribunal. He uses other political metaphors to articulate further aspects of a critique of reason. Taken together they are to show why certain procedures for orienting thinking or acting may be said to have authority. In particular they help us to understand one of the puzzles with which we began: Is not any supposed critique of reason unavoidably circular, and so question-begging?

In handling the issue of circularity Kant uses a political metaphor that is often condemned as inadequate or irrelevant in discussions of political as well as of discursive order. He suggests that reasoned communication and coordination can be modeled or symbolized by a debate. Reason's self-discipline is likened to free, critical and universal debate among fellow citizens who cannot bring power to bear to destroy what others assert or to support their own assertions.

At first thought the idea of modeling reason on free debate may seem to add nothing. First, we may suspect, this account too will only be negative instruction: Debates do not usually produce agreement; hence this image adds nothing to that of the "tribunal" of reason. Second, debates presuppose reason, so we cannot draw on the notion of debate to explain the authority of reason. Third, we may doubt that the prospects for uncoerced debate are any rosier than those for tribunals that do not rest on power relations.

Let us return to the task. When Kant subverts the Cartesian images of construction for his own purposes at the beginning of the "Transcendental Doctrine of Method", he suggests that the "building" of human knowledge can use only available "materials" and must follow a "plan" that is not antecedently given, but has to be devised and deployed by a plurality of agents who share a world, but who are short of principles for doing the sharing. This is why the basic task of constructing principles of discursive order is analogous to that of constructing principles of political order, and why politics provides metaphors for articulating the task, principles and limits of reason.

20

We now have some understanding of the *materials* out of which reasoning is to constitute its own authority. These materials include manifolds and forms of intuition, categories and empirical concepts. They may even include some algorithmic procedures (e.g., in logic or arithmetic). These materials will remain a rubbish heap unless those who are to make something of them converge on a plan. However, members of the work force do not have any antecedently prescribed plan: Not even methods of procedure for reaching a plan are antecedently inscribed in their consciousness. The most that can be said antecedently is that none of them can (if they are to arrive at any plan and to build even a modest structure) act in ways that will rule out arriving at a plan. If they are to have any sort of collaboration and construct any sort of "building", they must at least not act in ways that undermine the possibility of collaboration.

There are several respects in which debate provides an apt metaphor for such a process. First, debates link a plurality of speakers (or citizens), none of whom coerces the others. Second, debate is open-ended: At any stage previous assumptions can be queried, and at no stage are definitive answers established. The authority of principles reached in this way is only that they survive open-ended questioning, including questioning in terms of the standards they themselves promulgate. The vindication of such principles is recursive rather than foundational.

The metaphor of a "debate" goes beyond that of a "tribunal" not because it provides "positive" instruction (it does not), but because it displays the recursive character of the enterprise of critique of reason. Debate cannot survive the adoption of principles of destroying debate. The most fundamental principle for disciplining thought and action among any plurality is to reject principles for thought and action that cannot be shared. Reason's authority is established recursively, rather than resting on secure foundations; this authority is only negative, yet it constrains thought and action.

In a number of texts Kant embeds this recursive account of the authority of the most fundamental principle of reasoning in a possible history of the emergence of reason. Since history is undertaken retrospectively there is no contradiction in presuming standards of reasoning in giving an account of the emergence of such standards. The "inventory of materials" that constrain any possible plan can be depicted as the product of an evolutionary and historical story. The most rudimentary capacities to coordinate in beings whose coordination is not instinctually programmed are the raw materials for constituting reason's authority. Rudimentary capacities provide the context for the development of more elaborate capacities. In several essays, in particular his *Idea of a Universal History from a Cosmopolitan Point of View,* Kant sketches a speculative natural history of the emergence of human capacities, as well as a cultural history of their gradual development toward "Enlightenment". In the natural history his eye is on the evolutionary pressures provided by an unsocial sociability that forms the materials of reason, the capacities to coordinate of beings who cannot lead solitary lives, yet do not achieve instinctive coordination. In the cultural history he considers the task of deploying these materials by finding and agreeing on practical principles that can guide the coordination of a plurality of partially independent and mutually vulnerable beings who have at hand only the "materials" that evolutionary pressures have produced. He thinks that the historical task of finding the right plan for using these materials is still incomplete, and so seeks fellow workers and further effort. Hence the *Critique of Pure Reason* can itself be seen as an episode in the history of reason. Kant rashly – if not uniquely rashly – asserts that the task and history of human reason is almost complete: One more push and we will have made the transition to a fully enlightened age.

History looks backward, politics forward. Temporalized beings can understand reasoning only under the form of time; but they can look ahead as well as backward. Here we can see another way in which political metaphors are apt. Kant depicts the still incomplete task of constituting reason's authority as a political task. "Fellow workers" or "citizens" are not coordinated by instinct; no transcendent authority has inscribed the procedures of reason in them. They have to move toward finding a plan by which to satisfy their needs while taking account both of their limited materials and of the fact that they are several and so may disagree. They are not the externally disciplined slaves of a centrally planning despot. (There is bite in Kant's repeated use of the metaphor of despotism to characterize rationalism.) If there is to be any plan that is not based on despotic use of force, it must be an agreed plan. However, without procedures for reaching agreement there is nothing to be done except to refrain from preventing agreement. The only move that can be made toward the possibility of agreement in the absence of any procedures for agreeing is for each to act only on principles on which others at least can (thought they may not) agree to act.

This negative instruction is of course not an algorithm; it does not prescribe just what must be done in every circumstance if the possibility of sharing principles is to be left open. Neither agreement on a plan nor smooth collaboration is guaranteed. Yet even this meager principle of procedure has a great deal staked on it. (There is also bite in Kant's repeated characterization of those who reject the authority of reason as nomads, whose chaotic building projects collapse like the Tower of Babel: There must be a shared plan if there is not to be anarchy in thinking.) Any authority that reasoning can have must be constituted by those who reason; it cannot be imposed and it will not emerge from anarchy. The choice is stark:

freedom in thinking means the subjection of reason under no other laws than those it gives itself. Its opposite is the maxim of a lawless use of reason . . . if reason will not subject itself to the law it gives itself, it will have to bow under the yoke of laws which others impose . . . (*WOT*, VIII, 145; 303–4; cf. following paragraphs)

Reason's authority can be neither imposed nor anarchic. By elimination it must be self-imposed. Hence its vindication must be recursive, and those for whom it is (even partially) attainable must be (at least partially) capable of autonomy in the strict Kantian sense.

Debates may be inconclusive; indeed, if reason provides only negative instruction, it alone can never bring them to conclusions. Yet debates among those who share a world also have tasks. The third constraint Kant places on the construction of reason is that it must provide us a secure "home". Human needs, even the needs of human reasoning, are (as he repeatedly explains) practical. We may want speculative knowledge of a transcendent reality; but we find ourselves on "the plain of experience". The conception of reason's authority as constituted in the process of the self-discipline of thought and action must, even if it yields only negative instruction, provide at least for these needs. It may be that, as with other building projects, these needs could be met in many ways; but there are ways of thinking or acting, as there are ways of building, that are self-defeating. We get only negative instruction, and are left with perennial disagreements. That we find disagreement rather than disorientation testifies that there are standards of reason, rather than that there are not. If there were no standards of reasoning, the mutual (even if partial) comprehension on which disagreement rests would be impossible.

Once more we are led back to the pivotal role of the Categorical Imperative in the politics of reason. What is to be vindicated is not reason, considered in abstraction from any particular reasoners, but the reasoning of those who like ourselves have no preinscribed modes of coordination, and find that their native endowment provides neither algorithm nor instinct for acting or for thinking. What can such beings do? There is no maxim of reasoning whose antecedent authority can compel them; and yet they cannot share a world if there is no cognitive order. The most then that they can do is to reject basic principles of thought and action that are barriers to cognitive order. A minimal, negative step toward any solution must be to refrain from adopting plans that others cannot adopt. Those who are to be fellow workers must at least refrain from basing their action on basic principles that others cannot share. Those who act on such maxims are not guaranteed agreement, at all points; but if they wholly reject it, communication and interaction (even hostile interaction, let alone coordination) will be impossible. To act on this maxim is simply to make what Kant elsewhere calls the Categorical Imperative the fundamental principle of all reasoning and acting. It is to base action and thought only on maxims through which one can at the same time will that they be universal laws.

Kant's appeal to the image of a debate is not viciously circular. He does not imagine a prehistoric debate, nor one that is abstracted from all the conditions of debating. He considers only what we can say about the conditions of possible debate. Presumably there are always many ways by which a plurality of noncoordinated parties can communicate or interact. All of these ways, however, must meet at least the negative condition that they are not based on strategies of thought or action that are in principle unsharable. This is why the *supreme* principle of reasoning cannot be any rule of inference or algorithm for thinking or acting. Abstract rules or algorithms do not show why those whose thinking and acting is not already coordinated will agree on them or (if they happen to agree to the abstract rule) will agree on the initial conditions under which a given rule or algorithm may be deployed. Although we often need to think of reason in abstraction from acts of reasoning we cannot, unless we think that reasoning has a transcendent basis and is inscribed in each of us, think that specific rules and algorithms are what is fundamental to reason. What is fundamental must rather be a *strategy* for thinking and acting that does not defeat the possibility of action, interaction and communication. Any actual, historical plurality that follows this strategy no doubt comes to share many optional specific rules and algorithms and many views on the conditions and scope for their use. These dispensable and variable points of agreement may be no more than the established, perhaps establishment, modes of inquiry and conventional morality of a particular time and place.

In pointing to the Categorical Imperative as the supreme principle of reason Kant is true to his insistence that we can obtain only negative instruction. The Categorical Imperative is only a strategy for avoiding principles of thinking, communicating and acting that cannot be adopted by all members of a plurality whose principles of interaction, let alone actual interaction (let alone coordination!), are not established by any transcendent reality. The supreme principle of reason does not fix thought or action in unique grooves; it only points to limits to the principles that can be shared.

If the supreme principle of reason provides only limits, then its authority is indeed limited. It cannot dictate what reasoners can know or what they ought to do. Kant's answers to these questions are never developed merely from reason alone; knowledge is constrained by cognitive capacities other than reason and by the "materials" they provide for us, action by proposals for action that are the "material" submitted to the test of the Categorical Imperative and by casuistry in applying principles to cases. Although the limits on structuring the "material" of cognition and action that a plurality of uncoordinated knowers or agents must accept are broad, they are not arbitrary. Critique of reason is possible because there are constraints on the possible constructions of "fellow workers".

The politics of reason: the *sensus communis*

This account of the authority of reason, and of the grounds for thinking that the Categorical Imperative is the supreme principle of reason, helps show why Kant can reach apparently substantive conclusions while insisting that he offers and can offer only negative instruction. What has been vindicated at the end of the story is not a set of principles whose adoption will determine thought and action, but only principles that constrain adoptable sets of principles. How interesting a conclusion is this? The more familiar moral applications of the Categorical Imperative have often been charged with arid formalism. They work out the arguments by which certain possible maxims of action may be shown as not in principle available to all agents, and thus as requiring rejection by those who seek principles of action that can hold for a plurality. Many critics have held that they do not tell agents enough to count as action-guiding. If the Categorical Imperative fails to guide action, could it help guide thought or cognition?

Kant provides some suggestions on this point in his discussions of the *sensus communis* (*CJ*, V, 293ff.; *L*, IX, 57; 63), which articulate some ways in which the Categorical Imperative bears on practices of interpretation. The term *sensus communis* would be ill rendered as "common sense". The notion of *sense* is here used, as in the modern rather than the Aristotelian understanding of "common sense", without reference to sensation (as also in "sense of propriety" or "sense of truth"). But whereas "common sense" is used to refer to understandings that are actually shared, in an *actual* community or more widely, the *sensus communis* consists of three principles or maxims that constrain understandings, indeed practices of communication, that can be shared in any *possible* community. These maxims do not presuppose that standards or principles of communication are either antecedently established or actually shared: They articulate the self-discipline of thinking that will be required if there is to be communication among a plurality whose members are not antecedently coordinated, who form a merely possible community.

This more detailed account of the self-discipline of reason will once again provide only negative instruction. The maxims of the *sensus communis* are only a negative guide: They tell us only what we must *not* do in thinking or in communicating if a shared plan is to be possible.

The *sensus communis*, Kant writes, is

a critical faculty which in its reflective act takes account . . . of the mode of representation of everyone else, in order, *as it were*, to weigh its judgement with the collective reason of mankind . . . (*CJ*, V, 293)

He makes it clear that what is at stake here is not a requirement to accommodate to actual public opinion. It is the possible rather than the actual judgments of others that form the coordinates for the *sensus communis*. The Categorical Imperative, applied to reasoning itself, demands that we reason only on principles that others *can* (not "will" or "would") act on. To do so is to adopt three "maxims of common human understanding" (*CJ*, V, 294).

The first of these is (1) *to think for oneself*. Only those who think for themselves have any contribution to make to a debate or plan. Those who suppress

25

their own voices do not reason; they are mere voiceless echoes, whose parroted words cannot be taken as expressions of judgment or as acts of communication. Those who elide their own status as thinkers among other thinkers cannot adhere to the Categorical Imperative; they do not reason, and are doomed to disoriented consciousness;

To make use of one's own reason means nothing more than to ask oneself, with regard to everything that is to be assumed, whether he finds it practicable to make the ground of the assumption or the rule which follows from the assumption, a universal principle of the use of his reason. (*WOT,* VIII, 146n; 305n)

Those who reject this discipline no longer seek to interact or communicate; they are not committed to the maintenance or the development of any sharable modes of disciplining thought or action, and so may find their supposed reasoning impenetrable to others. Kant calls this maxim the "maxim of a never-*passive* reason" (*CJ,* V, 294). To adopt it is to refuse to submit to alien forces, such as the will of others, superstitution or prejudice. It is no algorithm for thought, but a "merely negative attitude" (*CJ,* V, 294n). Yet it "constitutes enlightenment proper" (*CJ,* V, 294n), and may be thought of as "the maxim of the self-preservation of reason" (*WOT,* VIII, 147n; 305n).

The second part of the *sensus communis* is the maxim (2) *to think from the standpoint of everyone else* (*CJ,* V, 294). Only those who try to think from the standpoint of everyone else and strive to listen to and interpret others and to see the point of their contributions are genuinely aiming to be "fellow workers" and to avoid maxims to which others cannot agree. Kant describes the task of thinking according to this "maxim . . . of *enlarged* thought" (*CJ,* V, 294) as one in which a thinker "reflects upon his own judgement from a *universal standpoint*" (*CJ,* V, 295). However, this universal standpoint is no preestablished Archimedean standpoint of reason; rather it is one that a thinker constructs "by shifting his ground to the standpoint of others" (*CJ,* V, 295). The reflexive and this-worldly character of a vindication of reason is here apparent: Reasoned thinking is governed not by transcendent standards but by the effort to orient one's thinking in ways that do not preclude its accessibility to others.

The third aspect of the *sensus communis* is the maxim (3) *always to think consistently* (*CJ,* V, 294). This is no trivial requirement of logical form, but rather a never-ending task. The set of judgments that we independently form, then revise as we shift our standpoint to take account of others' standpoints, will constantly change, and so may repeatedly fall into inconsistency. Hence Kant claims that this maxim is "the hardest of attainment" and "only attainable by the union of both the former" (*CJ,* V, 295). Once again the reflexive character of a vindication of reason is apparent.

The route Kant travels in providing a critique and vindication of reason is now, I hope, much clearer. He denies not only that we have access to transcendent meta-

26

physical truths, such as the claims of rational theology, but also that reason has intrinsic or transcendent vindication, or is given to consciousness. He does not deify reason. The only route by which we can vindicate certain ways of thinking and acting, and claim that those ways have authority, is by considering how we must discipline our thinking if we are to think or act at all. This disciplining leads us not to algorithms of reason, but to certain constraints on all thinking, communication and interaction among any plurality. In particular we are led to the principle of rejecting thought, action or communication that is guided by principles that others cannot adopt, and so to the Categorical Imperative.

Kant's negative instruction is clear: There is no method of building an edifice of human knowledge by relying on insight into things as they may be in themselves or on standards of reason disclosed in introspection. More generally, any thinking that follows an external discipline is not fully reasoned. Yet thinking that wholly dispenses with discipline falls into disorientation. If there is a discipline of thought or action that deserves to be thought of as authoritative and so to be called the discipline of reason, it must be self-imposed. Hence for us practical reasoning is fundamental. It is in choosing how to act, including how to think, to understand and to interpret, that we embody or flout the only principles that we could have reason to think of as principles of reason. It is also in thinking, communicating and acting that we discover that the most basic of these must enable us to accommodate the fact of our plurality and our lack (or at least ignorance) of any preestablished harmony between the modes of thought employed by different parties to a plurality. It is also in thinking, communicating and acting that we discover that we must discipline tendencies to rely on strategies of acting in ways that make others' adoption of like strategies impossible.

The connections between the two puzzles with which this essay set out are I hope now clear. Critique of reason is possible only if we think of critique as recursive and reason as constructed rather than imposed. The constraint on possibilities of construction is imposed by the fact that the principles are to be found for a plurality of possible voices or agents who share a world. Nothing has been established about principles of cognitive order for solitary beings. All that has been established for beings who share a world is that they cannot base this sharing on adopting unsharable principles. Presumably many specific conformations of cognitive and moral order are possible; in each case the task of the Categorical Imperative is not to dictate, but to constrain possibilities for acting and for cognition. Theoretical rationality constrains but does not determine what can be thought or believed, just as practical rationality constrains but does not dictate what may be done:

we should be able at the same time to show the unity of practical and theoretical reason in a common principle, since in the end there can only be one and the same reason, which must be differentiated solely in its application. (*G*, IV, 391)

2

The public use of reason

Liberals often think that diversity of belief and its expression should be tolerated if we are to respect either individuals or reason and truth themselves. Because they are "agnostic about the good for man", they hold that liberty for each to pursue his or her conception of the good in "self-regarding" matters is required, and that practices of toleration are important aspects of this liberty. They also often advocate practices of toleration as means by which reasoned and true beliefs can come to prevail over false beliefs. Each line of thought justifies practices of toleration as *means* to something that is seen both as logically independent and as of more fundamental value.

These familiar lines of thought are not the only possible liberal vindication of toleration. In Kant's writings toleration is not a derivative value, to be established only when the value of true and reasoned belief and of liberty in self-regarding matters has been established. His arguments for toleration of what he terms "the public use of reason" presuppose neither that there are antecedently given standards of rationality nor that any class of self-regarding individual actions is of special importance. For Kant the importance of (some sorts of) toleration is connected with the very grounding of reason, and so in particular with the grounding of practical reason. His arguments suggest that liberal political thinking can vindicate practices of toleration without commitment either to a strong form of individualism or to the view that we can distinguish "self-regarding" acts, and without claiming that reasoning either has a "transcendent" vindication or is groundless.

The themes of toleration and of the grounding of reason are brought together in many Kantian texts. The most important is the *Critique of Pure Reason,* in particular the section of the "Doctrine of Method" called "The Discipline of Pure Reason in Respect of Its Polemical Employment" (*CPR*, A739/B767–A769/B797). The same connection is stressed in many other places, including scattered passages in the second and third *Critiques,* in the *Logic* and in *Religion within the Limits of Reason Alone.* A number of shorter essays, including *What Is Enlightenment?* (1784), *What Is Orientation in Thinking?* (1786), *Idea of a Universal History from a Cosmopolitan Point of View* (1784), *The Conflict of the Faculties* (1798), *On the Common*

This chapter originally appeared in *Political Theory,* 14 (1986), 523–51. Copyright © 1986 Sage Publications, Inc., and reprinted by their permission.

Saying "This May Be True in Theory, but It Does Not Apply in Practice" (1793) and *Perpetual Peace* (1795), appear at first to have much to say about toleration, including the political aspects of toleration, and little about the grounding of reason. Yet here too the themes are often interwoven. The close connections between the short political essays and the central critical writings suggest not only that the essays are part of Kant's systematic philosophy, and not marginal or occasional pieces, but also perhaps that the entire critical enterprise has a certain *political* character. If this is the case, it is no accident that the guiding metaphors of the *Critique of Pure Reason* are political metaphors. If the discussion of reason itself is to proceed in terms of *conflicts* whose *battlefields* and *strife* are scenes of *defeat* and *victory* that will give way to a lasting *peace* only when we have established through *legislation* such *courts, tribunals* and *judges* as can weigh the issues and give *verdict,* then it is perhaps not surprising that Kant links his discussions of politics very closely to larger issues about the powers and limits of human reason. However, this is a large and for present purposes tangential issue.[1] The more immediate concern is to see how Kantian arguments link toleration to the very grounding of reason.

The grounding of reason

Kant's most basic move in seeking to explain the grounds and limits of human reason is his claim that practical uses of reason are more fundamental than theoretical uses of reason. He offers various lines of argument against the priority or independence of theoretical uses of reason. These include his claims that theoretical chains of reasoning are intrinsically incompletable, since they unavoidably lead to antinomies, as well as his particular form of explanation of the compatibility of human freedom and natural necessity.

Even if we were to accept these arguments, we would still be in the dark about the grounds of practical reason. Where does it gain its authority? It is not enough to say that *if* we reason theoretically, then we must also be able to or be resolved to reason practically. It seems rather that we should also be able to see *why* the standards we recognize as rational in practical matters are these standards, and not others. Yet how can this demand ever be met? We appear to be faced with a familiar dilemma. If the standards of practical reasoning are fundamental to all human reasoning, then any vindication of these standards is either circular (since it uses those very standards) or a failure (since it is not a vindication in terms of the standards said to be fundamental). What then can be said on behalf of standards of practical reasoning?

If there is anything to be said, it should, I think, leave us with some sense of

---

1 On this see Hans Saner, *Kant's Political Thought: Its Origins and Development,* esp. pp. 218 and 302ff.; as well as Hannah Arendt, *Lectures on Kant's Political Philosophy;* and Ronald Beiner's interpretive essay in the same volume.

why the standards to which it points are standards of *reason,* and so of the sort of authority that standards have. This may seem already too lofty a demand; but if we cannot meet it to any degree, then we are left with nothing convincing to say in the face of disagreement with others or uncertainty with ourselves. We need not suspect that there are rational methods for solving all possible practical problems – a universal practical algorithm – in order to fear that if there is *nothing* that has authority that can be said on behalf of some rather than other ways of approaching practical matters, then we are helpless in the face of diversity of practice. There is little comfort in appealing to the shared discourse of the like-minded when many deep problems of life reflect lack of like-mindedness.

When Kant turns to the problem of the grounding of reason, he often makes a limited but insistent claim on behalf of toleration. He asserts repeatedly that "the public use of reason should always be free". When we explore the sense of this claim and the arguments Kant advances for it, it turns out that he is concerned not (as it may initially seem) with a particularly diluted conception of toleration or liberal freedom, but with a particularly striking conception of the sort of vindication that practical reasoning, and so all reasoning, can have. It is a corollary of this conception that *some* sorts of toleration have a deeper importance than is usually claimed for *any* sort of toleration by liberal thinkers. It is therefore politically as well as philosophically important to see what Kant had in mind when he insisted that the public use of reason should be free.

Expression, communication and the proper object of toleration

Kant's emphasis on the toleration of the public use of reason can seem both weak and exaggerated. It will seem weak if we think of toleration as a response to the (merely) expressive use of reason – and unreason. There are two reasons why. First, his principle appears to afford no protection for uses of reason that are not public, and these for many liberals are uses that particularly need protection. Second, when toleration is understood as a response to expressions of opinion, Kant's principle appears to demand too little. If I am to tolerate others' expression of their opinions, whether in their religious ceremonies or their choice of life-style, or in more public matters such as their letters to the editor, it seems that all I need do is to refrain from interfering. Similarly, on this understanding of toleration, governments tolerate dissent provided they neither restrict nor hinder expression of opinion. Positive action is required only secondarily, when persons or institutions fail to tolerate. In such cases it may be necessary to restrict or restrain those who seek to intimidate or to silence. But the central requirement of toleration is that we do nothing.

If this is all that toleration demands, and we need do this much only for public uses of reason, Kant's insistence on the importance of toleration seems exaggerated. Toleration on this understanding is too negative a matter to be fundamental; it would be easy in theory and often not too difficult in practice, especially when we are called to tolerate matters we are not much concerned about. Such a view of toleration fuels a recurrent suspicion that toleration is the outward face of indifference.

But if we consider the part toleration plays in our lives less abstractly, the matter is not so simple. Doing nothing is not standardly a way of having no effect on others' possibilities for self-expression, given that the standard point of expression is communication. Doing nothing may convey disapproval and hostility. In extreme cases lack of response may reasonably be read as ostracism or rejection, as conveying the message that the other is not (or not fully) human. More commonly, doing nothing signals that what the other seeks to convey will be viewed as mere expression and not as a communication. It will indicate that any communication intended is a trivial and indifferent matter, not worthy of discussion or refutation, a merely private affair. When Marx, in *On the Jewish Question,* points out that political emancipation offers toleration of Jewish religious practice only on condition that the religious life be then regarded as a private matter, he points out that this constitutes a radical reconstrual and diminution of religious life, now to be seen as one more expression of private opinion, on a par with other spheres of private activity. More generally, once acts of communication are viewed primarily as acts of expression, it is not particularly controversial to argue that they should be tolerated.

Yet it is surely controversial to see the speaking, writing and related activities of human beings as primarily expressive, something that can in principle be purely private, indeed solitary, rather than as primarily communicative. Yet that is what we are doing as soon as we think of tolerating as a response to what others express, and so as a response to something that (further damaging effects on others apart) is private. What we communicate – whether by words, gestures, rituals or more complex patterns of activity – must be interpretable by some audience. A communication that meets only with noninterference is from a certain point of view already a failure. Expression is parasitic on communication, and all successful communication requires some sort of recognition or uptake by others, whether it consists in an understanding of the content communicated or merely in a recognition that the other seeks to communicate; and attempted communication requires the possibility of such recognition. We do not tolerate others' communications if we are *merely* passive and noninterfering. It is no accident that the forms and practices through which we express and communicate toleration of others' opinions (rules of order, standards of professional etiquette and of daily civility) embody clear signals of recognition of others' communications, even when there is disagreement or failure of understanding. Toleration of others' communications does not require us to endorse, or even fully to understand, what is communicated – if it did, there could be no toleration where there is lack of agreement, and toleration would lose its point. Once we see acts of communication rather than acts of expression as the proper objects of toleration, we can see why toleration is a demanding requirement. The basis of Kant's arguments for the toleration of public uses of reason and for its link to the grounds of reason is that he understands toleration as *a response to communication*. His position is articulated in *What Is Enlightenment?*.

What Is Enlightenment?

Kant's line of argument in *What Is Enlightenment?* has several puzzling features. He construes Enlightenment as an emergence from "self-incurred immaturity [*Unmündigkeit*]", a situation in which we fail to think and judge for ourselves, and defer to others:

> It is so convenient to be immature! If I have a book to have understanding in place of me, a spiritual adviser to have a conscience for me, a doctor to judge my diet for me, and so on, I need not make any efforts at all. (*WE*, VIII, 35; 54)

The escape from immaturity of all sorts is, however, a difficult if not impossible project for solitary individuals (*WE*, VIII, 36; 54; *IUH*, VIII, 18–19; 42–3). The habits of immaturity become second nature and are hard to slough off if unchallenged. But an entire public may, perhaps and gradually, overcome such habits and "disseminate the spirit of rational respect . . . for the duty of all men to think for themselves" provided only that they have "the most innocuous form of freedom" (*WE*, VIII, 36; 55), freedom to make public use of one's reason in all matters.

The notion of a *public* use of reason is here defined in terms of the *audience* whom an act of communication may reach. A private use of reason is (strangely!) "that which a person may make of it in a particular *civil* post or office"; here the audience is restricted (*WE*, VIII, 37; 55–6). Officers, clergy, civil servants, taxpayers must obey and not argue with the orders or doctrine or regulations that govern these roles. An appointed priest is "acting on a commission imposed from outside", and the use "he makes of his reason in the presence of his congregation is purely *private*" (*WE*, VIII, 38; 57). By contrast a public use of reason takes places when the same cleric "as a scholar addressing the real public (i.e. the world at large) . . . speaks in his own person" (*WE*, VIII, 38; 57). On Kant's view it is only the public use of reason in this sense that may, if tolerated, produce an enlightened people. Hence he commends Frederick the Great's ranking of intellectual above civil freedom, attributing to him the principle "*Argue as much as you like about whatever you like, but obey!*" (*WE*, VIII, 41; 59). He even suggests at one point that maximal civil freedom might be inimical to the best development of intellectual freedom, and that it is only within the "hard shell" of a restricted outward liberty that human capacities to think and to judge can mature into capacities to act freely (*WE*, VIII, 41; 59).

Three striking features of this line of thought are the very sharp distinction Kant appears to make between civil and intellectual freedom; the curious way in which the distinction between public and private is drawn; and the reasons given for ranking the toleration of public uses of reason so highly, and in any case above the toleration of private uses of reason. I shall comment briefly on the first two of these, and at greater length on the third.

Kant's distinction between civil and intellectual freedom appears too sharp because any use of reason involves some outward action, and so needs some civil freedom. Communication, whether public or private, needs a medium. We cannot communicate by universal telepathy, but need access to the media of our times. We need soapboxes and assemblies, publishers and libraries, and above all today the electronic media. Kant's celebration of the "freedom of the pen" is quite inadequate as an account of the social arrangements and technical resources needed if we are to succeed in communicating with the world at large, or even with a moderate audience. He says little about what is needed to secure access to the *means* of public (or more restricted) reasoning for all. However, this is not because he views intellectual freedom as a merely internal matter. He writes:

Certainly one may say, "Freedom to speak or write can be taken from us by a superior power, but never the freedom to think." But how much, and how correctly, would we think if we did not think as it were in common with others, with whom we mutually communicate! Thus one can well say that the external power which wrests from man the freedom publicly to communicate his thoughts also takes away the freedom to think – the sole jewel that remains to us under all civil repression and through which alone counsel against all the evils of that state can be taken. (*WOT*, VIII, 144; 303)

Intellectual freedom is from the start not merely freedom to engage in inward or solitary reflection. Kant does not provide us with an account of the material and social requirements for exercising intellectual freedom under various historical conditions; if he had, it would no longer have seemed "the most innocuous freedom". But the reason for this omission is that he is concerned with a more fundamental requirement for a communication to be public. *Whatever* means of communication are available, communications may fail to be public if they do not meet standards for being interpretable by others. No amount of publicity can make a message that is interpretable either by no others or only by some others into a fully public use of reason. Effective publicity is politically important; but it presupposes that what is to be communicated is publicizable.

To see what is required for a communication to be publicizable we need first to understand Kant's distinction between the public and the private. This may seem downright peculiar. The positions of clergy, officers, civil servants, taxpayers and so on are defined by state and church regulation. How then can communications made in filling these roles be construed as private? They are certainly not in any way personal. But Kant's conception of the private is never a conception of the merely individual or personal.[2] In speaking of the communications of officials as private he is not suggesting that these acts express the personal or individual opinions of officials, but pointing out that they address not "the world at large", but an audience that has been restricted and defined by some authority.

There are two aspects to this position. A communication that presupposes some authority other than that of reason may fail to communicate with those who are not subject to that authority; they can interpret it, if at all, only on the hypothesis of some claim that they reject. At some points in debates about such communications argument must stop and authority be invoked.[3] But a communication that does not presuppose such an authority, and so is in principle accessible to the world at large and can be debated without invoking authority, may, as it happens, actually be addressed to or understood by few. Publicizable communications may or may not receive full publicity.

For Kant publicizability is more fundamental than publicity. Communications that cannot, however disseminated, reach those who do not accept or assume some authority are not full uses of reason at all. Communications that presuppose no external authority are, even if they aim at and reach only a small audience, fit to be public uses of reason. Hence Kant regards communications between "men of learning" who are committed to reasoned inquiry as public (CF, VII, 19–20; 27–8; WE, VIII, 38; 57), although the circle of communication is small, whereas "enlightenment of the masses" needs publicity as well as publicizability (CF, VII, 89; 161; WE, VIII, 40; 58). For the same reasons he would see reasoned discussion between friends, or an inward process of reasoning, as fit to be public, though in no way made public; but would see all communication that presupposes authorities other than that of reason as neither public nor fully publicizable.

Toleration and authority of reason

Political progress ultimately requires communication that is both publicizable and made public. Only if we can communicate in ways that are generally interpretable is there any point in seeking an unrestricted audience. It is this thought that lies behind Kant's insistence that the *public* use of reason must always be free, and that links his defense of toleration to his account of the grounds of practical reason.

2 Cf. Thomas Auxter, "Kant's Conception of the Private Sphere", esp. pp. 299ff. and 305.
3 This is not to say that we cannot understand communication that presupposes authorities that we do not accept. Sociologists, historians and outsiders of all sorts do so constantly. They supply the missing premise that a certain authority is believed or trusted or accepted. Relative to the premise the communication makes sense; but the premise is not vindicated or accepted. This procedure works when the understanding sought is intellectual, and so conditional; but there remains a sense in which such communication does not fully engage those who reject the authority on which it is based – as insiders often complain about outsiders' accounts of their beliefs and practices.

His claim may strike one as markedly illiberal. Ronald Beiner has recently commented:

This precedence accorded to public over private prerogatives may appear as something of an inversion of traditional liberal priorities on the part of one of the fountainheads of liberal thought.[4]

However, the sources of this "inversion" lie deep within Kant's thinking. The priority that he assigns to the toleration of public uses of reason has its roots in central Kantian claims about the limits of theoretical reason and the possibility and grounds of practical reason, and the connection of both to the notion of a possible community.[5] I shall try to uncover some of these roots not only to show why Kant argues for an apparent "inversion" of traditional liberal priorities, but also to suggest that the traditional precedence accorded private uses of reason (and other private affairs) in much liberal thinking is less central to liberalism than is often assumed.

A public use of reason, we have seen, is in the first place one that could reach the world at large if suitably publicized. It must therefore assume no authority that could not be accepted by an unrestricted audience. Since "the world at large" accepts no common external authority, the only authority the communication can assume must be internal to the communication. (It cannot on Kant's account, and on many others, assume no authority whatsoever: "Lawless" communication ends in gibberish and loss of freedom to think [*WOT,* VIII, 145–6; 303–5].) The only authority internal to communication is, on Kant's view, reason.

What is spoken or written cannot count as a public use of reason merely because it is noised or displayed or broadcast to the world at large. Communication has also to meet sufficient standards of rationality to be interpretable to audiences who share no other, rationally ungrounded, authorities. There is a narrowness of focus in Kant's assumption that public uses of reason should address "the entire reading public", but no mistaking his thought that one who reasons publicly must address, and so be interpretable by, all others.

The basis and extent of shared standards of rationality and interpretability is, of course, the central concern of a critique of reason. In the first *Critique* Kant argues that the categories of the understanding, although indispensable to all experience and communication, are not sufficient either to structure our understanding and action or to satisfy our demand for a grounding of reason. Reference to the categorical structure of human understanding neither satisfies nor dispels our "natural" demand for *completeness* of reasons. It is not just that we do not seem to

---

4 Beiner, in Arendt's *Lectures on Kant's Political Philosophy,* p. 123.
5 Lucien Goldmann makes the theme of community central to his reading of Kant's thought and specifically to the enterprise of a critique of reason. See his *Immanuel Kant,* esp. pp. 21–2 and 152ff. This is plausible only if community is understood in a quite minimal sense. Kant is more interested in the conditions of possible community than in actual communities.

be in a position to answer questions such as "Where do the categories come from?" or "Could we have had different categories?" It is also that the only insight we gain into the authority of the categories is negative: Attempts to do without them end, so far as we know, in breakdowns of thought.[6]

To go further, Kant suggests, we must think about practical reasoning. Philosophy cannot merely "strive only after speculative knowledge", but must be the *"science of the highest maxims of the use of our reason"* (L, IX, 24; 28; CPR, Bx and A666/B694). We use certain Ideas of reason or maxims to regulate all our thinking and communicating. In using these Ideas of reason we *aim* at a systematic unity of experience, although we cannot legitimately bring it to completion. We use some Ideas of reason – the "maxims of speculative reason" (CPR, A666/B694; CJ, V, 182) – to guide our inquiries into nature, directing our thoughts toward unity and parsimony of explanation, which we cannot completely attain, but can approximate by striving to discern "the universal and true horizon" of natural inquiry (CPR, A659/B685). Finding ourselves restricted by a "private horizon", and determined by our "special powers of cognition, ends and standpoints" (L, IX, 41; 46), we can do no more than adopt the maxim "always to try rather to expand than to narrow one's horizon" (L, IX, 43; 48).

We use other Ideas of reason to regulate various aspects of our practical reasoning. The Postulates of Pure Practical Reasoning give a certain unity and closure to all our practical reasoning: "the concept of freedom is made the regulative principle of [practical] reason" (CPrR, V, 49; see also 133–4; CPR, A777–B805). Our judging of particular moral situations can be regulated by maxims of reflexive judging, by which we guide our construal or appraisal of actual moral situations in ways that may secure unity and congruence between our own judgments and those of others.[7]

The authority of these and other Ideas of reason is, however, neither self-evident nor given. Yet Kant does not think they are merely pragmatically necessary or conventionally established assumptions. The warrant that we have for following and trusting such procedures is that they are always subject to self-scrutiny and correction. The successful use of certain cognitive procedures, strategies and standards, including their successful reflexive use, where success is understood in terms of these very procedures, strategies and standards, confers authority:

6 I have sketched aspects of such a reading in Onora O'Neill, "Transcendental Synthesis and Developmental Psychology". It is perhaps tempting to think that the "cunning of reason" plays God in creating the categories of the understanding, and that all else is the work of man in the dialectical elaboration of maxims of reason. Reflection on a developmental account of cognitive capacities suggests that this is misleading. If the categories themselves have a developmental history, there is no one moment in human history or in the maturation of individual men and women at which dialectical development takes over from natural processes. The dualism between nature and culture cannot be sharp.

7 CJ, V, 179–86 and 293–6; for further discussion see Chapters 1 and 9 in this volume.

Reason must in all its undertakings subject itself to criticism; should it limit freedom of criticism by any prohibitions, it must harm itself, drawing upon itself a damaging suspicion. (*CPR*, A738/766)

Freedom in thinking means the subjection of reason under no other laws than those it gives itself. Its opposite is the maxim of a lawless use of reason . . . if reason will not subject itself to the law it gives itself, it will have to bow under the yoke of laws which others impose . . . (*WOT*, VIII, 145–6; 303–4)

We have here clear statements of Kant's reasons for thinking toleration of *public* uses of reason especially important. Restrictions of the public use of reason not only will harm those who seek to reason publicly, but also will undermine the authority of reason itself:

Reason depends on this freedom for its very existence. For reason has no dictatorial authority; its verdict is always simply the agreement of free citizens, of whom each one must be permitted to express, without let or hindrance, his objections or even his veto. (*CPR*, A738/B766)

One way of taking these passages suggests that the antithesis between public and private uses of reason is ill founded. For if reasoning cannot gain authority beyond the circles within which it guides communication – if its authority is, so to speak, retrospectively established rather than antecedently given – then private "uses of reason" would seem to be without any general authority, hence not really uses of reason at all. On such an understanding the authority of reason is an all-or-nothing affair: Either there is unimpeded communication between all, and authoritative standards of reasoning can emerge, or there are impediments to communication and no universally shared standards of reasoning can emerge, and what passes for private reasoning lacks authority.

This conclusion neglects the developmental framework of Kant's account of the grounds of reason. Enlightenment is a *process*. It is the emergence of increasingly prevailing, non-self-stultifying and authoritative standards. Even within the interstices of despotism and other traditional and less than rational polities, some authoritative standards of communicating can emerge. The commands of despots and their officers and officials, and the exhortations of preachers, can reach their intended audiences only if they meet some shared standards. Neither despots nor their commands can be in all respects arbitrary. Such uses of reason are not *wholly* private: Indeed, on the Kantian account a wholly private grounding of reason is no more a possibility than a Wittgensteinian private language. Despots can, however, retard the development of shared modes and practices of reasoning. Hence Kant appeals to those uses of reasoning that may even under despotism most closely approximate fully public uses of reason. In an age that is not yet enlightened the nearest-to-public uses of reason are those that aim beyond a restricted audience and point toward a universal debate. Incipiently public uses of

37

reason may be the source of fuller standards of reason and so (as despots have often realized) subversive of other authorities.

Toleration of public uses of reason is on this account necessary for the emergence and maintenance of the increasingly generally shared standards of reasoning that fully public communication requires. Practices of intolerance may damage the partial standards of reason on which restricted communication also depends. If we undermine the public use of reason by intolerance, all uses of reason are ultimately in jeopardy, including those that are private in the Kantian sense of being addressed to an audience restricted by some authority and those that are private in the sense of being personal. Reason, on this account, has no transcendent foundation, but is rather based on agreement of a certain sort. Mere agreement, were it possible, would not have any authority. What makes agreement of a certain sort authoritative is that it is agreement based on principles that meet their own criticism. The principles of reason vindicate their authority by their stamina when applied to themselves.

In Kant's view such self-criticism is best sustained in the form of free, critical and universal debate. Whereas the external authority of a "dictator" destroys the authority of reason, the debate of "fellow citizens" sustains it: "Reason is benefited by the consideration of its object from both sides" (*CPR*, A744/B772). Criticism, and the toleration that criticism requires, are fundamental for the authority of reason, and we are recommended to "allow . . . [our] opponent to speak in the name of reason, and combat him only with weapons of reason" (*CPR*, A744/ B772). In this way the powers and shortcomings of reason can best be revealed, its authority delimited and antinomies avoided. Reason's authority consists simply in the fact that the principles we come to think of as principles of reason are the ones that are neither self-stultifying nor self-defeating in use. The best way to find which principles have this character is to encourage the increasingly public use of reason. Indeed, if reason has no transcendent foundation, there is nothing else that we can do:

> it is indeed absurd to look to reason for enlightenment, and yet to prescribe beforehand which side she must necessarily favour. Besides, reason is already of itself so confined and held within limits by reason, that we have no need to call out the guard, with a view to bringing the civil power to bear upon that party whose alarming superiority may seem to us to be dangerous. In this dialectic no victory is gained that need give us cause for anxiety. (*CPR*, A747/B775)

We would deny reason and curtail its authority if we put some authority (such as state or church) above it. To accept and foster the authority of reason is to submit disputes to free and critical debate.

Toleration, at least of incipiently public uses of reason, has then a quite fundamental status in Kant's thought. Without it the authority of reason ebbs. Some degree of toleration is, it seems, a precondition for the emergence of any reasoning modes of life, and not merely for a just polity. The contention is not just that toleration and free discussion will lead to or are necessary for discoveries of truths (or will reduce false beliefs, or lead us to hold them less smugly). Nor is it that toleration and free discussion will be politically effective (or restrain tyrants or sustain individuals). Such instrumental justifications of toleration all *presuppose* that we have independent standards of rationality and methods of reaching truth. Kant's thought is rather that a degree of toleration must characterize ways of life in which presumed standards of reason and truth can be challenged, and so acquire the only sort of vindication of which they are susceptible. The development of reason and of toleration is interdependent: A measure of publicizability is needed for publicity; and publicity in turn is needed for further development of standards of publicizability. Practices of toleration help constitute reason's authority.

Nature, history and the source of reason

This developmental and historical framework is indispensable to Kant's account of the basis both of reason and of toleration. Where human reasoning is still subject to alien authorities of one or another sort, it is, though not wholly private, at best incipiently public. It becomes more public only as alien authorities are replaced by practices of toleration. Kant has some misplaced faith in the self-restraint of enlightened despots as a route of advance; but this is only a small aspect of a broader, speculative account of the natural and cultural history of reason. This account depicts reasoning capacities as emerging gradually. It maintains both that their initial appearance must precede any politically institutionalized forms of toleration (*IUH*, VIII, 18–9; 42–3), and that the process of emergence from "self-incurred immaturity" is incomplete even at late stages of human history. Kant speaks of his own age as an age of *enlightenment*, but not yet *enlightened* (*WE*, VIII, 40; 58). It is, in two senses, a critical stage in a long historical process.

The history of the development of reason in turn presupposes a long evolutionary process. The earliest beginning of capacities to reason could not depend on (partially) public debate, since any debate presupposes at least rudimentary capacities to reason. Kant offers a speculative account of the natural process by which such rudimentary capacities may have evolved. He sees the "unsocial sociability" of human beings as driving them toward shared forms of life and cooperation, which they can achieve only by communication. The "cunning of nature" provides only this minimum: "just enough for the most pressing needs of the beginnings of existence".[8] (In this, nature is wise, although we experience her as stepmotherly.)

8 *IUH*, VIII, 19–20; 42–3. See Yirmiahu Yovel, *Kant and the Philosophy of History*, esp. Chaps. 3 and 4 and Epilogue, for a detailed and critical account of the relation Kant envisages between the "cunning of nature" and his dialectical account of the development of reason. Yovel locates Kant's difficulty in giving an account of this transition in his underlying dualism and suggests that since this dualism introduces insoluble difficulties into the Kantian system, it is necessary to look

Only when sufficient capacities to reason have developed to link mankind in a "pathologically enforced social union" (*IUH*, VIII, 19–20; 43–5) can further advances become a historical undertaking based on the use of capacities already evolved.

So long as human progress is guided only by the "cunning of nature", toleration must be irrelevant for two reasons. First, Kant sees the natural antagonisms between human beings as providing the initial dynamics of progress. Premature toleration can only amount to noninterference. It damps antagonism and cannot play a dynamic role in developing human capacities. Second, toleration, construed as an appropriate and recognizing response to others' communications, cannot be practiced until capacities to communicate and reason are to some extent developed. Toleration fosters the development of reason only when this development has become a cultural task rather than a process of evolution. Only then can remaining "immaturities" be thought of as "self-incurred".

Still, the claim that the unenlightened are afflicted by self-incurred immaturity may seem a questionable exaggeration. Those whose reasoning capacities are incomplete have not chosen that they be so, but must lack insight into this incompleteness. What is "self-incurred" (if anything) is only the complacent acquiescence of a society, rather than of individuals, to the capacities it actually has. Those who live in conditions that are despotic or chaotic or barbarous may be able to do little to create a debate that extends practices of reasoning. At fortunate junctures of human history, intellectual and political activities may supplement or supersede the dynamics of unsocial sociability. When they do, modes of reasoning can be employed explicitly in their own scrutiny, and those that survive criticism can acquire such authority as reasoning can have, and can guide further theoretical and practical enterprises.

If the emergence of standards of reason is a gradual matter, there are excellent reasons to extend toleration to communications that in hindsight either appear irrational or advocate intolerance; for the standards by which such communications can be identified or criticized remain uncertain. However, this toleration cannot, without damage to prospects of establishing standards of reason, be extended to action that suppresses attempted communication of any sort. Kant holds rather that it is when a period of enlighten*ment* is reached that a debate in which modes and practices of reasoning are tested is most needed, and can be the dynamic for further progress toward enlightenment. At this stage intellectual freedom, understood broadly as practices of toleration, and not as mere freedom of

---

elsewhere. The two alternatives he identifies are a Hegelian conception of rationalized nature (which implausibly overlooks the finitude of human reason) and a naturalized conception of reason that forgoes any account of its authority. Despite Kant's sometimes overblown rhetoric of reason, a critique of reason decisively rejects the former. Insofar as he endorses a naturalistic account of reason, he does not take its cogency for granted, but thinks that something must be said about the authority of reason.

solitary thinking, has a certain priority; for its results are needed for further advances in reasoning and in political life. Kant thought the matter one of some urgency:

Reason does indeed stand in sore need of such dialectical debate; and it is greatly to be wished that the debate had been instituted sooner and with unqualified public approval. For in that case criticism would sooner have reached a ripe maturity, and all these disputes would of necessity at once have come to an end, the opposing parties having learned to recognize the illusions and prejudices which set them at variance. (*CPR*, A747/B775)

This picture of the rapid beneficial results of dialectical debate may not convince. A well-known result of debate is further debate, rather than the ending of all disputes. Why did Kant see the matter so optimistically? His line of argument again appears to stress the conditions for sharing standards of reasoning. He holds that without standards for resolving debates (whether by settling or by defusing them), communication itself would not be possible and the only "debates" would be spurious.

In a way this argument is the *positive* task of the whole of the "Doctrine of Method" of the first *Critique*. Whereas the "Transcendental Dialectic" has only the *negative* task of showing up illusory uses of "reason" that mesh us in antinomies, the "Doctrine of Method" reveals other, more productive, "modes of contention". It can be read as a contribution to the debate Kant thought overdue. It argues that if there is such a thing as the authority of reason (which we to some extent allow in the very act of joining debate with Kant), then not all modes of contention can be merely ways of disputing or quarreling: "there is . . . properly speaking no polemic [i.e., no mode of war] in the field of pure reason" (*CPR*, A756/B784, and cf. A750/B778). Where all modes of contention are mere polemic, there is no genuine debate, because neither party "can make his thesis genuinely comprehensible" (*CPR*, A750/B778). A *genuine* debate needs some mutual comprehension, not just a hostile talking past one another or a reliance on some external authority of greater or lesser scope, such as a state or church, or a dominant or powerful individual. Hence it affords the opportunity for discussing "the thoughts and doubts with which we find ourselves unable to deal" (*CPR*, A752/B780) and for testing and extending the principles of critical reasoning. The escape from arid and dogmatic modes of contention (which may mistakenly be thought modes of reasoning) comes not through "war" and the use of "dogmatic weapons", but through each party's willingness to "develop the dialectic that lies concealed within his own breast no less than in that of his antagonist" (*CPR*, A754/B782). The shared standards of debate that emerge, on which even skeptics must rely in communicating their thoughts, yield not mere communication, but with it some possibility for resolving disagreements or for revealing the sources of spurious disagreements.

This line of thought does not show that if reason's authority were fully established, *all* disagreement would be rationally resolvable. On the contrary, Kant's acknowledgment of the adequacy of incomplete standards of reasoning – of reason that falls short of being fully public – for much human communication suggests that even the fullest development of human reason might not make all disagreements resolvable, let alone guarantee that a time will come when all have been resolved. Kant's optimism may be doubly ungrounded. The resolution of all disagreements may be guaranteed neither in principle nor in practice. This should not surprise us: One of the achievements of twentieth-century reasoning has been to offer reasons for thinking the achievements of reason incompletable. Even if Kant's most ambitious and historically specific claims cannot be sustained, his arguments for the self-disciplining development of reason's standards by processes of reasoning offer a way between the cliffs of a transcendent vindication of reason and the whirlpools of relativism. His remedy for the "endless disputes of a merely dogmatic reason" (*CPR,* A752/B780), stripped of some of its more specific speculations about the history of reason, is a critique of pure reason, which,

arriving at all its decisions in the light of fundamental principles of its own institution, the authority of which no one can question, secures to us the peace of a legal order, in which our disputes have to be conducted solely by the recognised methods of *legal action . . .* [and] are . . . ended by a *judicial sentence* which, as it strikes at the very root of the conflicts, effectively secures an eternal peace. (*CPR,* A751–2/B779–80)

Reason's authority, like other human authorities, is humanly instituted. But it is not on that account arbitrary or in any sense merely a convention. On the contrary, it cannot be questioned, because intelligible questioning presumes the very authority it seeks to question. Although the great architectonic is a plan for a human edifice, it is not one we can coherently reject; were we to try to do so we would be left disoriented nomads, condemned to solitary and thoughtless silence. Even the project of rejection would exceed our powers.

Freedom and maxims of communication

Even if we find appealing Kant's attempt to vindicate the authority of reason without a transcendent starting point, many questions about his picture of the authority and history of reason, and of the grounds of toleration, may strike us as inadequately answered. Why should he think that the debate in the course of which principles of reasoning emerge and are secured in social practices has an end? Has he sufficient reasons for thinking that this end is approaching and that we have, in the late eighteenth or in the late twentieth century, reached even an age of enlightenment? How do we know that there are not many different non-self-defeating systems of human reasoning? And if there are, in what sense can we still speak of the authority of any of them? Is toleration of the public use of reason only a necessary condition of the emergence of a developed system of reason, or is it sufficient? If it is not, what else is needed?

Comprehensive discussion of these questions would have to include accounts of the sense in which reason constitutes a unity or system, of the possibilities of alternative histories of reason, and of grounds for holding or doubting that various aspects of human reason are completable. Such an account would have to ask whether there are alternative Ideas of reason, and if there are, whether the shared categorial basis of human understanding makes it possible to arbitrate between them. Much more would need to be said about the extent and forms of toleration required for the development of aspects of reason at various stages. We would need to understand what sort of authority a particular account of the history of reason may have. I shall leave these and other large questions aside and try to say something more contextual about the way in which this vindication of reason is in the first place a vindication of *practical* reasoning. In particular I shall try to show that Kant offers us the appropriate complement to a discursive grounding of reason in his reasoned grounding of practices of discourse. Reason's authority and toleration are interdependent.

The division Kant makes between the natural emergence of some cognitive capacities and the dialectical development of others in human communication is fundamental to his picture. Communication is action, and hence at least to some extent freely undertaken rather than a natural product. It takes place between beings who are at least partially separate from one another, and at least partially free and rational. This picture does not deny that human communication has an animal and evolutionary basis; indeed, Kant's developmental account of reason fits well with an evolutionary view of cognition. But no noncultural account of human communication would be complete. Human communication is not a set of repertoires whose emergence reflects only the evolution of the species and the maturation of individual organisms, but has a history. Neither are the principles of communicating that emerge in the course of this history given from any source that transcends human life. They have to develop and be instituted in the course of human communication. There is neither a natural nor a preestablished harmony in the conversation of mankind.

Because the structure of human communication is not preestablished, its conduct is a *practical* problem. We are not guaranteed coordination with others, so we must ask which maxims or practical principles can best guide us when we seek to communicate, and must try to avoid principles that could not regulate communication among a plurality of separate, free and potentially reasoning beings. If we find such "principles of communication", their justification must be recursive; they will simply be principles by which practices of communication can be maintained and developed rather than stultified.

This view has a startling corollary. If reasoning has only a discursive and recursive grounding, and lacks transcendent vindication, then even the "supreme principle of practical reason", the Categorical Imperative, has no greater authority than that it is a principle capable of guiding the interactions, including the communicating, of beings whose coordination is not naturally guaranteed. The Categorical Imperative states essential requirements for a *possible* community (not an actual community) of separate, free and rational beings.

This is quite explicit in the Formula of the Kingdom of Ends, and not far below the surface in the other formulations. The idea of acting on maxims fit to be universal law, which is the core of the Formula of Universal Law, invokes the notion of a plurality of free and rational agents who act only in ways that do not preclude others' doing likewise. The idea of treating all others as ends, which is the core of the Formula of the End-in-Itself, invokes the notion of a plurality of agents who control their action to achieve coordinated respect for one another's freedom and rationality. These standards can be applied reflexively to the process in which they are established. They must be applied reflexively if they lack transcendent vindication and are yet to have the authority of principles of reason. Incipiently free and rational beings, who lack transcendent principles of practical reasoning, can and must regulate their communicating by maxims that do not undermine or stultify their incipient communication. There is nothing else they can do if their communicating is neither transcendently nor (fully) naturally coordinated. In its application to maxims of communication, as to other maxims, the Categorical Imperative is no more than the test of whether what is proposed is action on a maxim that *could* be shared (not "is shared" or "would be shared") by a plurality of at least partially free and rational beings.

Confirmation for this reading of the authority of the Categorical Imperative and its close connection with practices of toleration can be found in Kant's comments on communication. Although the notorious four examples of applications of the Categorical Imperative of the *Groundwork* do not include any specific maxim of communication (some false promising may be failure in communicating), in other works Kant says a good deal both about unacceptable and about morally required maxims of communication.

One initially plausible, but on reflection impossible, maxim of communication, which he discusses in scattered passages in the first *Critique,* is that of polemical debate (at other points he speaks of contention, of quarreling, of eristic dispute). Could we make the fundamental guideline of our communicating parallel to a maxim of war making, with the aim of victory? If such a maxim were fundamental, no holds would be barred. Victory would take priority over comprehension itself. But the victory that rests on incomprehension is not a victory *in debate or communication.* The aim of discussion or debate cannot reduce to victory; it can at best be victory by securing the other's agreement or understanding or conviction, or perhaps "agreement to differ". However, if these are the aims of discussion, communication must be guided by maxims that have some regard to others' being able to follow the communication. Achieving another's *compliance* in debate does not amount to winning the debate[9] (intimations here of the master–slave dialectic). A maxim of coercion in debate is no more universalizable than other maxims of coercion.

Another alluring, but on reflection impossible, maxim of communication to which Kant turned his attention (in a form few of his admirers find adequate)[10] is that of falsehood. Leaving aside his unsatisfactory resolution of dilemmas posed by would-be murderers who ask for vital information, it appears that a maxim of falsehood in communication *could not* serve as a universal principle for communications among a plurality of rational beings, or beings who are becoming rational. For if falsehood became the maxim of "communications" among such beings, comprehension itself would cease, and so also the possibility of communication. This is not to say that a maxim of *selective* falsehood would be an impossible one for regulating the communicating of a plurality of partially free and rational beings. Plenty of actual communities get on well with a universally shared convention of falsehood in response to intimate inquiries or about punctuality or in relations with strangers. But the very possibility of recognizing what is said in such contexts as falsehood presupposes comprehensibility, and thus also that standards of truth telling obtain more generally in those communities.

Restraint of polemic and lying may be necessary guidelines for tolerating one another's communicating; but they are only the beginnings of practices of toleration. In the *Critique of Judgment* and the *Logic* Kant offers more extensive accounts of maxims of communication that must be adopted in a possible community of rational beings. He there speaks of

a critical faculty which in its reflective act takes account . . . of the mode of representation of everyone else, in order, *as it were,* to weigh its judgment with the collective reason of man-kind, and thereby avoid the illusion arising from subjective and personal conditions. (*CJ*, V, 294–5; cf. *L*, IX, 41; 46)

Kant terms this faculty a *sensus communis,* for which "common sense" has served as the standard but misleading translation. Since he glosses *sensus communis* as "public sense" and contrasts it with a *sensus privatus,* I shall use the term "public sense."[11]

To exercise this faculty is to adopt certain further maxims as guides in our thinking and communicating; maxims that Kant terms "maxims of common human understanding". The three maxims that he cites are intended to guide different aspects of our thinking and communicating.

---

9 See Saner, *Kant's Political Thought,* Pts. II and III, for detailed discussion of Kant's view on requirements for genuine debate.
10 See *SRL,* VIII; and also Christine Korsgaard, "The Right to Lie: Kant on Dealing with Evil".
11 Arendt proposes the translation "community sense"; this too is not entirely apt. See *Lectures on Kant's Political Philosophy,* p. 70.

The maxim that should guide our understanding is "To think for oneself"; it is "the very motto of enlightenment" (*WOT,* VIII, 146n; 305n). Kant describes this maxim suggestively as the "maxim of never *passive* reason" and a "maxim of *unprejudiced* thought". In *What Is Orientation in Thinking?* he formulates it thus:

to ask oneself with regard to everything that is to be assumed, whether he finds it practicable to make the ground of the assumption, or the rule which follows from the assumption, a universal principle of the use of his reason. (*WOT,* VIII, 145; 303)

Kant also calls it the "maxim of the self preservation of reason". To adopt this maxim is to seek to form one's *own* judgment and not merely to be led by others' judgments. It is, in a minimal sense, to act for oneself in matters of understanding. Clearly, if there is to be genuine communication and debate, all parties must be guided by such a maxim; otherwise understanding and agreement will be spurious, mere echoings of what the other or the many assert. Genuine communication occurs only between beings who are at least partially separate. Hence total failure to preserve a measure of separateness from those with whom one supposedly communicates is self-defeating. Nobody communicates with an echo. This is why the cleric who makes a public use of reason in *What Is Enlightenment?* must speak in his *own* voice: Total lack of self-respect defeats the possibility of communicating with another, since speaker and audience are no longer distinct.

This maxim does not presuppose any strong form of individualism. It demands only that there be a plurality of parties to any debate, whose thinking and judging are to some extent independent. Where nobody thinks for him- or herself there is no plurality of viewpoints to be heard and debated. Toleration then becomes pointless. Acting on this maxim is, Kant suggests, a difficult matter when "others are always coming and promising with full assurance that they are able to satisfy one's curiosity" (*CJ,* V, 294n). The social pressures to stop thinking for oneself are always great; if we entirely succumb to them, we can no longer take part in any discussion or debate.

The second maxim that Kant believes should guide our judging of particular situations is "To think from the standpoint of everyone else" (*CJ,* V, 294), which he calls "the maxim of enlarged thought". One who adopts it

detaches himself from the subjective personal conditions of his judgment, which cramp the minds of so many others, and reflects upon his own judgment from a *universal standpoint* (which he can only determine by shifting his ground to the standpoint of others). (*CJ,* V, 294n)

Without a transcendent viewpoint, taking a universal or detached view cannot be a matter of adopting any neutral, Archimedean standpoint, but only one of seeking to see one's own initial judgments from the standpoints of others. One who adopts a maxim of enlarged thought must therefore listen to what others are actually judging and communicating. There is no lofty position above the debate, as perhaps there might be if human reason had a transcendent source. There is only the position of one who strives to reach and understand the perspectives of others, and to communicate with rather than past them. Only communication that conforms to the maxim of enlarged thought can reach "the world at large". This is what the cleric who reasons publicly in *What Is Enlightenment?* must do if his communication is to be fit to reach "the world at large". Practices of toleration that include respect for others and their no doubt partial and private understanding are as fundamental to communication as is self-respect.

The third maxim of public sense may seem trivial compared to the first two. It is the "maxim of consistent thought": "always to think consistently" (*CJ*, V, 294). But once we think of the principles of human reason not as an antecedently given system, but as one that is gradually developed, then we can also see that achieving consistency is an unending and exacting task, whose limits remain unclear to us. Some local degree of consistency may indeed be a trivial presupposition of all thought, but achieving a systematic consistency is not. Kant indeed thought this maxim "the hardest of attainment" (*CJ*, V, 295) and wrote in the second *Critique*, "Consistency is the highest obligation of a philosopher and yet the most rarely found" (*CPrR*, V, 24). If reason is to achieve consistency between the understanding and judgments of a plurality of inquirers, then the maxim of consistent thought is in effect a maxim of seeking to render whole bodies of thought coherent, and so appropriately the maxim of an unending philosophical task.

Looking at these maxims from the standpoint of the Categorical Imperative, we can see why they must be among the obligatory principles of human communication. If there is a possible form of communication between beings who are separate and whose coordination is not naturally given or preestablished, then those beings must guide their attempts at communicating by principles that neither erode their own thinking nor fail to seek to understand and to follow the thinking of others, nor shrink from the task of working through and integrating a constantly revised set of judgments to achieve consistency. The grounding of principles of reasoning in incipient communication is mirrored by the grounding of developing communication in principles of reasoning. The supreme principle of practical reason both emerges from and disciplines human communication. Its breach, whether by failure to judge for oneself or by indifference to others' communications or to consistency, damages not only particular communications, but also the practices of reasoning on which possibilities of communicating rest. However, if reason itself is both secured and disciplined by practices of toleration in communication, there are the deepest reasons for seeking and maintaining those practices. Those who flout reasoned maxims of communication risk damage to shared standards of reasoning, which are essential for addressing the world at large and to some extent required even by those who seek to address only their own sect or friends or the politically or religiously or otherwise like-minded. Noninterference may be all that is needed to *express* oneself to the world at large;

but developed practices of toleration are needed if *communication* with the world at large is to be possible.

Toleration and politics

We now have a sketch of Kant's picture of the maxims on which our communicating must be based if we aim to develop standards of reasoning that could be used to address "the world at large". Because the overall picture of human reason that emerges is a historical picture, we can also see why toleration of actual communication and attempted communication has been and remains vital for the emergence of forms of life in which reasoning is highly developed, and in particular for the development of political forms of life. "Freedom of the pen" and more complex practices of toleration are indispensable in any society that does not forgo intellectual and political progress. Lack of toleration for incipiently public uses of reason blocks the only route by which revised or more widely shared standards for debate and communication can be established, or maintained. Intolerance brings unreasoned authority to bear on communication. Wherever intolerance is practiced, whether by state or church or other bodies or individuals, those whose thinking and communicating are suppressed are silenced not by reason but by authorities that lack reasoned vindication. When these authorities govern us, the authority of reason is diminished, and our distance from a reasoned form of life and politics grows.

In Kant's view even despotism, if enlightened, can provide the context for some maturation of reasoning capacities. Because "enlightened" despots practice some forms of toleration, they may permit practices of communication within which standards of reasoning progress. But it seems unlikely that human capacities to reason can attain their fullest development in such restricting polities. Debates that take place by courtesy of a despot may not be even incipiently public in the Kantian sense. Since by Kant's own standards we will not reason or even think correctly unless we think in common with others (*WOT,* VIII, 145; 303), our reasoning must remain defective while we live in defective polities. There is no direct route from Frederick the Great's Prussia to the establishment of fully public standards of reasoning or to a just polity. Nor is it clear that Kant has grounds within his own account of the history of reason for ranking intellectual ahead of civil freedom even in the short run, or for an age of enlighten*ment*. Reasoning capacities that mature within the hard shell of a restricted outward liberty may prove warped when the hard shell crumbles.

Until a just polity emerges, uses of reason can be public only in the sense of approximating to maxims of communication that would fit communicative acts to be understood by the world at large, if such unrestricted communication were possible. However, the claim that it is more urgent for *public* uses of reason to be free will not be vacuous so long as we can distinguish uses of reason that come closer to being universally communicable from uses that depend more on external authority. So long as universal communication remains impossible, many uses of reason will be not even incipiently public, but rather irremediably private, in the sense that they embody principles of reasoning that fit them for communication only with some restricted audience. Arguments for toleration of public or incipiently public uses of reason cannot show whether all such private uses of reason must also be tolerated.

However, Kant does not see any reasons to restrict (relatively) private uses of reason. On the contrary, he argues that the constitution of a just polity allows "*the greatest possible human freedom* in accordance with laws by which *the freedom of each is made to be consistent with that of all others*" (*CPR*, A316/B373; cf. *MEJ*, VI, 230). Even so, the difference between public and private uses of reason remains important. Failure to tolerate public and incipiently public uses of reason undercuts all possibility of development of standards of debate and of moves in the direction of a just polity. Some private uses of reason, by contrast, may hinder or prevent communication with the world at large, and so may hinder the emergence of public standards of reasoning and of a just polity. There are no good reasons for tolerating any private uses of reason that damage public uses of reason. For example, communications and expressions that denigrate or mock or bully others, or more generally fail to respect them, may make it harder or impossible for some to think for themselves, and so to follow the maxim of Enlightenment. Communications and expressions that foment divisions between persons and groups may make it harder to follow the maxim of enlarged thought. Hence some forms of censorship and restriction of private uses of reason may be acceptable (indeed required) when (but only when) they are needed to foster or sustain capacities for communication with the world at large. Kantian liberalism can provide reason for specific restraint and censorship where their absence would lead to forms of defamation or harassment that damage capacities for agency or for recognition of others' agency.[12]

Kant's constant stress in his more political writings is not so much on the aims or intentions we must have in communicating as on the standards we must achieve and the practices these standards presuppose. If our communicating is to be genuine, it must, so far as possible, meet shared standards of interpretability. It must be able to bear the light of publicity, even if perhaps a particular communication is directed at a small audience or understood by none, or by few (*TP*, VIII, 33–4; 84–5; *CF*, VII, 19–20; 27; 29). It is only the public uses of reason that can converge toward a self-regulating and self-correcting system, and so provide conditions for development toward a just polity. While standards of

12 Here one might find the basis for liberal arguments in favor of restricting supposedly "self-regarding" expression of opinion that may damage others' self-respect and capacities for agency. In certain circumstances there might be grounds for certain sorts of restriction on (for example) practices of sexual and racial stereotyping. See Onora O'Neill, "Practices of Toleration".

reasoning are developing, those patterns of reasoning that come closest to being public can pave the way for others that come closer, enabling all uses of reason, including those addressed to a small circle, to converge toward standards of universal communicability. But while those standards are only approximated, many uses of reason must remain relatively private in the sense that they can in principle be used to communicate only with some restricted group, defined by another, rationally ungrounded, authority. These deprived and partial private uses of reason may sometimes help to establish more complete and public standards of reason. But there is no guarantee that they will always do so. Since they are at least partly shielded from refutation and correction by one or another nonrational authority, such reasonings may embody principles that could not survive open scrutiny and are not generally indispensable for progress toward a more comprehensive or more generally shared rationality or the possibility of a just polity.

Toleration in the Kantian picture is then not merely a political virtue or a practice that would have to be part of any achieved just polity. It is the only matrix within which a plurality of potentially reasoning beings can constitute the full authority of reason and so become able to debate without restrictions what a just political constitution might be.

3

Reason and autonomy in *Grundlegung* III

Much of the difficulty of Kant's *Grundlegung* arises from shifts of framework within each chapter. The third chapter shifts *from* a metaphysic of morals *to* a critique of pure practical reason. This complicated shift is hardly discussed in the text, yet it is the crux of the chapter. In this essay I draw on other Kantian texts, in particular on the *Critique of Pure Reason,* to elucidate the point and outcome of the shift of framework. Much that I shall say is tentative: a proposal for reading the chapter rather than detailed commentary. I shall try to make it definite enough for criticism to have points of focus.

In the preface to *Grundlegung* we are told that "a metaphysic of morals has to investigate the Idea and principles of a possible *pure* will" rather than "the activities and conditions of human willing as such" (*G,* IV, 390). For much of Chapter II and in Chapter III up to page 450, Kant stays within the framework of a metaphysic of morals. He presents the Categorical Imperative and analyzes the connection between freedom and morality in abstraction from claims about actual rational beings.[1] Even if it convinces, we will still be unsure about human rationality, human freedom or human duties. No doubt we will share the common rational understanding of morality of Chapter I; but Kant will not have vindicated this common understanding. The shift to a metaphysic of morals in Chapter II may turn out to be a blind alley for human beings. A metaphysic of morals may lack application to human beings. To show that the discussion of Chapter II and of the first part of Chapter III is relevant to *us,* an entirely different framework is needed.

The brief prefatory comments on critique of practical reason offer a tantalizing clue. Kant writes that a complete critique of practical reason "should be able at the same time to show the unity of practical and theoretical reason in a common principle, since in the end there can only be one and the same reason" (*G,* IV, 391). A successful critique of practical reason should apparently show that there is a single supreme principle for practical and for theoretical reason. The *Grundlegung* is clear

---

This chapter originally appeared in *Grundlegung zur Metaphysik der Sitten: Ein kooperative Kommentar,* ed. Otfried Höffe, Vittorio Klostermann, Frankfurt, 1989.

1 The examples of duties are an exception. They evidently mention specifically human possibilities and institutions. This need not trouble us if we think that the examples are illustrative. Illustrations are commonly determinate in ways that the texts they illustrate are not.

enough that the supreme principle of practical reason is the Categorical Imperative. Could the Categorical Imperative be the supreme principle of all reason? Does this thought even make sense?

I shall propose a reading of *Grundlegung* III that presents the Categorical Imperative as the supreme principle of all reason. It has the corollary that freedom and autonomy are at the heart not just of morality but of all reasoning. This reading will, I hope, help to show what can and what cannot be done to vindicate reason, and how reason and autonomy are connected. The claim that the Categorical Imperative is the supreme principle of human reason, I shall argue, both offers a coherent view of Kant's larger enterprise and sheds some light on the last chapter of *Grundlegung*.

The agenda is simple, if a bit presumptuous. First I shall recapitulate the conditional claims of the early part of Chapter III, and note what remains to be established if these conditionals are to be relevant to us. Then I shall rehearse Kant's account of the connections between critique, autonomy and the authority of reason, drawing largely on the *Critique of Pure Reason*. These considerations will be used to throw light on the critical passages of Chapter III on the two standpoints (*G*, IV, 450 onward). The initial claims about freedom, autonomy and morality are reconsidered in the light not of the preceding account of morality but of Kant's conception of critique and of the authority of reason. To present this line of thought compactly I have avoided all but the most glancing engagement either with the *Critique of Practical Reason* or with the secondary literature. The result is less a commentary than a proposal for organizing a commentary.

The gap between rationality and freedom

The analysis of freedom at the start of the third chapter makes only conditional claims. Kant characterizes will as "a kind of causality belonging to living beings so far as they are rational" (*G*, IV, 446). This definition leaves it open whether the human will is free and how freedom may be connected to rationality. Kant distinguishes causality that works by natural necessity or the influence of "alien causes" from causality that works by freedom.[2] Freedom is initially defined negatively as the property by which a will is "able to work independently of *determination* by alien causes" (*G*, IV, 446). The distinction between natural necessity and freedom is clearly drawn; but until we understand what an "alien" cause is, the criteria for its application are unclear. In particular Kant offers no argument to

2   It is important not to attribute to Kant the claim that we can distinguish events that are naturally caused from others that are not. He holds that all events are part of some objective sequences and can be given a naturalistic explanation. His view is that naturalistic explanation cannot be the whole story – not that there are some events about which it has nothing to say. See Chapter 4 in this volume.

show that human beings, or other supposedly rational beings, have wills that can work independently of alien causes.

The second move of the chapter connects the "negative" with a "positive" conception of freedom (*G,* IV, 446). Positive freedom is more than independence from alien causes. It would be absent in lawless or random changes, although these are negatively free, since they depend on no alien causes. Since will is a mode of causality it cannot, if free at all, be merely negative free, so it must work by nonalien causality. Free will (if it occurs) must be (capable of being) positively as well as negatively free; it must be a capacity for *self-determination* or *autonomy* (*G,* IV, 447). Once again the distinctions are well drawn, but the criteria for their application are unfixed.

The third move of the chapter identifies the positive conception of freedom – self-determination or autonomy – with conformity to the Categorical Imperative (*G,* IV, 447). Kant's reasoning is compressed, indeed sketchy; but the thought, at least in its moral interpretation, is familiar. It was presented in more explicit form in Chapter II, in the discussion of the Formula of Autonomy, which runs, "Never to choose except in such a way that in the same volition the maxims of your action are also present as universal law" (*G,* IV, 440).[3] The thought is roughly that *if* there are beings who can choose freely, in the sense that their choosing can be lawlike yet not determined by alien causes, they must be capable of imposing lawlikeness on their actions, that is, of acting on universalizable maxims. However, the crucial connections between rationality and autonomy are not made explicit at the beginning of Chapter III. Kant assumes a background understanding that the supreme principle of practical reason links the requirement of autonomy to an ability to choose universalizable maxims.

Kant views the initial claims of Chapter III as "mere analysis of the concept of freedom" (*G,* IV, 447). All that he claims to have shown is that *if* rational beings are free, they are not simply negatively free, but (capable of) autonomy, and that *if* (capable of) autonomy, they are subject to the principle of morality, that is, to the supreme principle of practical reason. These supposedly analytic claims can seem deeply unconvincing. Why is not conformity to reason, even to a supposed supreme principle of practical reason, just another mode of heteronomy? Why does Kant take conformity to desires for heteronomy, and conformity to reason for autonomy? Why are desires but not reasons to be seen as "alien"? Does not calling the supreme principle of practical reason an "imperative" suggest that reason too is alien? Autonomy in many modern accounts is construed empirically as action on reflectively endorsed desires, or as avoiding specific sorts of social and personal

---

3 The treatment of autonomy in Chapter II is, however, incomplete: Kant states at *G,* IV, 440, that proof that autonomy is the sole basis of ethics needs a critique of practical reason and "does not belong in the present chapter".

dependence.[4] What reason is there to prefer the stricter and stranger Kantian conception of autonomy?

These questions are not answered immediately. We can, however, discern aspects of an answer. Most pertinently we can begin to see why, if autonomous action is to be independent of everything "alien", it must be action determined by reason. Independence from "alien" causes, taken strictly, must be independence from contingent or variable events, including those that are intimately part of agents. Such events depend on the play of natural forces or (possibly) on random occurrences, and so ultimately on indisputably "alien" causes. Maxims of autonomous action, by contrast, must hold equally for all rational agents, whatever their peculiar contingent and variable characteristics, and so must be universalizable.[5] Their authority, if they have any, cannot derive from any contingency of human life but only from the requirements of reason, whatever those may be.

From these claims, however, we can draw only a conditional conclusion about reason: If reason has any authority, that authority will hold indifferently for all rational beings. We do not learn *what* the principle(s) of reason are or *why* they have authority. Equally, we can draw only a conditional conclusion about human rationality and freedom: *If* we are rational in the required sense, then we are also free and so capable of autonomy and bound by morality. If we are not rational in the required sense, but only in some other (e.g., purely instrumental) sense,[6] then there will be a gap between our rationality and our freedom, and the Kantian conception of autonomy will be irrelevant to us.

Kant is well aware that the gap between rationality and freedom has not been closed. We have still, he points out, "to prove that freedom too is a property of the will of all rational beings" (*G*, IV, 447). Unless and until this can be done he can only *assert* or *maintain* but not demonstrate or ground human freedom. Kant uses the first person in two striking and uncharacteristic assertions[7] to show that these claims are ones that he cannot vindicate (at least at this stage): "Now I assert [*Ich sage nun* . . .] that every being who cannot act except *under the Idea of freedom* is by this alone – from a practical point of view – really free" (*G*, IV, 448). The emphasis is doubled: "And I maintain [*Nun behaupte ich* . . .] that to every rational being possessed of a will we must also lend the idea of freedom as the only

4 This view can be traced back at least to J. S. Mill. It has recently been refined by Harry Frankfurt, "Freedom of the Will and the Concept of a Person", since when it has become standard fare in English-language writing on autonomy.

5 This is not to say that they demand *uniformity* of action; *universalizable* principles demand uniform action only for like cases. Conditional universalizable principles demand action only of those who meet the condition.

6 In *Grundlegung* I Kant argued that there cannot be beings with merely instrumental rationality (*G*, IV, 396). This argument is conducted within the framework of common rational knowledge of morality. Its conclusion remains in doubt since that framework is later shown to be insufficient.

7 Cf. *G*, IV, 428: "Now I say [*Nun sage ich* . . .] that man, and in general every rational being, *exists* as an end in himself . . ." This too is a moment where Kant needs to anticipate the results of a critique of practical reason.

one under which he can act" (*G*, IV, 448). Assertion is not argument; but it may be enough for practical purposes. If indeed we can act and judge only "under the Idea of freedom", we must insist upon looking at ourselves as free whether or not we can show we are. In particular we must look at our reasoning itself as autonomous: "Reason must look upon itself as the author of its own principles independently of alien influences. Therefore as practical reason, or as the will of a rational being, it must be regarded by itself as free" (*G*, IV 448).

However, the practical indispensability of viewing ourselves as free is no proof of human freedom. Could not the fact that we must think we are free when we act and judge be a profound illusion? Many have thought that it is. Kant reminds us that "alleged experiences of human nature" (*G*, IV, 447) cannot prove human freedom. So long as the connection between reason and freedom is not established, the links between freedom, autonomy and morality are merely a series of analyses and the moral skeptic need not be shaken. The skeptic may hold that reason is inert, available for theoretical purposes but a mere slave of the passions in practical matters. Kant is adamant about the limitations of his analytic arguments. Freedom has not been demonstrated: "we have been quite unable to demonstrate freedom as something actual in ourselves and in human nature" (*G*, IV, 448). Nor has morality. We have no insight into *"how the moral law can be binding"* (*G*, IV, 450). For all we know, our inability to act or judge except under the Idea of freedom reflects some quirk or illusion of human nature and nothing fundamental about rational beings as such. The analysis had led us into "a kind of circle, from which, as it seems, there is no way of escape" (*G*, IV, 450). Since analysis traps us in a circle, no move is possible without a radical shift of argumentative strategy.

Critique, autonomy and the authority of reason

It is only in the passages after page 450 that Kant argues that human beings are free agents, in a sense that makes their actions imputable and the Categorical Imperative relevant to them. Neither his articulation of our common moral consciousness in Chapter I, nor the abstract analysis of principles of obligation for rational beings that a metaphysic of morals offers, has shown, *or could have shown,* that *we* are agents of the required sort. Yet unless we are free agents in the required sense the entire moral theory will lack practical significance for us. To go further we must enter the different framework of a critique of practical reason.

A critique of practical reason could take us no further than a metaphysic of morals if it were simply a more abstract way of arguing. However, this is not the difference between them. Rather it is a matter of starting point. A critique of (practical) reason reconsiders the *standpoint* from which argument is conducted. Kant writes that "One shift [*Auskunft* – perhaps "departure" or "way out"], however, still remains open to us" (*G*, IV, 450). The only way out of the circle is to "enquire whether we do not take one standpoint when by means of freedom we conceive ourselves as causes acting *a priori*, and another standpoint when we contemplate ourselves with reference to our actions as effects which we see before our eyes" (*G*, IV, 450). The critical turn considers how we can shift our very starting points. Only by making such a shift can we exit from the circle of analysis.

Here we see immediately the connection to the fundamental movement of the *Critique of Pure Reason*, the Copernican turn, which Kant also characterizes as a matter of viewing things from a double point of view (*CPR*, Bxix[n]). To undertake a critique (whether of pure reason, or specifically of pure practical reason) is not to attain an unconditional transcendent vantage point, but to take a critical view of the starting point, or condition, of one's own previous thinking. Critique rests on the ability to shift starting points, and so to gain some distance and independence from a given starting point.

In the *Critique of Pure Reason* Kant sees criticism of reason as undertaken from the standpoint of those who find themselves apparently able to reason, yet led into antinomies in their reasoning, from which they are able to escape only by disciplining their reasoning. From the start Kant insists that critique of reason must be a reflexive process: "reason has insight only into that which it produces after a plan of its own" (*CPR*, Bxiii). The plan that he proposes is to shift perspective: "We must therefore make trial [*Versuch*] whether we may not have more success in the tasks of metaphysics if we suppose that objects must conform to our knowledge" (*CPR*, Bxvi). The entire "Doctrine of Elements" of the first *Critique* is offered as the first part of such a "trial" or experiment. It offers no account of reason's authority. The whole familiar dissection of sensibility and understanding is intrinsically incomplete. Although we may receive a manifold of intuition that we synthesize under empirical concepts and judge according to the categories of the understanding, these acts of judgment rely on as yet unvindicated uses of reason. After seven hundred pages we have only "an inventory of materials" [*Bauzeug;* elsewhere *Stoff*] (*CPR*, A707/B735). It is the task of the "Doctrine of Method" to move toward an account of the authority of reason. The next part of the "trial" must be to see what can be said in vindication of reason.

In the "Doctrine of Method" Kant offers a recursive account of the authority of reason. In a post-Copernican world, with no absolute *up* or *down*, we cannot have a foundationalist account of the grounds of reason (whatever that might be). A critical grounding of reason works by showing what it takes to orient thinking and acting by principles that do not fail even if used universally and reflexively. The key idea behind the notion of a critique of pure reason is that we can find standards of reasoning by considering how we can and must discipline our thinking. However, this discipline is not to be thought of as externally imposed: Rather it is *self-discipline* or *autonomy* in thinking.

These points have a firm textual basis. The "Doctrine of Method" initially characterizes discipline as "the compulsion by which the constant tendency to disobey certain rules is restrained and finally extirpated" (*CPR*, A709/B737). Kant notes: "that reason, whose proper duty it is to prescribe a discipline for all other endeavours, should itself stand in need of such a discipline may indeed seem strange" (*CPR*, A710/B738). Yet this strange requirement is the key to Kant's account of the authority of reason. Our thinking needs "a discipline, to restrain its tendency towards extension beyond the narrow limits of possible experience and to guard it against extravagance and error" (*CPR*, A711/B740), and "the whole philosophy of pure reason has no other than this strictly negative utility" (*CPR*, A711/B740). Reason, the discipline of all disciplines, can only be and must be *self-*disciplined: The subordination of thinking or practice to other supposed authorities (state, church, experts, personal preferences) is not reason, but the abrogation of reason.[8] Reason's discipline cannot be alien; it must be autonomous.

The task of closing the gap between reason and autonomy (which the analytic passages left open) can now be seen in a new light. This gap is to be closed not by establishing that human beings are rational, and then proving that they are free, and hence also (given the analytic argument) autonomous. Kant's strategy is the reverse. He argues not from reason to autonomy but from autonomy to reason. Only autonomous, self-disciplining beings can act on principles that we have grounds to call principles of reason. Reason has no transcendent authority; it can only be vindicated by critique, and critique itself is at bottom no more than the practice of autonomy in thinking. Autonomy does not presuppose but rather constitutes the principles of reason and their authority:

Reason must in all its undertakings subject itself to criticism; should it limit freedom of criticism by any prohibitions, it must harm itself, drawing upon itself a damaging suspicion. Nothing is so important through its usefulness, nothing so sacred, that it may be exempted from this searching examination, which knows no respect for persons. Reason depends on this freedom for its very existence. For reason has no dictatorial authority; its verdict is always simply the agreement of free citizens, of whom each one must be permitted to express, without let or hindrance, his objections or even his veto. (*CPR*, A738/B766)

Because the authority of reason can only be established by autonomous self-discipline in thought and action, attempts to lean on other authorities backfire:

it is indeed absurd to look to reason for enlightenment, and yet to prescribe beforehand which side she must necessarily favour. Besides, reason is already of itself so confined and held within limits by reason, that we have no need to call out the guard, with a view to bringing the civil power to bear upon that party whose alarming superiority may seem to

---

8   These passages throw light on Kant's insistence that the kernel of Enlightenment is not reason but autonomy. Cf. *WE*, VIII, 33; and Onora O'Neill, "Enlightenment as Autonomy: Kant's Vindication of Reason".

us to be dangerous. In this dialectic no victory is gained that need give us cause for anxiety. (*CPR*, A747/B775)

A large part of the "Doctrine of Method" is rebuttal of supposed alternative accounts of the authority of reason. The rationalist conception of reason as mathematical method is doubly wrong: Philosophy cannot be done *more geometrico*, nor mathematics *more analytico*. Equally, an eristic conception of reason as intrinsically polemical cannot be vindicated. The only hope, if we are to discern principles that have authority either for thinking or for acting, is a discipline, a "negative instruction" that rejects as pseudorational principles that make thinking conditional on some "alien", rationally ungrounded authority. Such principles have authority only on condition that the "alien" authority on which they depend is accepted. The only unconditional principles that have authority are those that appeal to nothing except disciplined autonomy in thinking. Criticism, which has destroyed the authority of traditions, can sustain the authority of reason not by *polemic* with supposed rival authorities (churches, civil powers, etc.), let alone by dependence on discredited authorities, but only by relying on principles that demand no more than that criticism be conducted in and survive their own terms. Such principles have no transcendent authority; we grant them provisional authority and rely on them because they survive all self-criticism and depend on nothing alien. The authority of reason differs from that of civil and other powers, whose antagonisms are destructive. Reason is self-disciplining, but not self-destroying.

In *What Is Orientation in Thinking?* Kant articulates the fundamental strategy of autonomy in thinking. He begins with the claim that there is no alien, transcendent authority in thinking. The choice is between autonomy and lawlessness, reason and madness: "Freedom in thinking means the subjection of reason under no other laws than those it gives itself. Its opposite is the maxim of a lawless use of reason" (*WOT*, VIII, 145; 303–4). But lawlessness ends in servitude: "if reason will not subject itself to the law it gives itself, it will have to bow under the yoke of laws which others impose . . ." (*WOT*, VIII, 145; 303–4). These dilemmas are dramatic; but they do not show anything about the "law" that reason can give itself. Which principles have unconditional authority in thinking and acting? Where could self-discipline either in thinking or in acting begin? At least one negative point can be made. One corollary of refusal to bow under an alien yoke is that what count as the principles of reason cannot hinge on variable and contingent matters, all of which, however intimately human, are alien causes. Would-be reasoners must then at least adopt the strategy of not acting on principles that accept such alien authorities. They must act only on maxims on which others whose contingent circumstances and characters differ can also act.

In adopting this merely negative strategy for guiding thought and action, reasoners – or potential reasoners – adopt the principle that we know in other contexts as the Categorical Imperative. The Categorical Imperative is the supreme principle of reasoning not because it is an algorithm either for thought or for action,[9] but because it is an indispensable strategy for disciplining thinking or action in ways that are not contingent on specific and variable circumstances. The Categorical Imperative is a fundamental strategy, not an algorithm; it is the fundamental strategy not just of morality but of all activity that counts as reasoned. The supreme principle of reason is merely the principle of thinking and acting on principles that can (not "do"!) hold for all. Hence to reason is "to ask oneself, with regard to everything that is to be assumed, whether he finds it practicable to make the ground of the assumption . . . a universal principle of the use of his reason" (*WOT,* VIII, 146n; 305n). Both in thinking and in acting the self-discipline of reason is a matter of asking whether the ground of the assumption can be a universal principle. The supreme principle of reason both emerges from and disciplines human thought, action and communication. There is no gap between reason and autonomy because the authority of reason is grounded in autonomy.

Critique and the two standpoints

This account of the connections between critique, autonomy and reason provides a background for understanding the shift to a critique of practical reason in *Grundlegung* III. After page 450 Kant adopts a critical approach to the enterprise of specifically practical reasoning. He focuses no longer on the analytic connections between concepts but on the distinct starting points that are open to us. He begins with the reminder that empirical knowledge, both of the world and of ourselves, is knowledge of appearances and is incomplete. Appearances cannot be everything. Hence we not only may but must form the conception of an intelligible, that is, nonempirical, "world". However, he also reiterates that this intelligible world cannot be an object of knowledge (see also *CPR,* A255/B311). He apparently repudiates both the thought that such a nonempirical world is illusory and the thought that it is a distinct, supernatural reality. He eschews both empirical idealism and transcendental realism, and speaks rather of the two standpoints from which a rational being can regard himself: "*first* – so far as he belongs to the sensible world – to be under laws of nature (heteronomy); and *secondly* – so far as he belongs to the intelligible world – to be under laws which, being independent of nature, are not empirical but have their ground in reason alone" (*G,* IV, 452). Kant's claim is that human agents (and presumably any other

---

9 But surely, it may be objected, the principles of reason should be algorithms. They should include – perhaps consist of – elementary rules of inference and algorithms of practical reason, if there any any. This objection forgets that algorithms are not self-deploying. When we reconsider rules of inference we are considering an aspect of reasoning that can be abstracted; but abstracted rules of inference and decision procedures alone cannot guide a single thought or act. The authority of algorithms presupposes rather than provides the authority of reason.

finite rational agents) not only *may* but *must* adopt both standpoints, and must shift between them: "when we think of ourselves as free, we transfer ourselves into the intelligible world as members . . . when we think of ourselves as under obligation, we look upon ourselves as belonging to the sensible world and yet to the intelligible world at the same time" (*G,* IV, 453). Neither standpoint is eliminable; the standpoint of the intelligible world is indeed required to grasp that of the sensible world: "*the intelligible world contains the ground of the sensible world and therefore also of its laws* . . ." (*G,* IV, 454). Kant insists that, despite the apparent contradiction, the two standpoints are compatible: Nature and freedom are equally necessary and "not merely *can* get on perfectly well together, but must be conceived as *necessarily combined* in the same subject" (*G,* IV, 456).

These passages are highly controversial. Kant himself concedes that reason is in a tight corner. One tempting reading suggests that in talking of "intelligible" and "sensible" worlds Kant assumes the very transcendent metaphysics that he otherwise repudiates, and so lapses into rationalism. Yet if his views of self-knowledge undercut the possibility of knowledge of an ontologically distinct intelligible world, how can he offer any two-worlds story? Surely such an account can be neither true nor knowable from a Kantian perspective, and in any case offers an ontologically extravagant and psychologically implausible account of atemporal agency. There is much to be said against such readings both on textual and on wider grounds. Although the metaphors of the intelligible and the sensible world continually invite an ontological interpretation that fits their Platonic and Leibnizian heritage, Kant repeatedly distances himself from such interpretations, and insists that he hinges his argument on *two standpoints* and not *two worlds.* He puts the matter unambiguously: "The concept of the intelligible world is thus only *a point of view* which reason finds itself constrained to adopt outside appearances *in order to conceive itself as practical*" (*G,* IV, 458; cf. 462 and *CPR,* A5/ B9, A255/B310ff.). Indeed, it is not only the intelligible world that cannot be a transcendent reality. The core of transcendental idealism is the denial that the sensible world either is or reveals a transcendent reality. Our understanding of Kant's use of the term *world* must be firmly restrained if we are not to slide into transcendent realism. Nature is "the sum of all appearances" (*CPR,* B163), and "appearances do not exist in themselves" (*CPR,* B164).

Yet there are also strong reasons to interpret the term *world* as referring to an ontologically distinct realm. For how else are we to make sense of the crucial notion of a standpoint? A standpoint, surely, is a position in some space. Without the space there will be no standpoints. How can the intelligible world be *only* a point of view?

It will not be adequate to read Kant as holding that the two standpoints, far from being or depending on ontologically distinct worlds, are mere illusion, so that the duality of standpoints reflects a merely subjective necessity – a psychological compulsion. This approach would abandon all hope of making sense of the critical portions of *Grundlegung*. Here and elsewhere Kant repudiates empirical idealism as firmly as he repudiates transcendent realism.

A careful reading of the criticial sections of *Grundlegung* III suggests a way between the view that the intelligible and sensible standpoints are transcendent realities and the view that either is illusion. Kant uses the vocabularies of "sensible world" and "intelligible world" and of the naturalistic and practical standpoints more or less interchangeably. But it is the latter vocabulary that is used to anchor the former. Rather than taking the two standpoints as standpoints within two worlds, hence needing an independent account of those two worlds, we are to take the two worlds as differentiated by the inability of human reason to form a comprehensive picture of its objects. From the first sentence of the first *Critique* we are warned of the predicament of a reason that aspires to tasks that it cannot achieve: Reason's failure is that it cannot give a unified account of nature and freedom. *The metaphor of the intelligible world signals the finitude, not the transcendence, of human reason.*

Kant in fact argues for three points. He claims that both standpoints are indispensable; that the theoretical standpoint, and the knowledge of nature it permits, are unavailable without the practical; and finally that the two are compatible.

Why does Kant hold that neither way of viewing ourselves is dispensable? (Many dualities in human self-consciousness are quite dispensable.) Why, in particular, does he not think (with many others) that the naturalistic standpoint is the only important one? We are perhaps not inclined to reconsider the status of the naturalistic standpoint when we read Chapter III of the *Grundlegung*. Since the initial, analytical passage of the chapter proposes interesting conditional connections between freedom, autonomy and morality, we are (quite reasonably) eager to discover whether the antecedents of those conditionals are true. We want to know whether we human beings are free agents with the capacity for autonomy, so that morality with all its implications binds us. In reading the third chapter we readily take for granted that we must look upon ourselves as belonging to the sensible world, and assume that we must vindicate freedom in theoretical terms. A return to the perspective of the first *Critique* can be revealing at this juncture because the *naturalistic* standpoint both on ourselves and more generally is in question there. Neither the status nor the scope of causal explanation is established at the start of the first *Critique*.

The naturalistic standpoint is in question in the first *Critique* because it leads to antinomies when extended indefinitely. When we try to treat it as a comprehensive viewpoint, it proves self-undermining. We cannot form a coherent account of a spatiotemporal totality that is causally ordered. Although the empirical use of reason must strive for completeness in naturalistic understanding, the completeness is only a regulative ideal, and not attainable (*CPR*, A565/B593). A naturalistic account of the world lacks closure. Causal explanations of the natural world work only on condition that naturalism and causal explanations are not the whole story. The only way to adopt the naturalistic standpoint without being led into antinomies is to acknowledge the restricted scope of naturalistic explanation, which provides the framework for understanding the world as it appears to us, but cannot explain that the world should so appear. Hence naturalistic explanations cannot cover things as they are in themselves; if they could, the antinomies would be fatal to the coherence of naturalistic explanation. Consideration of the antinomies and the consequently restricted scope of naturalistic understanding suggests why Kant should have held that the ultimate grounds of "the sensible world" must lie beyond that "world". However, we have no intellectual grasp of things as they are in abstraction from the naturalistic standpoint. The "intelligible" grounds of nature elude our theoretical inquiries.

These considerations may show why Kant thought that those who view matters from a naturalistic standpoint must acknowledge some other standpoint. But do they vindicate human freedom and agency? Have we grounds for asserting practical as well as transcendental freedom? It may be the case that (as a matter of anthropological fact) we conceive ourselves from two standpoints and that (as a matter of necessity) the naturalistic standpoint provides an incomplete view. If so, why should we think a specifically practical standpoint indispensable? Why should we "transfer ourselves to the intelligible world" or think of *ourselves* as able to act in independence of alien causes? Why should not the duality of standpoints be a merely anthropological phenomenon, unconnected with the deeper reasons why our theoretical knowledge is incompletable? Why should we understand *ourselves* as part of the "intelligible world" that naturalistic understanding presupposes? Might not that "intelligible world" be not merely inaccessible to human cognition, but also irrelevant to human action, for which (despite our fragmented self-understanding) we can best account in naturalistic terms?

Once again it may be helpful to look at the claims of *Grundlegung* III in the light of the first *Critique,* where claims to know that nature is causally ordered are in question. The argument of the second analogy may provide a key to the claim that the practical standpoint is no illusion. Kant argues that the basis for claiming that events are causally ordered − that they have a necessary order − is that we can distinguish merely subjective from objective sequences of perceptions. This distinction cannot be based on any direct apprehension of objective time, which we lack. Rather, the distinction between objective sequences (which are causally explicable) and other sequences (which are not) must be drawn *within* experience. The elements of merely subjective sequences could have been perceived in another order: In Kant's example a sequence of house perceptions might be perceived in various orders. In objective sequences the order of perception is (in certain respects) outside the control of the perceiver: In Kant's example a sequence of perceptions of a moving ship cannot be (wholly) rearranged by the perceiver (*CPR,* A192−3/B237−8). We distinguish a sequence of perceptions as objective and open to causal explanation when we cannot vary their order. We understand what it means for the order of perceptions to lie beyond our control when we contrast cases where we have (some) control over the sequence of perceptions. If we could not make this contrast, we could not distinguish empirical reality and fantasy. In a fantasy world all sequences are dreamlike; we cannot distinguish self from world, or our own doings from what happens; *and the basis for naturalistic explanations of an objective world is lost.* When succession is objective, by contrast, "I cannot arrange the apprehension otherwise than in this very succession" (*CPR,* A193/B238); and we realize that "this compulsion is really what first makes possible the representation of a succession in an object" (*CPR,* A197/B242).

The second analogy, in short, argues that the grounds of objective sequence, hence of naturalistic explanation, lie in the possibility of distinguishing what we control from what is beyond our control. Agency is here taken to be the presupposition of causal judgment. The second analogy invokes practical freedom – not the mere spontaneity of understanding, which is revealed *within* theoretical knowledge – to account for the possibility of causal explanation.[10] It follows that if the theoretical standpoint is indispensable to us, the practical standpoint must also be so. This argument from the second analogy provides the additional move that explains why Kant maintains in *Grundlegung* III not only that the sensible *world* has its ground in the intelligible *world,* but specifically that *we* cannot think of ourselves merely as members of the sensible world. The reason that we must "transfer" *ourselves* to the intelligible world is that if we are not agents, we will never have reasons to think of ourselves as confronting a natural world that is causally determined, and so resists our control. If we take the "speculative standpoint" for granted, we will not see that if we are to have empirical or scientific knowledge, we not merely may but must be free agents. For we will fail to note that the naturalistic view is available only to those who are free and capable of autonomy.

This is why Kant concludes in the critical sections of *Grundlegung* III that although no (theoretical, naturalistic) *explanation* of freedom is possible, still "to argue freedom away is as impossible for the most abstruse philosophy as it is for the most ordinary human reason" (*G,* IV, 456). It is impossible because freedom is presupposed by theoretical understanding.

Morality, autonomy and reason

Grundlegung III ends at "the extreme limit of all moral enquiry" (*G,* IV, 462). Kant contends that if we press on with a critical consideration of our very starting

---

10 Cf. *G,* IV, 452, where Kant stresses the distinction between spontaneity of understanding and the higher spontaneity of reason. The former produces only concepts "whose sole service is *to bring sensuous ideas under rules*"; this spontaneity is shown in the indeterminacy of judgment. The latter "manifests its highest function in distinguishing the sensible and intelligible worlds . . . and so in marking out limits for understanding itself". The argument of the second analogy spells out some limits of understanding; it shows that practical freedom is presupposed by cognition within which spontaneity of understanding is possible.

points, we find that freedom (and so, by the analytic argument of the beginning of Chapter III), autonomy and morality, which are fundamental to the practical standpoint, are also presupposed by theoretical understanding. This does not constitute an unconditional argument that the practical standpoint is indispensable; but it is a powerful consideration for those who accept the theoretical standpoint.

Critique of reason leads us face to face with the conditional character of all reason: We can demonstrate neither a transcendently real world nor the actuality of human freedom: "it is an . . . essential *limitation* of the same reason that it cannot have insight into the *necessity* either of what is or what happens, or of what ought to happen, except on the basis of a *condition* under which it is or happens or ought to happen" (*G*, IV, 463). Put in other terms: All reasoning must have some standpoint, and what it establishes is conditional on that standpoint. Kant has not shown unconditionally that we cannot be skeptics about freedom and morality. But he has raised the stakes: If we are skeptics about the practical standpoint, we will also have to be skeptics about knowledge and science.

Yet despite the conditional character of human reason we can see why reason, unlike desires, is not an alien cause. Desires come and go, are contingent, varied and naturally caused. Only while a desire (or other alien cause) lasts does it affect deliberations. To speak of desires as alien is just to stress this contingency. Reason, by contrast, depends on nothing separable from an agent. It is merely autonomy in thinking and acting, considered in the abstract. Without autonomy there can be neither practical nor theoretical reasoning. There is no gap between reason and autonomy, because nothing counts as reason except the principles of self-discipline or autonomy that cannot be wholly dispensed with in any thinking or acting. Of course, *finite* rational beings can reject autonomy sporadically. Both evil and error are to be expected. Hence reason, although grounded in autonomy, presents itself to us as an imperative. It does so because we are finite, not because its authority is external or alien.

The Kantian grounding of reason, as of morality, cannot be foundationalist. Anything that could count as foundations would have to be transcendent, and so alien. Once we make the Copernican turn we cannot expect any such foundations to be available. Kant's strategy is rather to give a constructivist account of the authority of reason, whose supreme principle is no more than the maxim or strategy of refraining from acting or thinking on principles that cannot be adopted by all potential agents, regardless of their variable characteristics.

Postscript: a conjecture

If this is a plausible way of reading *Grundlegung* III, why did Kant apparently come to think otherwise? Why in writing the *Critique of Practical Reason* did he assign to morality and freedom the status of "facts of reason [*Facta der Vernunft*]"?

He would hardly have forgotten if he thought he had so recently done all that could be done to vindicate morality and freedom! So mustn't he have concluded that the argument had failed and that neither could be vindicated without appeal to an unvindicated, transcendent fact? Perhaps. However, if reason's authority is constructed, in the way I have suggested, then reason is precisely and unavoidably *factum,* and not unvindicated and unvindicable *datum.* Those who see the "fact of reason" passages as reversion to transcendent realism assume that the "fact" is given or posited; but if it is made or constructed, the distance between *Grundlegung* and the *Critique of Practical Reason* may not be so great. A great deal of textual spadework would be needed to show whether this conjecture can be made convincing.

4

Action, anthropology and autonomy

What accounts for the gap between Kant's practical philosophy and contemporary would-be Kantian writing on ethics? No doubt it is partly that modern protagonists of "Kantian" ethics are mainly, some of them exclusively, interested in rights, which for Kant are one element in a broader picture. Perhaps the gap also reflects reluctance to take on the full sweep of Kant's thought, and the hope that this can be avoided by detaching the parts that appeal. However, the main source of divergence lies, I believe, in reliance upon radically differing conceptions of action and autonomy. Both Kant and his would-be followers admire freedom, rationality and autonomy; but their understandings of these terms are hugely different.

Much contemporary work in ethics and political philosophy, including "Kantian" writing, relies on a family of broadly empiricist theories of action in which reasons and desires, or preferences, are the key elements. Theories of action of this type are designed to meet two needs. On the one hand they are meant to *explain* acts as the product of certain desires and beliefs. On the other hand they are meant to provide models of rational choice that can *guide* action in the efficient pursuit of (intrinsically arbitrary) desires or preferences. An instrumental conception of practical reasoning is seen as a corollary of the causal explanations to which theoretical reasoning aspires. A unified theory of action can serve both purposes. On such an account agents are those who rationally pursue their desires or preferences; autonomous agents are those who do so with a relatively high degree of self-control or independence. Self-control and independence are matters not of independence from the agent's own preferences, but of pursuit of those preferences with a high degree of organization, foresight or reflection. Autonomy is seen as a disposition or ability to pursue preferences, which engages preferentially with second-order or reflectively evaluated preferences, but which does not invoke any conception of reason other than internal coherence and an instrumental account of practical rationality. On such views agency can be credited to (some forms of) animal as well as to human life; but autonomy is achieved only within (stretches of) human life.[1]

1   J. S. Mill is the source of many accounts of autonomy within a broadly empiricist theory of action; the most frequently cited recent work is Harry Frankfurt, "Freedom of the Will and the Concept of a Person." On the whole, recent writing in English on autonomy is eager to offer an account of autonomy while remaining noncommittal about its metaphysical basis. Autonomy is

4. ACTION, ANTHROPOLOGY AND AUTONOMY

On Kant's view no single account of action can serve for all purposes:

> a rational being . . . has . . . two points of view from which he can regard himself . . .
> *first* – so far as he belongs to the sensible world – to be under laws of nature (heteronomy);
> and *secondly* – so far as he belongs to the intelligible world – to be under laws which, being
> independent of nature, are not empirical but have their ground in reason alone. (*G,* IV,
> 452)

We should then expect to find two accounts of action. The first, theoretical account would consider acts as natural events and would aim to explain their occurrence; it would view action as intrinsically heteronomous. The second, practical account would consider acts as expressing certain determinations of the will, and moral action as expressing certain sorts of determination of the will. It would view action as (more or less fully) autonomous insofar as it reflects certain sorts of determinations of the will.

On many accounts this dualism is a catastrophe. Thomas Hill has recently summarized the picture to which such accounts of Kant's position apparently converge as follows:

> We are strange hybrids sometimes governed by freely acknowledged rational principles and
> sometimes in the grip of natural forces beyond rational control; and what switches us from
> the one mode to the other is inexplicable. It could not be a free choice because to be capable
> of free choice is to be in one mode rather than the other.[2]

On such readings (which Hill rejects) a "two-worlds" picture fails to connect the sensible and intelligible worlds, or to explain how agents "shift" between them. It apparently can allow only for acts that are beyond rational control and so not imputable, and for acts that are governed by reason and so (on Kant's account) not merely imputable but fully moral. It then seems that Kant's theory of action rules out the possibility of immoral yet imputable action. Many commentators[3] point out that Kant later addressed this problem. In his later writings he distinguished explicitly between the exercise of free choice (*Willkür*) and its exercise in accordance with practical reason (*Wille*). Only action based on *Wille* is fully moral, and only it is autonomous in Kant's distinctive sense of the term. Looked at carefully, even the text of *Grundlegung* draws this distinction and so allows for the possibility of action that is freely chosen yet immoral. However, even if we can discern a way for Kant to pigeonhole immoral yet freely chosen action, larger issues remain. These large issues are the concern of this chapter.

to play a central role in discussions of political theory, education, medical ethics and many other fields. It is seen as an ideal of character rather than as a property of particular acts. For recent works see Robert Young, *Personal Autonomy: Beyond Negative and Positive Liberty;* and Richard Lindley, *Autonomy.*

2 See Thomas E. Hill, Jr., "Kant's Argument for the Rationality of Moral Conduct", p. 7.

3 In addition to Hill see John R. Silber, "The Ethical Significance of Kant's *Religion*"; Bernard Carnois, *The Coherence of Kant's Doctrine of Freedom;* Allen W. Wood, "Kant's Compatibilism"; and Michael Rosen, "Kant's Anti-determinism".

Action from the standpoint of the sensible world

The previous chapter provides a framework for distinguishing Kant's two accounts of action. The two standpoints are to be thought of not as ontologically distinct realms between which human agents must switch, but as distinct, indispensable, yet mutually irreducible frameworks of thought. The causal understanding at which theoretical reasoning aims is premised upon the supposition that the knowers who seek it can act freely; the actions that agents perform assume a causally ordered and knowable world that provides the arena for action. Most of what Kant has to say about action is said from the standpoint of agency and freedom; but the other standpoint is never denied.

In the discussion of the antinomies of pure reason in the first *Critique* Kant insists repeatedly that from the empirical standpoint human action must be considered part of the natural world, and subject to natural causation.

In its empirical character, therefore, this subject, as appearance, would have to conform to all the laws of causal determination. To this extent it could be nothing more than a part of the world of sense, and its effects, like all other appearances, must be the inevitable outcome of nature . . . all its actions must admit of explanation in accordance with the laws of nature. (*CPR*, A540/B568)

In principle human action is explicable and predictable like other natural events:

if we could exhaustively investigate all the appearances of men's wills, there would not be found a single human action which we could not predict with certainty, and recognise as proceeding necessarily from its antecedent conditions. (*CPR*, A550/B578)

We can "institute a physiological investigation into the motive causes of his action" (*CPR*, A550/B578). In practice no natural science of human action is attainable. Kant even doubts whether elementary biological processes – grass growing – can be explained mechanistically (*CJ*, V, 400).

However, for purposes of understanding his account of action this is not the important limitation. The important limitation is that all naturalistic explanations – even the most impressive explanations of some future neuroscience – are conditional explanations of the "appearances of men's wills". In a certain sense they are incomplete, for they can never explain that any natural law should take the form that it does. Even the most exhausting investigation cannot be exhaustive. Any explanations offered in terms of events and their effects is incomplete because it presupposes an account of the form of certain principles. Putting this in an old-fashioned way we might say that explanations under the heading of efficient causality presuppose explanations under the heading of formal causality. In Kant's terminology empirical relations presuppose intelligible relations, or, in the words he uses in the last chapter of *Grundlegung*.

The intelligible world contains the ground of the sensible world and therefore also of its laws. (G, IV, 453)

Action from the standpoint of the intelligible world

The intelligible world is not a transcendent realm beyond this world, but the system of formal conditions that our understanding of the empirical world presupposes; it is precisely *intelligible,* not *supersensible:*

Whatever in an object of the senses is not itself appearance I entitle *intelligible.* (CPR, A538/B566)

Unlike our understanding of natural objects, which is restricted to their empirical aspects, our conception of ourselves must have a dual character. We must not only see ourselves as parts of nature with a certain incompletely known empirical character; we must also see this empirical character as presupposing another, unknowable but *intelligible character.* This is the central claim (CPR, A539/B567ff) of the most difficult of all Kant's thoughts about the atemporal character of human agency; I shall take a circumspect view of the deep issues that these passages raise.

What is it that makes an aspect of character intelligible? Why should not the presuppositions of empirical character be simply obscure and unintelligible, the limit not only of human knowledge but also of intelligibility? What demands that we see ourselves as having intelligible as well as empirical character? The argument of the last chapter suggests the following answer: The enterprise of naturalistic explanation itself presupposes freedom; freedom cannot be merely negative nondetermination by "alien" causes, but must include the capacity for self-determination or autonomy; the exercise of autonomy, in thinking and in acting, is what we call reason. The outward mark of reason is that the thoughts and actions it guides are intelligible. When we view ourselves from the standpoint of the intelligible world, we view our actions not as events caused by prior events in accordance with some vastly complex and scantily known set of natural laws; we view our acts, performed and prospective, as bearing the marks of reason, as having determinate and intelligible form, rather than as the effects of determining causal antecedents. Intelligibility is not a matter of being *explicable* in the terms of theoretical reason; it is a matter of conforming (to some extent) to the standards of reason. To try to explain intelligibility would be a sort of category mistake:

To explain why in the given circumstances the intelligible character should give just these appearances and this empirical character transcends all the powers of our reason, indeed all its rights of questioning, just as if we were to ask why the transcendental object of our outer sensible intuition gives intuition in *space* only and not some other mode of intuition. (*CPR*, A557/B585)

Kant never claims to demonstrate or explain freedom, or identify any efficient causes of intelligible character (*G*, IV, 458ff.). He reminds us that his intention "has not been to establish the *reality* of freedom" (*CPR*, A558/B586), and that were we to "yield to the illusion of transcendental realism, neither nature nor freedom would remain" (*CPR*, A543/B571). Kant's resolution of the conflict between freedom and determinism is to see the entire domain of natural events as determined by efficient causes, but the formal presuppositions of free acts (including activities of causal explanation!) as (in another sense) determined by intelligible causes.

Finite reason and intelligible action

Kant does not and cannot offer a single model of human action that can both serve for empirical explanation and guide choice. What account of action can he offer for the latter purpose? Clearly, if the grounds of empirical character and action are to be *intelligible,* this account of action must focus on intelligibility. It must focus not on acts as natural events, but on the propositional content that acts express.

Kant will therefore clearly repudiate a Hobbesian, physicalist picture of act-individuation that insists that "life is but a motion of limbs". In fact, many who advocate an empiricist account of action do not assume physicalism (there are exceptions, of course, behaviorist psychologists being the obvious case). At least for practical purposes they are likely to think that actions are packaged in intelligible "options". The intelligibility of "options" is a tacit presupposition of many models of rational choice. Others will insist that such a limited view of intelligibility still brackets too much. Intelligible options, they may suggest, are intelligible only against a background of a certain form of life or tradition.[4] Our ways of construing actions presuppose a *Sittlichkeit,* which constitutes a determinate and (locally) intelligible language. However, many of those who insist that intelligible action presupposes an intelligible tradition will go no further. They will deny that intelligibility can cross borders.

Kant goes further. On his account intelligibility demands more than that actions fall under descriptions that are current and understood in a given social milieu.

---

4   See Alasdair MacIntyre, *After Virtue: A Study in Moral Theory.* This view is generally held by historicist and by Wittgensteinian writers.

Kant's account of the intelligibility of action begins with the claim that acts must have maxims, or underlying practical principles (see Part II). It is these maxims that determine the will (*Willkür*), but not, of course, in the way that efficient causes determine anything. Like other aspects of intelligible character, these maxims are not objects of knowledge. All that we can *know* are their empirical aspects, "the appearances of men's wills"; however, for practical purposes any intelligibility of action is secured by the choice of maxims.

The appropriate question to put to Kant then would be why he thinks that the intelligibility of action requires more than its intelligibility relative to a certain language or tradition. Could it not be the case that human action is intelligent and intelligible, but does not have to be intelligible to those who do not share "our" ways of thought and life? In particular, if we are (as Kant insists) *finite* rational beings, then will not the intelligibility of our action also be limited? Or, put in a familiar and more recent idiom, will not human action be ultimately absurd, since its intelligibility must (in the end) be relative to groundless standards?

To answer these questions we need to understand what Kant means when he speaks of "finite rational beings". As is well known, and as often seems unhelpful, Kant's practical philosophy is presented as relevant not just to human beings, but to "finite rational nature as such":

the metaphysic of morals is really pure moral philosophy, with no underlying basis of anthropology or other empirical conditions. (*CPR*, A842/B870; cf. *G*, IV, 389; cf. 410, 425, 427)

This pure moral philosophy cannot be derived from, but only applied to, the human case:

it does not borrow in the slightest from acquaintance with him (in anthropology), but gives him laws *a priori* as a rational being. (*G*, IV, 389; cf. *MM*, VI, 216)

However, although moral philosophy can abstract from anthropology, it cannot abstract from finitude. For the concept of duty is central to morality, and is defined in terms of

a good will exposed, however, to certain subjective limitations and obstacles. (*G*, IV, 397)

The will of a nonfinite rational being would not be "exposed to subjective limitations and obstacles"; for such a will nothing could count as an imperative or as an obligation, and morality would be redundant.

Kant always sets the case of human agency in the framework of a wider spectrum of possible types of agency. This spectrum includes *at least* the following: animals or other nonrational agents; finite rational wills in general, among whom human willing is the familiar case; and at the far end of the spectrum the even more special, and puzzling, case of the holy will.[5]

At the lower end there are nonrational beings, who are not free agents in that they cannot act independently of alien causes. The action of such *arbitria bruta* can be explained theoretically (by those who are free agents) as caused by certain desires, drives, inclinations and the like. Their actions are not imputable, and practical reasoning is irrelevant to them. We impute neither empirical nor intelligible character to such nonrational beings.[6] Here the familiar empiricist model of rational choice is appropriate, and Kant invokes it. The antecedents of animal action are events; their explanation is a matter of finding causal laws that link those prior events to the acts that are performed. And here practical reasoning is simply out of the question. Brutes cannot and do not have to conceive themselves from two standpoints.

Finite rational beings are classified as free agents. They are like the animals in experiencing desires, impulses, inclinations, but unlike animals in that their action is chosen. Kant speaks of finite rational agents as having an *arbitrium liberum sed sensitivum,* or *freie Willkür* (*MM*, VI, 213). Because they have *arbitria libera,* such beings can act independently of alien causes. The desires and inclinations and other "pathological" processes they undergo are experienced, but do not cause them to act. If such beings gratify their occurrent desires, it is because they choose to do so. Kant does *not* classify finite rational wills as *arbitria libera sed bruta,* which would (incoherently) attribute both determination by natural desires and freedom from such determinations to human willing.

Finitude and instrumental rationality

In what specific ways are finite rational beings finite? A very tempting view, which fits well with contemporary models of rational choice, is to think that they are finite in rationality in that they are fallible and can reason instrumentally, but lack more comprehensive rational capacities. We can combine this view with insistence that acts must be (at least locally) intelligible, by holding that standards of instrumental rationality, but nothing more, must be part of *any* intelligible tradition. When means taken and ends sought drift apart, action and lives

5 Are Kant's holy wills embodied? If so, they too are part of nature, subject to alien causes and to temptation. So, contrary to Kant's claims, morality is not redundant for them. Or are they disembodied? If so, they are not part of nature and it is not clear how they could distinguish changes that merely come about from those that they bring about. Mere conformity to a disembodied will cannot show that a change is their doing – as opposed to the intervention of an ever-benevolent power. If the thought experiment of the holy will cannot be rescued from this impasse, it may show that once Kant has adopted the anthropological perspective of the Copernican turn, he can no longer think finitude away – even for an aside.

6 Does Kant compress too much here? Is there as sharp a demarcation between the free, intelligible and rational, albeit finite, beings (such as ourselves) and the animals as he suggests? We often impute maxims to animals – noting that we anthropomorphize as we do so.

become unintelligible. On this view instrumental rationality would be the core of finite rationality and integral to any intelligible tradition.

This is not Kant's position. Not only does he deny that reason is or ought to be the slave of the passions; he actually insists that there are and can be no merely instrumental reasoners. One point where this argument appears is in the first chapter of *Grundlegung*, where he insists that for any organic being, where "the real purpose of nature" is "his *preservation*, his *welfare*, or in a word his *happiness*" (*G*, IV, 395), reason of any sort would be not only redundant, but counterproductive:

the whole rule of his behaviour would have been mapped out for him far more accurately by instinct . . . nature would have prevented reason from striking out into a *practical use* and from presuming, with its feeble vision, to think out for itself a plan for happiness and for the means to its attainment. Nature would herself have taken over the choice, not only of ends, but also of means, and would with wise precaution have entrusted both to instinct alone. (*G*, IV, 395)

The argument used here has restricted significance, for it assumes a certain teleological biology that can be invoked appropriately within the framework of our "common rational knowledge of morality", which the first chapter of *Grundlegung* assumes, but which Kant does not establish. It conclusion, however, is of the greatest interest, although seldom stressed. Kant's claim is that any practical reasoner – even a finite rational being – can do more than calculate means to ends. The favored empiricist conception of practical rationality is not merely not the only one: *It is never found in isolation.* The only beings who can reason instrumentally are free agents. The rational choosers of empiricist accounts of practical reason are not special cases: They are missing cases. Either human beings must lack even instrumental capacities to reason – they must be *arbitria bruta* – or they must have more than instrumental capacities to reason. In *Grundlegung* Kant leaves this question open until the last chapter, where he argues that we are indeed reasoners with more than instrumental capacities. Because the first hypothesis, that we are merely *arbitria bruta*, can provide no basis for the theoretical uses of our reasoning powers, it is the second that must be taken seriously:

in spite of regarding myself from one point of view as a being that belongs to the sensible world, I shall have to recognize that, *qua* intelligence, I am subject to the law of the intelligible world. (*G*, IV, 453)

Indeed,

theoretical reason had to assume at least the possibility of freedom in order to fill one of its own needs. (*CPrR*, V, 4)

Kant does not take for granted that we have at least a limited mode of rationality – the capacity to reason instrumentally – and then argue that in addition "pure reason can of itself be practical". He insists that either we have no capacities to reason, or else reason's function must be "to produce a *will* which is *good,* not as a *means* to some further end, but *in itself"* (*G,* IV, 396).

Finitude and anthropology

These claims throw a great deal of doubt on any interpretation of Kant's account of finite rationality that centers on instrumental rationality, but do not show what other interpretation should be put in its stead. Clues can be gleaned from Kant's numerous asides about other possible types of finite rational agent, and from our limited knowledge of the specific character of human finitude. He notes in the *Anthropology:*

It seems, then, that the problem of indicating the character of the human species is quite insoluble; for to set about solving it, we should have to compare two *species* of rational beings through *experience,* and experience does not present us with a second such species. (*A,* VII, 321)

This lack explains a good deal about the discrepancy between the stated ambition of *Grundlegung* to present an account of principles of obligations for finite rational beings as such and its actual use of notorious examples that not merely draw on specifically human duties, but apparently presuppose a narrow and determinate social order, with institutions like money, shops, debtors, theaters and the other amenities of life in Königsberg. The problem of the moral philosopher is that all the illustrations of obligations have to be drawn from the case of the finite rational being with which we are acquainted. Like a biologist studying a phylum of which a lone species survives, the moral philosopher is always drawing on a special case for illustrations. Kant clearly acknowledges that principles of duty might have very different import for other species of finite rational being. For example, he imagines rational beings who, unlike us, "can have no thoughts they do not utter" and suggests that for them moral relations would be quite different (presumably they would have almost no prospect of deliberately deceiving one another) (*A,* VII, 332).

These discussions, and the many other passages in which Kant is preoccupied with the thought that human beings may not be the only sorts of finite rational being, provide some evidence of his understanding of finite rationality (e.g., *IUH,* VIII, 23n; 47n; and most strikingly *CPR,* A825/B853). We are to construe "finite rational beings" not as "beings whose rationality is finite", but as "finite beings who are rational". The thought that a finite rational being is one who can reason only instrumentally is misplaced, both because Kant casts doubt on the possibility of that mode of finitude, and because he gives us clear evidence that he has in mind that it is, so to speak, the being rather than simply the rationality of "finite rational beings" that is limited.

Autonomy and finitude

These moves clear the ground for disentangling Kant's conception of autonomy from contemporary ones. Autonomy viewed within the framework of many, including empiricist, theories of action is not to be identified with rationality. On such accounts, to be autonomous is a matter of being (relatively) independent of something on which action is often dependent: Children may become autonomous of their parents; mature persons are autonomous when not too dependent on others' help or good opinions; colonies become autonomous when they no longer depend on the imperial power. Instrumental rationality is necessary for autonomy, so conceived, but it is not sufficient. Such independence is often coveted and admired, and yet it is not obvious why it is admirable. The high esteem in which such forms of autonomy are held is also often put into question – for example, recently by communitarian and feminist critics of "abstract" accounts of morality and justice, who point out that there is much to be said for interdependence, affiliation and the social virtues.[7] Autonomy as now commonly construed is a matter of achieving a particular self-sufficiency and independence; it may have little or no intrinsic connection with conceptions of the good, the right or the rational. No doubt autonomy, so construed, *may* have instrumental importance as an efficient means to human happiness, as John Stuart Mill urges so eloquently in *On Liberty*. But this is a contingent matter. In many situations this sort of autonomy will cost rather than constitute our happiness, and its connection with morality is often obscure.

Many discussions of Kant assume that he too is committed to this perilous conception of autonomy. Nobody has put it more vividly than Iris Murdoch:

We are still living in the age of the Kantian man, or Kantian man-god. Kant's conclusive exposure of the so-called proofs of the existence of God, his analysis of the limitations of speculative reason, together with his eloquent portrayal of the dignity of rational man, has had results which might possibly dismay him. How recognizable, how familiar to us, is the man so beautifully portrayed in the *Grundlegung,* who confronted even with Christ turns away to consider the voice of his own conscience and to hear the voice of his own reason. Stripped of the exiguous metaphysical background which Kant was prepared to allow him, this man is with us still, free, independent, lonely, powerful, rational, responsible, brave, the hero of so many novels and books of moral philosophy. The *raison d'être* of this attractive but misleading creature is not far to seek . . . since he is not a Hegelian (Kant, not Hegel, has provided Western ethics with its dominating image) his alienation is without cure. He is the ideal citizen of the liberal state, a warning held up to tyrants. He has the virtue which the age requires and admires, courage. It is not such a very long step

---

7　As well as MacIntyre, *After Virtue,* see Michael Sandel, *Liberalism and the Limits of Justice;* Michael Walzer, *Spheres of Justice: A Defence of Pluralism and Equality;* Carol Gilligan, *In a Different Voice: Psychological Theory and Women's Dependence;* Eva Feders Kittay and Diane Meyers, eds., *Women and Moral Theory;* Carol McMillan, *Women, Reason and Nature;* and Nell Noddings, *Caring: A Feminine Approach to Ethics and Moral Education.*

from Kant to Nietzsche, and from Nietzsche to existentialism and the Anglo-Saxon ethical doctrines which in some ways closely resemble it. In fact Kant's man had already received a glorious incarnation nearly a century earlier in the work of Milton: his proper name is Lucifer.[8]

This is a grand accusation, and misplaced. Kant's conception of autonomy is quite different. Autonomy is not the special achievement of the most independent, but a property of any reasoning being. The capacity for autonomy goes with the capacity to act on principles even when inclination is absent, with being able to adopt maxims of action that do not sit well with our desires. Kantian autonomy is not existentialist radical freedom; it is not even a diluted version of existentialist freedom. On Kant's understanding such freedom, if found, would be a "lawless", merely "negative" freedom and the antithesis of autonomy.

Murdoch's version of Kantian man is a finite rational being who (supposedly) selects maxims of action. Freedom so conceived is an exercise of *Willkür*, but there is no room for *Wille;* it is negative freedom from alien causes without anything that can count as positive freedom, or autonomy as Kant understood it. On such a view of freedom, the intelligibility of action ultimately fails: The freely chosen acts of such beings are in the end absurd, lawless, unintelligible. This position can hardly be more different from one that locates freedom and autonomy in the capacity to think of oneself as a member of the "intelligible world".

On Kant's view in *Grundlegung* III, there is no possibility of *Willkür* – of freedom from alien causes – for those who do not also have the capacity for *Wille* – for autonomy. To be free from alien causes is not to surrender to arbitrariness and unintelligibility, but to seek to ground action in something that is not alien. This standard cannot be fully achieved merely by immersion in a culture and its traditions. One whose supposedly intelligible character had no other basis would lack autonomy. If the repudiation of alien authorities is not to end in arbitrary and unintelligible action, it must be self-disciplined. On Kant's account autonomy, in thought or in action, is a matter of submitting only to those standards that are required if there is not to be submission to alien standards. Hence the fundamental maxim of autonomy, as of morality, is to act only on maxims through which one can at the same time will that they be universal laws. This meager principle is merely a commitment not to base action on anything contingent or arbitrary that would limit its intelligibility.

Despite the complexity of this account, autonomy so conceived is a prosaic vision, as well as a demanding one. If human choice (*Willkür, arbitrium liberum*) is not determined (efficiently) by sensuous impulses (*MM,* VI, 212), it must be determined (intelligibly) by principles of action. If these principles are to render action intelligible, they must do more than align it with the categories of some given social order. The power of choice must include a power of self-determination

8   Iris Murdoch, *The Sovereignty of Good,* p. 80.

that rejects *both* subordination to anything contingent, variable, external, *and* nondetermination. Full self-determination can then only be acting on a law that refers to nothing contingent and variable, that is, on a principle that can be acted on by any finite rational being, whatever that being's specific empirical characteristics. Self-determination is a matter not of radical freedom but of capacity to act on the Categorical Imperative. This is the "power of pure reason to be of itself practical" (*MM*, VI, 213). It is a power that is limited both in human beings and in other finite rational beings:

since the maxims of men, based on subjective grounds, do not of themselves agree with that objective ground, pure practical reason can lay down this law only as an imperative . . . (*MM*, VI, 213)

Hence the other face of Kantian autonomy is morality, and not the independence from morality that Murdoch sees in Kant. Neither autonomy nor morality is fully achieved in the lives of finite beings. Nor do we know when and how well they are achieved. The outward, empirical face of human character is only an indication of underlying intelligible character. Hence much human action will be intelligible only relative to certain premises about desires and inclinations, forms of life and traditions. Kant thinks that that we do not know whether *fully* moral and autonomous rational acts have ever been performed. Knowledge, however, is not the aim of practical reasoning. In seeking to make our actions intelligible we do not need proof of success: We need only seek to align our action with that which would be done by one whose maxim was fully autonomous. When empirical character is such that it could be the appearance of a fully autonomous intelligible character, there is no more that finite rational beings can do to achieve autonomy.

Although many contemporary admirers of autonomy claim Kantian ancestry, their inheritance shows other, perhaps incompatible, strains. The arguments by which Kant links autonomy to reason and to morality cannot be reconstituted within a broadly empiricist account of action and freedom. Those who want to show that autonomy is integral to morality and rationally justified may find that in the end they cannot duck the larger systematic and metaphysical issues.

PART II

Maxims and obligations

5

Consistency in action

Universality tests in autonomous and in heteronomous ethics

Many recent discussions of universality tests, particularly those in English, are concerned either with what everybody wants done or with what somebody (usually the agent; sometimes an anonymous moral spectator) wants done either by or to everybody. This is true of the universality tests proposed in Singer's Generalization Argument, in Hare's Universal Prescriptivism and generally of various formulations of Golden Rules as well as of Rule Utilitarianism. Since universality tests of these sorts all make moral acceptability in some way contingent upon what is *wanted* (or, more circumspectly expressed, upon what is preferred or found acceptable or promises the maximal utility), they all form part of moral theories that are *heteronomous,* in Kant's sense of that term. Such theories construe moral acceptability as continent upon the natural phenomena of desire and inclination, rather than upon any intrinsic or formal features of agents or their intentions. If we rely on any of these proposed criteria of moral acceptability, there will be no types of act that would not be rendered morally acceptable by some change or changes in human desires.

By contrast Kant's proposed universality test, the Categorical Imperative, contains no reference either to what everybody wants done or to what somebody wants done either by or to everybody. Kant's first formulation of the Categorical Imperative, the so-called Formula of Universal Law, runs:

Act only on that maxim through which you can at the same time will that it should become a universal law. (*G,* IV, 421)

We are invited here to consider that we *can* will or intend, what it is *possible* or *consistent* for us to "will as a universal law" (not what we *would* will or *would* find acceptable or *would want* as a universal law). Since the principle contains no reference to what everybody or anybody wants, nor to anything that lies beyond the agent's own capacity to will, it is part of a moral theory for agents who, in Kant's sense of the term, act *autonomously.* The principle asserts that such agents need only to impose a certain sort of consistency on their actions if they are to

This chapter originally appeared in *Universality and Morality: Essays on Ethical Universalizability,* ed. N. Potter and M. Timmons, Reidel, 1985, pp. 159–86.

avoid doing what is morally unacceptable. It proposes an uncompromisingly rationalist foundation for ethics.

Nevertheless, Kant interpretation, particularly in English, is rich in heteronomous readings of the Formula of Universal Law and in allegations that (despite claims to the contrary) it is impossible to derive nontrivial, action-guiding applications of the Categorical Imperative without introducing heteronomous considerations.[1] Textual objections apart (and they would be overwhelming objections), such heteronomous readings of Kant's ethics discard what is most distinctive and challenging in his ethical theory. These are the features of his theory on which I intend to concentrate. I want to challenge the view that Kantian ethics, and nonheteronomous ethical theories in general, must be seen as either trivially empty or relying covertly on heteronomous considerations in order to derive substantive conclusions. To do so I shall try to articulate what seem to me to be the more important features of a universality test for agents who, in a certain sense of the term, can act autonomously, that is, without being determined by their natural desires and inclinations.

I shall take Kant's Formula of Universal Law as the canonical case of such a universality test, and shall argue that it neither is trivially formalistic nor requires supplementing with heteronomous considerations if it is to be action-guiding. However, my main concern here is not to explicate Kant's discussion of his universality test, nor to assess the difficulty or adequacy of his various moves. I shall say nothing about his vindication of the Categorical Imperative, nor about his powerful critique of heteronomy in ethics, nor about his conception of human freedom. By setting aside these and other more strictly textual preoccupations I hope to open the way for a discussion of some features of universality tests for autonomous agents that have an interest that goes far beyond a concern with reading Kant accurately. I hope to show that Kant's formula, taken in conjunction with a plausible set of requirements for rational action, yields strong and interesting ethical conclusions that do not depend on what either everybody or anybody wants, and hence that reason can indeed be practical.

Over the last twenty years theorists have shed considerable light on the underlying structure of heteronomous ethical theories (as well as on other, particularly economic and political, decisions) by drawing on studies of the formal aspects of decision making under various conditions that have been articulated in various models of rational choice. In such discussions it is generally taken for granted that

1 Heteronomous readings of Kant's ethics include Schopenhauer's in *On the Basis of Morality,* but are most common in introductory works in ethics. Recent examples include William K. Frankena, *Ethics,* p. 25; Gilbert Harman, *The Nature of Morality,* p. 73; and D. D. Raphael, *Moral Philosophy,* p. 76. Allegations that Kant, despite his intentions, must invoke heteronomous considerations if he is to reach substantive conclusions can notoriously be found in J. S. Mill's *Utilitarianism,* p. 4, but are also now more common in more general discussions of Kant's ethics. Examples include C. D. Broad, *Five Types of Ethical Theory,* p. 130; and Marcus Singer, *Generalization in Ethics,* p. 262.

rational choosing is in some way or other contingent upon a set of desires or preferences.[2] I shall suggest that a similar concentration on certain requirements of rationality that are not contingent upon desires or preferences can help to provide a clearer picture of the underlying structure and strength of an ethical theory for autonomous beings.

The sequence of argument is straightforward. The following section provides an explication of Kant's Formula of Universal Law and of some of the ways in which it affects the character of an ethic for autonomous beings. The section entitled "Inconsistency without universalizing" discusses some ways in which action can fall into inconsistency even when the question of universalizing is not raised. The three sections that follow show how requirements for rational intending can be conjoined with Kant's universality test to yield determinate ethical conclusions.

Maxims and moral categories

The test that Kant's Formula of Universal Law proposes for the moral acceptability of acts has two aspects. In the first place it enjoins us to *act on a maxim;* secondly it restricts us to action on those maxims *through which we can will at the same time that they should be universal laws.* It is only the latter clause that introduces a universality test. However, for an understanding of the nature of this test it is essential in the first place to understand what Kant means by "acting on a maxim". For, contrary to appearances, this is not a trivial part of his criterion of morally acceptable action. Because a universality test for autonomous beings does not look at what is wanted, nor at the results of action, but merely demands that certain standards of consistency be observed in action, it has to work with a conception of action that has the sort of formal structure that can meet (or fail to meet) standards of consistency. Only those acts that embody or express syntactically structured principles or descriptions can be thought of as candidates either for consistency or for inconsistency. Mere reflexes or reactions, for example, cannot be thought of as consistent or inconsistent; nor can acts be considered merely instrumentally as means for producing certain outcomes. In requiring action on a maxim Kant is already insisting that whatever is morally assessable should have a certain formal structure.

A maxim, Kant tells us, is "a subjective principle of action"; it is "a principle on which the subject *acts*" (*G,* IV, 421n; cf. 401n). A maxim is therefore the principle of action of a particular agent at a particular time; but it need not be "subjective" in the sense that it seeks to fulfill that particular agent's desires. In speaking of maxims as subjective principles Kant is not adopting any sort of

---

2 Even such a wide-ranging and reflective discussion of rational choice theory as Jon Elster's in
Ulysses and the Sirens discusses no nonheteronomous conceptions or aspects of rational choice.

heteronomous standard, but means to propose a standard against which the principles agents propose to act on, of whatever sort, may be tested. The Categorical Imperative provides a way of testing the moral acceptability of what we propose to do. It does not aim to generate plans of action for those who have none.

Although maxims are the principles of action of particular agents at particular times, one and the same principle might be adopted as a maxim by many agents at various times or by a given agent on numerous occasions. It is a corollary of Kant's conception of human freedom that we can adopt or discard maxims, including those maxims that refer to our desires.

On the other hand, acting on a maxim does not require explicit or conscious or complete formulation of that maxim. Even routine or thoughtless or indecisive action is action on *some* maxim. However, not all of the principles of action that a particular agent might exemplify at a given time would count as the agent's maxim. For principles of action need only incorporate *some* true description of an agent and *some* true description of the act and situation, whether these descriptions are vacuous and vague or brimming with detail. But an agent's maxim in a given act must incorporate just those descriptions of the agent, the act and the situation upon which the doing of the act depends.

An agent's maxim in a given act cannot, then, be equated simply with intentions. For an agent's intentions in performing a given act may refer to incidental aspects of the particular act and situation. For example, in making a new visitor feel welcome I may offer and make him or her some coffee. As I do so there will be innumerable aspects of my action that are intentional – the choice of mug, the addition of milk, the stirring – and there will also be numerous aspects of action that are "below the level of intention" – the gesture with which I hand the cup, the precise number of stirs and so on. But the various specific intentions with which I orchestrate the offer and preparation of coffee are all ancillary to an underlying principle. *Maxims are those underlying principles or intentions*[3] *by which we guide and control our more specific intentions.* In this particular example, had I lacked coffee I could have made my visitor welcome in other ways: The specific intention of offering and making coffee was subordinate to the maxim of making a visitor welcome. Had I had a quite different maxim – perhaps to make my visitor unwelcome – I would not in that context have acted on just those specific intentions. In another context, for example, in a society where an offer of coffee would be understood as we would understand an offer of hemlock, the same or similar specific intentions might have implemented a maxim of making unwelcome.

The fact that maxims are underlying or fundamental principles has important

---

3 I would not now use the term *intention* here, or as I used it throughout this essay. Replacing it with (*underlying*) *practical principle* allows the same points to be made in more general form, and makes it easier to stress the extent to which maxims, unlike certain intentions, can be hidden from those whose maxims they are. Chapters 6–8 in this volume lean less heavily on the term.

implications.[4] It means in the first place that it may not be easy to tell on which maxim a given act was performed. For example, a person who helps somebody else in a public place may have the underlying intention of being helpful – or alternatively the underlying intention of fostering a certain sort of good reputation. Since the helpful act might equally well be performed in furtherance of either underlying intention, there may be some doubt as to the agent's maxim. Merely asking an agent what his or her maxim is in such a situation may not settle the issue. The agent might be unsure. Both agents and others can work out that if the action would have been performed even if nobody had come to know of it, then the underlying principle would not have been to seek a certain sort of reputation. But an agent may after all be genuinely uncertain what his or her act would have been had he or she been faced with the possibility of helping, isolated from any effects on reputation. Isolation tests can settle such issues (G, IV, 398–9; 407) – if we know their outcome; but since most such tests refer to counterfactual situations we often don't know that outcome with any great certainty. Further, isolation tests provide only a *negative* test of what an agent's maxim is not. Even those who have not adopted a maxim of seeking a good reputation may still be unsure whether they have adopted the maxim of helpfulness. They may perhaps wonder whether the underlying intention was not to preserve a certain sort of self-image or to bolster their sense of worth. Kant remarks on the opacity of the human heart and the difficulty of self-knowledge; he laments that for all we know there may never have been a truly loyal friend (G, IV, 407–8; DV, VI, 440; 445–6). And he does not view these as dispellable difficulties. Rather, these limits to human self-knowledge constitute the fundamental context of human action. Kant holds that we can know what it would be to try to act on a maxim of a certain sort, but can never be sure that what we do does not reflect further maxims that we disavow. However, the underlying intentions that guide our more specific intentions are not in principle undiscoverable. Even when not consciously formulated they can often be inferred with some assurance, if not certainty, as the principles and policies that our more specific intentions express and implement.

On a certain view of the purpose of a universality test, the fact that the maxim of a given action is neither observable nor always reliably inferable would be a most serious objection. For it would appear to render the outcome of any application of a universality test of dubious moral importance – since we might mistakenly have applied the test to a principle other than the agent's maxim. Further, even if the maxim had been correctly formulated, whether by the agent or by others, the maxim itself might reflect mistaken beliefs or self-deception in the agent, or the agent's act might fail to live up to its maxim. How then could

4 However, the claim that maxims are underlying or fundamental intentions or principles should not be collapsed into the claim, which Kant makes in *Religion within the Limits of Reason Alone*, that for any agent (rather than "for any act") at a given time there is one fundamental maxim, to which all other principles that we might think maxims are ancillary.

any test applied to the agent's maxim be expected to classify acts into moral categories such as the right and the forbidden? For these categories apply to the outward and observable aspects of action. It is after all common enough for us to think of acts that are at least outwardly right (perhaps even obligatory) as nevertheless reflecting dubious intentions (I aim to kill an innocent, but mistakenly incapacitate the tiger who is about to maul him), and of acts whose intentions are impeccable as issuing tragically in wrong action (I aim for the tiger but dispatch the innocent).

The answer Kant gives to this problem is plain. It is that rightness and wrongness and the other "categories of right" standardly used in appraisal of outward features of action are *not* the fundamental forms of moral acceptability and unacceptability that he takes the Categorical Imperative to be able to discriminate.[5] Since the locus of application of Kant's universality test (and perhaps of any nonheteronomous universality test) is agents' fundamental principles or intentions, the moral distinction that it can draw is in the first place an intentional moral distinction, namely that between acts that have and those that lack moral worth. In an application of the Categorical Imperative to an agent's maxim we ask whether the underlying intention with which the agent acts or proposes to act – the intention that guides and controls other more specific intentions – is consistently universalizable; if it is, according to Kant, we at least know that the action will not be morally unworthy, and will not be a violation of duty.

The fact that Kant is primarily concerned with judgments of moral worth is easily forgotten, perhaps because he speaks of the Categorical Imperative as a test of *duty,* while we often tend to think of duty as confined to the *outward* aspects of action. It is quite usual for us to think of principled action as combining both duty and moral worthiness, which we regard as separate matters (e.g., showing scrupulous respect for others), or alternatively as revealing a moral worthiness that goes beyond all duty (e.g., gratuitous kindness that we think of as supererogatory). Correspondingly, it is quite usual for us to think of unprincipled action as in any case morally unworthy but still, in some cases, within the bounds of duty (e.g., the case of a could-be poisoner who mistakenly administers a life-saving drug). This is quite foreign to Kant's way of thinking, which sees the *central* case of duty as that of action that has moral worth, and regards as *derivative* that which accords merely in external respects with morally worthy action. On Kant's view the would-be poisoner who inadvertently saves life has violated a duty by acting in a morally unworthy way.

By taking an agent's fundamental or underlying principle or intention as the point of application of his universality test Kant avoids one of the difficulties most

5 See *G,* IV, 397–8: "the concept of *duty,* which includes that of a good will . . ." The persistence of the view that Kant is primarily concerned with right action perhaps reflects the modern conception that duty *must* be a matter of externals more than it reflects the Kantian texts. Cf. Onora Nell (O'Neill), *Acting on Principle,* and Chapters 6–8.

frequently raised about universality tests, namely that it seems easy enough to formulate *some* principle of action for any act, indeed possibly one that incorporates one of the agent's intentions, which can meet the criterion of any universality test, whatever the act. Notoriously some Nazi war criminals claimed that they were only "doing their job" or only "obeying orders" – which are after all not apparently morally unworthy activities. The disingenuousness of the claim that such acts were not morally unworthy lies in the fact that these Nazis were not only obeying orders, and indeed that in many cases their specific intentions were ancillary to more fundamental intentions *or principles* that might indeed have revealed moral unworthiness in the agent. (Such fundamental intentions or principles might range from "I'll do whatever I'm told to so long as it doesn't endanger me" to a fundamental maxim of genocide.) The fact that we can formulate *some* universalizable surface intention for any action by selecting among the agent's various surface intentions is no embarrassment to a universality test that is intended to apply to agents' maxims, and offers a solution to the problem of relevant descriptions.

It is equally irrelevant to a universality test that applies to maxims that we may be able to find some nonuniversalizable intentions among the more specific intentions with which an agent implements and fills out any maxim. If in welcoming my visitor with a cup of coffee I intentionally select a particular cup, my specific intention clearly cannot be universally acted on. The very particularity of the world means that there will always be aspects of action, including intentional aspects, that could not be universally adopted or intended. Kant's universality test, however, as we shall see, construes moral worth as contingent not on the universalizability or otherwise of an agent's specific intentions but on the universalizability of an agent's fundamental or underlying intention or principle.[6]

For Kant, then, the Categorical Imperative provides a criterion in the first place for duties to act on underlying intentions or principles that are morally worthy. It is only as a second and derivative part of his ethical theory that he proposes that the Categorical Imperative also provides a test of the outward wrongness and rightness of acts of specific sorts. He proposes in the *Groundwork* that acts that accord in outward respects with acts done on morally worthy maxims of action should be seen as being "in conformity with" or "in accord with" duty. The claim that we can provide a *general* account of which specific actions conform to the outward expressions of morally worthy maxims is highly controversial. We have already noted that there are many ways in which ancillary intentions may be devised in undertaking action on a given maxim, and there may be no

---

6   The points mentioned in this and the preceding paragraphs suggest why a focus on maxims may make it possible to bypass a variety of problems said to plague universality tests when applied to principles that are "too general" or "too specific"; these problems include invertibility, reiterability, moral indeterminacy, empty formalism and the generation of trivial and counterintuitive results. See Singer, *Generalization in Ethics;* and Nell (O'Neill), *Acting on Principle.*

single specific intention that is indispensable in all circumstances for action on a given maxim. Hence it is not generally clear what outward conformity conforms to. Kant appears to accept that the notion of outward conformity to duty is empty in many cases of duties of virtue, which are not sufficiently determinate for any particular more specific intentions to be singled out as required. He speaks of such duties as being "of wide requirement". But he also speaks of duties of narrow or strict requirement, and includes among these duties of justice and certain duties of respect to ourselves and to others.[7] Hence he takes it that there could in principle be a merely outward conformity to these strict or "perfect" duties. Whether this claim is justified depends on the success of his demonstration that the underlying maxims of justice and respect have determinate specific implications for all possible human conditions. If they do not, then there will be no wholly general account of the requirements of justice and respect for all possible situations. It is then at any rate not obvious that we can derive a standard for the outward rightness of acts from a standard for the moral worth of underlying intentions or principles. This is a major problem that I intend to set on one side in order to explore the implications of a universality test that applies to underlying intentions or principles and therefore aims, at least primarily, at a test of the moral worth rather than the outward rightness of actions.

The fact that Kant's universality test focuses on maxims, and so on the moral worth of action, implies that it is a test that agents must seek to apply to their own proposals for action. This is not, however, because agents are in a wholly privileged epistemological position with respect to their own underlying intentions. No doubt others may often have some difficulty even in discerning all of an agent's surface intentions, and may be quite unsure about the underlying intention. But Kant does not regard the agents' vantage points as affording infallible insight into their own intentions – self-consciousness is not transparent – and would not deny that on occasion others might arrive at a more accurate appreciation of an agent's underlying intention or principle than the agent could reach.

The reason why a universality test in a nonheteronomous ethical theory is primarily one for the use of agents rather than of moral spectators is that it is only an agent who can adopt, modify or discard maxims. Although a test of the outward moral status of acts might be of most use and importance to third parties (legislators, judges, educators – those of us who pass judgment on others), because it may be possible (or indeed necessary) to prevent or deter or praise or punish in order to elicit or foster outward action of a certain sort, it is difficult if not impossible for outward regulation or pressure to change an agent's maxim.

---

7   Kant does not then see all acts that are specifically required by strict or perfect duties as matters of justice. Some duties of virtue also have (limited) strict requirements, such as refraining from mockery or detraction or otherwise damaging others' self-respect. These are indispensable elements of any way of enacting maxims of respect. Cf. *DV*, VI, 421ff. and 463ff.; Nell (O'Neill), *Acting on Principle*, pp. 52–8; and Barbara Herman, "Mutual Aid and Respect for Persons".

Surface conformity can be exacted; intentional conformity is more elusive (*DV,* VI, 380–1). Precisely because we are considering what a universality test for autonomous beings must be like, we must recognize that the test is one that we can propose to but not impose upon moral agents.

Inconsistency without universalizing

This account of acting on a maxim shows at least how action can be construed in a way that makes consistency and inconsistency possible, and provides some grounds for thinking that a focus on maxims may avoid some of the difficulties that have arisen in attempts to apply universality tests unrestrictedly to principles of action of all sorts. This opens the way for showing how action on a nonuniversalizable maxim is inconsistent and for considering whether such inconsistency constitutes a criterion of moral unworthiness. Before dealing with these topics it will be useful to run over some of the many ways in which action on a maxim may reveal inconsistency even when universalizing is not brought into the picture.

It is of course true that any act that is performed is possible, taken in itself. But it does not follow that the intentions that are enacted are mutually consistent. There are two sorts of possibilities here: In the first place there may be an internal inconsistency within an agent's maxim; in the second place there may be contradictions between the various specific intentions an agent adopts in pursuit of that maxim, or between some of these specific intentions and the agent's maxim. These two sorts of contradiction correspond closely to the two types of contradiction that Kant thinks may arise when attempts to universalize maxims fail, and that he characterizes as involving, respectively, "contradictions in conception" and "contradictions in the will" (*G,* IV, 424). Since I am also interested in charting the inconsistencies that can arise independently of attempts to universalize, as well as in those that arise when universalizing fails, I shall use the rather similar labels *conceptual inconsistency* and *volitional inconsistency* to distinguish these two types of incoherence in action. A consideration of the different types of incoherence that maxims may display even when the question of universalizability is not raised provides a useful guide to the types of incoherence that nonuniversalizable maxims display.

A maxim of action may in the first place be incoherent simply because it expresses an impossible aspiration. An agent's maxim might be said to involve a conceptual inconsistency if the underlying intention was, for example, both to be successful and to be unworldly, or alternatively, to be both popular and reclusive, or both to care for others and always to put his or her own advantage first, or both to be open and frank with everybody and to be a loyal friend or associate, or both to keep a distance from others and to have intimate personal relationships. Agents whose underlying maxims incorporate such conceptual inconsistencies do not, of course, succeed in performing impossible acts; rather, the pattern of their actions appears to pull in opposite directions and to be in various ways self-defeating. At its extreme we may regard such underlying incoherence in a person's maxim, and consequent fragmentation of the person's action, as tragic or pathological (and perhaps both), since there is no way in which he or she can successfully enact the underlying intention. In other cases we may think of the pattern of action that results from underlying conceptual incoherence as showing no more than ambivalence or presenting conflicting signals to others, who are consequently at a loss about what they should expect or do, finding themselves in a "double bind".

However, not all cases of disjointed action constitute evidence of an internally inconsistent maxim. For it may well be that somebody adopts some accommodation of the potentially inconsistent aspects of an underlying intention. For example, somebody may adopt the maxim of being competitive and successful in public and professional life but of disregarding such considerations in private life; or of being obedient and deferential to superiors but overbearing and exacting with all others. Provided such persons can keep the two spheres of action separated, their underlying intentions can be internally consistent. Hence one cannot infer an inconsistency in someone's underlying intentions merely from the fact that he or she exhibits tendencies in opposing directions. For these tendencies may reflect a coherent underlying intention to respond or act differently in different types of context or with different groups of people. A nonuniversalizable maxim embodies a conceptual contradiction only if it *aims* at achieving mutually incompatible objectives and so cannot under any circumstances be acted on with success.

A focus on maxims that embody contradictions in conception pays no attention to the fact that maxims are not merely principles that we can conceive (or entertain, or even wish) but principles that we *will* or intend, that is to say, principles that we adopt as *principles of action*. Conceptual contradictions can be identified even in principles of action that are never adopted or acted upon. But a second and rather different type of incoherence is exhibited in some attempts to will maxims whose realization can be quite coherently envisaged. Willing, after all, is not just a matter of wishing that something were the case, but involves committing oneself to doing something to bring that situation about when opportunity is there and recognized. Kant expressed this point by insisting that rationality requires that whoever wills some end wills the necessary means insofar as these are available.

Who wills the end, wills (so far as reason has decisive influence on his actions) also the means which are indispensably necessary and in his power. So far as willing is concerned, this proposition is analytic: for in my willing of an object as an effect there is already conceived the causality of myself as an acting cause – that is, the use of means; and from the concept of willing an end the imperative merely extracts the concept of actions necessary to this end. (G, IV, 417)

This amounts to saying that to will some end without willing whatever means are indispensable for that end, insofar as they are available, is, even when the end itself involves no conceptual inconsistency, to involve oneself in a volitional inconsistency. It is to embrace at least one specific intention that, far from being guided by the underlying intention or principle, is inconsistent with that intention or principle.

Kant, however, explicitly formulates only *one* of the principles that must be observed by an agent who is not to fall into volitional inconsistency. The Principle of Hypothetical Imperatives, as expressed in the passage just quoted, requires that agents intend any indispensable means for whatever they fundamentally intend. Conformity with this requirement of coherent intending would be quite compatible with intending no means to whatever is fundamentally intended whenever there is no specific act that is indispensable for action on the underlying intention. Further reflection on the idea of intending the means suggests that there is a *family* of Principles of Rational Intending, of which the Principle of Hypothetical Imperatives is just one, though perhaps the most important one. The following list of further Principles of Rational Intending that coherent intending (as opposed to mere wishing or contemplating) apparently requires agents to observe may not be complete, but is sufficient to generate a variety of interesting conclusions.

First, it is a requirement of rationality not merely to intend all *indispensable* or *necessary* means to that which is fundamentally intended but also to intend some *sufficient* means to what is fundamentally intended. If it were not, I could coherently intend to eat an adequate diet, yet not intend to eat food of any specific sort on the grounds that no specific sort of food is indispensable in an adequate diet.

Second, it is a requirement of rationality not merely to intend all necessary and some sufficient means to what is fundamentally intended but also to seek to make such means available when they are not. If it were not, I could coherently claim to intend to help bring about a social revolution but do absolutely nothing, on the grounds that there is no revolutionary situation at present, settling instead for rhetoric and gesture rather than politics. But if I do this, I at most wish for, and do not intend to help to bring about, a social revolution.

Third, it is a requirement of rationality not merely to intend all necessary and some sufficient means to whatever is fundamentally intended but also to intend all necessary and some sufficient *components* of whatever is fundamentally intended. If it were not, I could coherently claim to intend to be kind to someone to whom, despite opportunity, I show no kindness in word, gesture or deed, merely because acting kindly is not the sort of thing that requires us to take means to an end, but the sort of thing that requires that we act in some of the ways that are *constitutive* of kindness.[8]

---

8 Kant's discussions of duties of virtue in any case suggest that he would count the necessary constituents or components of an end, and not merely the instrumentally necessary acts, as means to that end.

Fourth, it is a requirement of rationality that the various specific intentions we actually adopt in acting on a given maxim in a certain context be mutually consistent. If it were not, I could coherently claim to be generous to all my friends by giving to each the exclusive use of all my possessions.

Fifth, it is a requirement of rationality that the foreseeable results of the specific intentions adopted in acting on a given underlying intention be consistent with the underlying intention. If it were not, I could coherently claim to be concerned for the well-being of a child for whom I refuse an evidently life-saving operation, on the grounds that my specific intention – perhaps to shield the child from the hurt and trauma of the operation – is itself aimed at the child's well-being. But where such shielding foreseeably has the further consequence of endangering the child's life, it is clearly an intention that undercuts the very maxim that supposedly guides it.

There may well be yet further principles that fully coherent sets of intentions must observe, and possibly some of the principles listed above need elaboration or qualification. The point, however, is to reveal that once we see action as issuing from a complex web of intentions, many of which are guided by and ancillary to certain more fundamental intentions or principles under particular conditions, the business of intending coherently and avoiding volitional inconsistency becomes a demanding and complex affair.

Reflection on the various Principles of Rational Intending reveals a great deal about the connections between surface and underlying intentions to which a rational being must aspire. Underlying intentions to a considerable extent express the larger and longer-term goals, policies and aspirations of a life. But if these goals, policies and aspirations are willed (and not merely wished for), they must be connected with some set of surface intentions that express commitment to acts that, in the actual context in which agents find themselves, provide either the means to or some components of any underlying intentions, or at least take them in the direction of being able to form such intentions, without at any point committing them to acts whose performance would undercut their underlying intentions. Wherever such coherence is absent we find an example of intending that, despite the conceptual coherence of the agent's maxim, is volitionally incoherent. In some cases we may think the deficiency cognitive – agents fail despite available information to appreciate what they need to do if they are indeed to act on their maxims (they may be stupid or thoughtless or calculate poorly). In other cases we might think of the deficiency as primarily volitional: agents fail to intend what is needed if they are to will their maxims and not merely to wish for them to be realized. Each of these types of failure in rationality subdivides into many different sorts of cases. It follows that there are very many different ways in which agents whose intentions are not to be volitionally inconsistent may have to consider their intentions.

Perhaps the most difficult of the various requirements of coherent willing is the last, the demand that agents not adopt specific intentions that in a given context may undercut their own maxims. There are many cases in which agents can reach relatively clear specific intentions about how they will implement or instance their maxims, yet the acts they select, though indeed selected as a means to or component of their underlying intentions, backfire. It is fairly common for agents to adopt surface intentions that, when enacted, foreseeably will produce results that defeat their own deeper intentions. Defensive measures generate counterattack; attempts to do something particularly well result in botched performances; decisive success in battle is revealed as Pyrrhic victory. It is perhaps unclear how long a view of the likely results of their action agents must take for us not to think action that leads to results incompatible with its underlying intention is irrational. But at the least the standard and foreseeable results of an action should not undercut the underlying intention if we are to think of an agent as acting rationally. Somebody who claims to intend no harm to others, and specifically merely intends to share a friendly evening's drinking and to drive others home afterward, but who then decides on serious drinking and so cannot safely drive, cannot plausibly claim to intend merely the exuberant drinking and bonhomie and not the foreseeable drunkenness and inability to drive safely. Given standard information, such a set of intentions is volitionally incoherent. For it is a normal and foreseeable result of exuberant drinking that the drinker is incapable of driving safely. One who intends the drinking also (given normal intelligence and experience) intends the drunkenness; and hence cannot coherently also intend to drive others home if the underlying intention is to harm nobody.[9]

This brief consideration of various ways in which agents' intentions may fail to be consistent shows that achieving consistency in action is a difficult matter even if we do not introduce any universality test. Intentions may be either conceptually or volitionally incoherent. The demand that the acts we perform reflect conceptually and volitionally coherent sets of intentions therefore constitutes a powerful constraint on all practical reasoning. This conclusion provides some reason for thinking that when these demands for consistency are extended in the way in which the second aspect of Kant's Formula of Universal Law requires, we should

---

9 The fifth requirement of rational intending clearly deals with the very nexus of intentions on which discussions of the Doctrine of Double Effect focus. That doctrine claims that agents are not responsible for harm that foreseeably results from action undertaken with dutiful intentions, provided that the harm is not disproportionate, is regretted, and would have been avoided had there been a less harmful set of specific intentions that would have implemented the same maxim in that situation. (The surgeon foresees, and regrets, the pain unavoidably inflicted by a lifesaving procedure). Although the Doctrine of Double Effect holds that agents are not to be held responsible for such action, it allows that they do, if "obliquely" rather than "directly", intend it. It is compatible with the Doctrine of Double Effect to insist that an agent whose oblique intention foreseeably undercuts the action for the sake of which what is directly intended is done, acts irrationally. Where the fundamental intention is so undercut by a supposedly ancillary aspect of action, proportionality is violated, and the attribution of the fundamental intentions may be called in question.

expect to see patterns of reasoning that, far from being ineffective or trivial, generate powerful and interesting results.

Inconsistency in universalizing

The intuitive idea behind the thought that a universality test can provide a criterion of moral acceptability may be expressed quite simply as the thought that if we are to act as morally worthy beings, we should not single ourselves out for special consideration or treatment. Hence whatever we propose for ourselves should be possible (note: not "desired" or "wanted" – but at least *possible*) for all others. Kant expresses this commonplace thought (it is, of course, not his argument for the Categorical Imperative) by suggesting that what goes wrong when we adopt a nonuniversalizable maxim is that we treat ourselves as special:

> whenever we transgress a duty, we find that we in fact do not will that our maxim should become a universal law – since this is impossible for us – but rather that its opposite should remain a law universally: we only take the liberty of making an *exception* to it for ourselves (or even just for this once) . . . (*G*, IV, 424)

It is evident from this understanding of the Formula of Universal Law that the notion of a plurality of interacting agents is already implicit in the Formula of Universal Law. It is not the case that Kant introduces these notions into his ethics only with the Formula of the Kingdom of Ends, which would imply that the various formulations of the Categorical Imperative could not be in any way equivalent. To universalize is from the start to consider whether what one proposes for onself *could* be done by others. This seems to many too meager a foundation for ethics but not in itself an implausible constraint on any adequate ethical theory.

Clearly enough, whatever cannot be consistently intended even for oneself also cannot be consistently intended for all others. The types of cases shown to be conceptually or volitionally inconsistent by the methods discussed in the previous section are a fortiori nonuniversalizable. This raises the interesting question whether one should think of certain types of cognitive and volitional failure as themselves morally unworthy. However, I shall leave this question aside in order to focus on the types of failure in consistent intending that are *peculiar* to the adoption of nonuniversalizable intentions.

I shall therefore assume from now on that we are considering cases of maxims that are in themselves not conceptually incoherent, and of sets of underlying and surface intentions that are not themselves volitionally inconsistent. The task is to pinpoint the ways in which inconsistency emerges in some attempts to universalize such internally consistent intentions. The second part of Kant's Formula of Universal Law enjoins action only on maxims that the agent can at the same time will as universal laws. He suggests that we can imagine this hypothetical willing by working out what it would be like "if the maxim of your action were to become through your will a universal law of nature".[10] To universalize maxims agents must satisfy themselves that they can both adopt the maxim and simultaneously will that others do so. In determining whether they can do so they may find that they are defeated by either of the two types of contradiction that, as we have already seen, can afflict action even when universalizing is not under consideration. Kant's own account of these two types of incoherence, either of which defeats universalizability, is as follows:

We must *be able to will* that a maxim of our action should become a universal law – this is the general canon for all moral judgement of action. Some actions are so constituted that their maxim cannot even be *conceived* as a universal law of nature without contradiction, let alone be *willed* as what *ought* to become one. In the case of others we do not find this inner impossibility, but it is still impossible to *will* that their maxim should be raised to the universality of a law of nature, because such a will would contradict itself. (*G*, IV, 424)

Kant also asserts that those maxims that when universalized lead to conceptual contradiction are the ones that strict or perfect duty requires us to avoid, whereas those that when universalized are conceptually coherent but not coherently willable are opposed only to wider or imperfect duties.[11] Since we probably lack both rigorous criteria and firm intuitions of the boundaries between perfect and imperfect duties, it is hard to evaluate this claim. However, it is remarkably easy to display contradictions that arise in attempts to universalize maxims that we might think of as clear cases of violations of duties of justice and self-respect, which Kant groups together as perfect duties; and it is also easy to show how contradictions emerge in attempts to universalize maxims that appear to exemplify clear violations of duties of beneficence and self-development, which Kant groups together as imperfect duties. By running through a largish number of such examples I hope to show how groundless is the belief that universality tests need supplementing with heteronomous considerations if they are to be action-guiding.

---

10 This is the so-called Formula of the Law of Nature. Cf. *G*, IV, 421, and also 436: "maxims must be chosen as if they had to hold as universal laws of nature"; see also *MM*, VI, 225: "Act according to a maxim which can, at the same time, be valid as a universal law." In this discussion I leave aside all consideration of the relationships between different formulations of the Categorical Imperative, and in particular the differences between those versions that are stated "for finite rational beings" (typics) and those that are formulated in ways that make them relevant strictly to the human condition. These topics have been much discussed in the literature: H. J. Paton, *The Categorical Imperative;* John Kemp, *The Philosophy of Kant;* Robert Paul Wolff, *The Autonomy of Reason;* Bruce Aune, *Kant's Theory of Morals.*

11 *G*, IV, 424; *MM*, IV, Introduction; *DV*, VI, esp. 389; see also Chapters 11 and 12 in this volume.

Contradictions in conception

A maxim that may lead to contradictions in conception when we attempt to universalize it often does not contain any conceptual contradiction if we merely adopt the maxim. For example, there is no contradiction involved in adopting the maxim of becoming a slave. But this maxim has as its universalized counterpart – the maxim we must attempt to "will as a universal law" – the maxim of everybody becoming a slave.[12] But if everybody became a slave, there would be nobody with property rights, hence no slaveholders, and hence nobody could become a slave.[13] Consider alternatively a maxim of becoming a slaveholder. Its universalized counterpart would be the maxim of everybody becoming a slaveholder. But if everybody became a slaveholder, then everybody would have some property rights; hence nobody could be a slave; hence there could be no slaveholders. Action on either of the nonuniversalizable maxims of becoming a slave or becoming a slaveholder would reveal moral unworthiness: It could be undertaken only by one who makes of himself or herself a special case.

Contradictions in conception can also be shown to arise in attempts to universalize maxims of deception and coercion. The maxim of coercing another has as its universalized counterpart the maxim that all coerce others; but if all coerce others, including those who are coercing them, then each party both complies with others' wills (being coerced) and simultaneously does not comply with others but rather (as coercer) exacts their compliance. A maxim of coercion cannot coherently be universalized and reveals moral unworthiness. By contrast, a maxim of coordination can be consistently universalized. A maxim of deceiving others as convenient has as its universalized counterpart the maxim that everyone will deceive others as convenient. But if everyone were to deceive others as convenient, then there would be no trust or reliance on others' acts of communication; hence nobody could be deceived; hence nobody could deceive others as convenient.

An argument of the same type can be applied to the maxim that is perhaps the most fundamental for a universality test, namely the maxim of abrogating judgment. One whose maxim it is to defer to the judgment and decisions of others – to choose heteronomy[14] – adopts a maxim whose universalized counterpart is that everyone defer to the judgments and decisions of others. But if everyone defers to the judgments and decisions of others, then there are no decisions to provide the starting point for deferring in judgment; hence it cannot be the case that everybody defers in judgment. Decisions can never be reached when everyone merely

12   For further discussion of the notion of the universalized counterpart of a maxim see Nell (O'Neill), *Acting on Principle*, pp. 61–3.

13   For an application of the Formula of Universal Law to the example of slavery see Leslie A. Mulholland, "Kant: On Willing Maxims to Become Laws of Nature".

14   To see why Kant thinks the abrogation of autonomy would be the most fundamental of failings see his *What Is Enlightenment?* and Barry Clarke's discussion of "elective heteronomy" in "Beyond the Banality of Evil".

affirms, "I agree." A maxim of "elective heteronomy" cannot consistently be universalized.

Interpreters of Kant have traditionally made heavier weather of the contradiction in conception test than these short arguments suggest is necessary. There have perhaps been two reasons why. One is clearly that Kant's own examples of applications of the Categorical Imperative are more complex and convoluted than these short arguments suggest.[15] But even if detailed analysis of these examples is necessary for an evaluation of Kant's theory, it is clarifying to see whether a contradiction in conception test works when liberated from the need to accommodate Kant's particular discussion of examples.

But a second reason why the contradiction in conception test has seemed problematic to many of Kant's commentators is perhaps of greater importance for present concerns. It is that whereas many would grant that we can detect contradictions in attempts to universalize maxims simply of slaveholding or coercing or deceiving or deference, they would point out that no contradiction emerges if we seek to universalize more circumspect maxims, such as "I will hold slaves if I am in a position of sufficient power" or "I will deceive when it suits me and I can probably get away with it" or "I will defer in judgment to those I either admire or fear." Still less do contradictions emerge when we aim to universalize highly specific intentions of deception or deference, such as "I will steal from Woolworths when I can get away with it" or "I will do whatever my parish priest tells me to do."

However, the force of this objection to the claim that the contradiction in conception test can have significant moral implications is undercut when we remember that this is a test that applies to agents' maxims, that is, to their underlying or fundamental intentions or principles, and that as a corollary it is a test of moral worth. For what will be decisive is what an agent's fundamental intention or principle in doing a given act really is. What counts is whether the expression of falsehood expresses a fundamental attempt to deceive, or whether agreement with another (in itself innocent enough) expresses a fundamental refusal to judge or think for oneself. For an agent cannot truthfully claim that an underlying intent, plan or principle was of a very specific sort unless the organization of other, less fundamental, intentions reveals that it really was subject to those restrictions. Precisely because the Categorical Imperative formulates a universality test that applies to *maxims,* and not just to any intention, it is not rebutted by the fact that relatively specific intentions often can be universalized without conceptual contradiction. Conversely, further evidence for the interpretation of the notion of a maxim presented in the section entitled "Maxims and moral categories" is that it leads to an account of the Categorical Imperative that is

15 See the various works of commentary listed in footnote 10 above; Jonathan Harrison, "Kant's Examples of the First Formulation of the Categorical Imperative"; and John Kemp, "Kant's Examples of the Categorical Imperative".

neither powerless nor counterintuitive. However, for the same reason (that it applies to maxims and not to intentions of all sorts) the Categorical Imperative can most plausibly be construed as a test of moral worth rather than of outward rightness, and must always be applied with awareness that we lack certainty about what an agent's maxim is in a given case. This is a relatively slight difficulty when we are assessing our own proposed maxims of action, since we at least can do no better than to probe and test the maxim on which we propose to act (but even here we have no guarantee against self-deception). But it means that we will always remain to some extent unsure about our assessment of others' acts. Kant after all insists that we do not even know whether there *ever* has been a truly morally worthy act. But that is something we do not need to know in order to try to perform such acts. Self-deception may cloud our knowledge of our own maxims; but we are not powerless in self-guidance.

Contradictions in the will

Just as there are maxims that display no conceptual incoherence until attempts are made to universalize them, so there are maxims that exhibit no conceptual incoherence even when universalized, but that are shown to be volitionally inconsistent when attempts are made to universalize them. Such maxims cannot be "willed as universal laws"; attempts to do so fail in one way or another to meet the standards of rationality specified by the group of principles that I have termed Principles of Rational Intending. For to will a maxim is, after all, not just to conceive the realization of an underlying intention; that requires no more than speculation or wishing. Willing requires also the adoption of more specific intentions that are guided by, and chosen (in the light of the agent's beliefs) to realize, the underlying intention, or, if that is impossible, as appropriate moves toward a situation in which such specific intentions might be adopted. Whoever wills a maxim also adopts more specific intentions as means to or constituents of realizing that underlying intention, and is also committed to the foreseeable results of acting on these more specific intentions. Since intending a maxim commits the agent to such a variety of other intentions, there are various different patterns of argument that reveal that certain maxims cannot be willed as universal laws without contradiction.

Clearly the most comprehensive way in which a maxim may fail to be willable as a universal law is if its universal counterpart is inconsistent with the specific intentions that would be necessary for its own realization. Universalizing such a maxim would violate the Principle of Hypothetical Imperatives. The point is well illustrated by a Kantian example.[16] If I seek to will a maxim of nonbeneficence as

a universal law, my underlying intention is not to help others when they need it,

16   Cf. *DV*, VI, 447–64, for Kant's discussions of love and social virtues.

and its universalized counterpart is that nobody help others when they need it. But if everybody denies help to others when they need it, then those who need help will not be helped, and in particular I will not myself be helped when I need it. But if I am committed to the standards of rational willing that constitute the various Principles of Rational Intending, then I am committed to willing some means to any end to which I am committed, and these must include willing that if I am in need of help and therefore not able to achieve my ends without help, I be given some appropriate help. In trying to universalize a maxim of nonbeneficence I find myself committed simultaneously to willing that I not be helped when I need it and that I be helped when I need it. This contradiction, however, differs from the conceptual contradictions that emerge in attempts to universalize maxims such as those considered in the last section. A world of nonbenevolent persons is conceivable without contradiction. Arguments that reveal contradictions in the will depend crucially upon the role of the various Principles of Rational Intending – in this case on the Principle of Hypothetical Imperatives – in constraining the choice of specific intentions to a set that will implement all underlying intentions. It is only because *intending* a maxim of nonbeneficence as a universal law requires commitment to that very absence of help when needed, to which all rational intending requires assent, that nonbeneficence cannot coherently be universalized.

A second Kantian example,[17] which provides an argument to volitional incoherence, is a maxim of neglecting to develop any talents. A world of beings who develop no talents contains no conceptual incoherence. The maxim of an individual who decides to develop no talents, though imprudent, reveals no volitional inconsistency. For it is always *possible* that others fend for the imprudent, who will then find means available for at least some action. (It is not a fundamental requirement of practical reason that there should be means available to whatever projects agents adopt, but only that they should not have ruled out all action.) However, an attempt to universalize a maxim of neglecting talents commits one to a world in which no talents have been developed, and so to a situation in which necessary means are lacking not just for some but for any sort of complex action. An agent who fails to will the development, in self or others, of whatever minimal range of talents is required and sufficient for a range of action, is committed to internally inconsistent sets of intentions. Such agents intend both that action be possible and that it be undercut by neglect to develop even a minimal range of talents that would leave some possibility of action. This argument shows nothing

---

17 Cf. *DV*, VI, 443–7, for discussion of the duty not to neglect to develop talents (the "duty to seek one's own perfection"). "Talents" here are to be understood not as any particularly unusual accomplishments, but as any human powers that (unlike natural gifts) we can choose either to cultivate or to neglect. Kant tends to think the most important talents are second-order ones (e.g., self-mastery, self-knowledge) and that we can do little to develop these in others. Both restrictions seem to me unnecessary. See Onora O'Neill, *Faces of Hunger: An Essay on Poverty, Development and Justice*, Chap. 8, for development of these thoughts.

about the development of talents that may be required or sufficient for any *specific* projects, but only points to the inconsistency of failing to foster such talents as are needed and sufficient for action of some sort or other. It is an argument that invokes not only the Principle of Hypothetical Imperatives but also the requirement that rational beings intend some set of means sufficient for the realization of their underlying intentions or principles.

These two examples of arguments that reveal volitional inconsistencies show only that it is morally unworthy to adopt maxims either of systematic nonbeneficence or of systematic neglect of talents. The duties that they ground are relatively indeterminate duties of virtue. The first of these arguments does not specify whom it is morally worthy to help, to what extent, in what ways or at what cost, but only that it would be morally unworthy to adopt an underlying intention of nonbeneficence. Similarly, the second argument does not establish which talents it would be morally worthy to develop, in whom, to what extent or at what cost, but only that it would be morally unworthy to adopt an underlying intention of making no effort to develop any talents. The person who adopts a maxim either of nonbeneficence or of nondevelopment of talents cannot coherently universalize the maxim, but must either make an exception of himself or herself, and intend, unworthily, to be a free rider on others' beneficence and talents, or be committed to some specific intentions that are inconsistent with those required for action on the maxim.

Another example of a maxim that cannot consistently be willed as a universal law is the maxim of refusing to accept help when it is needed. The universalized counterpart of this underlying intention would be the intention that everyone refuse to accept help when it is needed. But rational beings cannot consistently commit themselves to intending that all forgo a means that, if ever they are in need of help, will be indispensable for them to act at all.

A further example of a nonuniversalizable maxim is provided by a maxim of ingratitude, whose universalized counterpart is that nobody show or express gratitude for favors received. In a world of non-self-sufficient beings a universal maxim of ingratitude would require the systematic neglect of an important means for ensuring that help is forthcoming for those who need help if they are to realize their intentions. Hence in such a world nobody could coherently claim to will that those in need of help be helped. Yet we have already seen that to will that all in need of help be refused help is volitionally inconsistent. Hence, willing a maxim of ingratitude also involves a commitment to a set of intentions not all of which can be consistently universalized. The volitional inconsistency that overtakes would-be universalizers of this maxim arises in two stages: The trouble with ingratitude is that, practiced universally, it undercuts beneficence; the trouble with nonbeneficence is that it cannot be universally practiced by beings who have at least some maxims, yet (lacking self-sufficiency) cannot guarantee that their own resources will provide means sufficient for at least some of their projects.

The hinge of all these arguments is that human beings (since they are adopters of maxims) have at least some maxims or projects, which (since they are not self-sufficient) they cannot always realize unaided, and so must (since they are rational) intend to draw on the assistance of others, and so must (if they universalize) intend to develop and foster a world that will lend to all some support of others' beneficence and talents. Such arguments can reveal the volitional inconsistencies involved in trying to universalize maxims of entirely neglecting the social virtues – beneficence, solidarity, gratitude, sociability and the like – for beings who are rational yet not always able to achieve what they intend unaided. It follows from this point that the social virtues are very differently construed in Kantian and in heteronomous ethics. An ethical theory for nonheteronomous agents sees the social virtues as morally required, not because they are desired or liked but because they are necessary requirements for action in a being who is not self-sufficient. The content of the social virtues in this framework cannot be spelled out in terms of the provision of determinate goods or services or the meeting of certain set needs or the satisfaction of a determinate set of desires. Rather, the content of these virtues will always depend on the various underlying maxims and projects, both individual and collaborative, to which agents commit themselves. What will constitute beneficence or kindness or care for others will depend in great part on how others intend to act.

Contradictions in the will and further results

The patterns of argument that can be used to show underlying antisocial intentions morally unworthy make use of various Principles of Rational Intending in addition to the Principle of Hypothetical Imperatives. In particular they draw on the requirements that rational agents intend not merely necessary but also sufficient means to or components of their underlying intentions or maxims, and that they also intend whatever means are indirectly required and sufficient to make possible the adoption of such specific intentions. However, the particular features of the fifth Principle of Rational Intending – the Principle of Intending the Further Results – have not yet been displayed. Attempts to evade this Principle of Rational Intending lead to a peculiar sort of volitional inconsistency.

Good examples of arguments that rely on this principle can be developed by considering cases of maxims that, when universalized, produce what are frequently referred to as "unintended consequences". For example, I can adopt the underlying intention of improving my economic well-being, and the specific intention of doing so by competing effectively with others. The maxim of my action can be consistently universalized: There is no conceptual contradiction in intending everyone's economic position to improve. The specific intention of adopting competitive strategies is not inconsistent with the maxim to which it is ancillary; nor is universal action on competitive strategies inconsistent with universal economic advance (that indeed is what the invisible hand is often presumed to achieve). But if an agent intends his or her own economic advance to be achieved solely by competitive strategies, this nexus of intentions cannot consistently be willed as universal law, because the further results of universal competitive activity, by itself, are inconsistent with universal economic advance. If everyone seeks to advance by these (and no other) methods, the result will not put everybody ahead economically. A maxim of economic progress combined with the specific intention of achieving progress merely by competitive strategies cannot be universalized, any more than the intention of looking over the heads of a crowd can be universally achieved by everyone in the crowd standing on tiptoes.[18] On the other hand, a maxim of seeking economic advance by means of increased production can be consistently universalized. It is merely the particular specific intention of advancing economically by competitive strategies alone that leads to volitional inconsistency when universalized. Competitive means are inherently effective only for some: Competitions must have losers as well as winners. Hence, though it can be consistent to seek individual economic advance solely by competitive methods, this strategy cannot consistently be universalized. Once we consider what it would be to intend the consequences of universal competition – the usually *unintended* consequences – we can see that there is an inconsistency not between universal competitive activity and universal economic progress, but between the *further results of intending only universal competitive activity and universal economic progress.* Economic progress and competitive activity might each of them consistently be universal; indeed, it is possible for them to coexist within a certain society. (Capitalist economies do experience periods of general economic growth.) Nevertheless, there is a volitional inconsistency in seeking to achieve universal economic growth *solely by way* of universal adoption of competitive strategies.

This argument does not show that either the intention to advance economically or the intention to act competitively cannot be universalized, but only that the composite intention of pursuing economic advance solely by competitive tactics cannot be universalized. It does not suggest that either competition or economic progress is morally unworthy, but only that an attempt to achieve economic progress solely by competitive methods and without aiming at any productive contribution is not universalizable and so is morally unworthy.

Similarly, there is no inconsistency in an intention to engage in competitive activities of other sorts (e.g., games and sports). But if such competition is ancillary to an underlying intention to win, then the overall intention is not universalizable. Competitive games must have losers. If winning is not the overriding aim in such activities, if they are played for their own sake, the activity is consistently universalizable. But to play competitively with the fundamental

18 See F. Hirsch, *The Social Limits to Growth.*

intention of winning is to adopt an intention that makes of one's own case a necessary exception.

Conclusions

The interest of a Kantian universality test is that it aims to ground an ethical theory on notions of consistency and rationality rather than upon considerations of desire and preference. Kant's universality test meets many of the conditions that any such universality test must meet. In particular it focuses on features of action that are appropriate candidates for assessments of coherence and incoherence, namely the maxims or fundamental intentions that agents may adopt and the web of more specific ancillary intentions that they must adopt in a given context if their commitment to a maxim is genuine. Although Kant alludes specifically to conceptual inconsistencies and to those volitional inconsistencies that are attributable to nonobservance of the Principle of Hypothetical Imperatives in attempts to universalize intentions, there is in addition a larger variety of types of volitional inconsistency that agents who seek to subject their maxims to a universality test (and so not to make an exception of their own case) must avoid. A universality test applied to maxims and their ancillary, more specific, intentions can be action-guiding in many ways without invoking any heteronomous considerations.

However, precisely because it applies to intentions or principles, a universality test of this sort cannot generally provide a test of the rightness or wrongness of the specific outward aspects of action. It is, at least primarily, and perhaps solely, a test of the inner moral worth of acts. It tells us what we ought to avoid if we are not to act in ways that we can know are in principle not possible for all others. Such a test is primarily of use to agents in guiding their own moral deliberations, and can only be used most tentatively in assessing the moral worth of others' action, where we are often sure only about specific outward aspects of action and not about the maxim. This point will not be of great importance if we do not think it important whether an ethical theory enables us to pass judgment on the moral worth of others' acts. But specific outward aspects of others' action are unavoidably of public concern. The considerations discussed here do not reveal whether or not these can be judged right or wrong by Kant's theory. Kant no doubt thought that it was possible to derive specific principles of justice from the Formula of Universal Law; but the success of this derivation and of his grounding of *Rechtslehre* is beyond the scope of this chapter.

The universality test discussed here is, above all, a test of the mutual consistency of (sets of) intentions and univeralized intentions or principles. It operates by showing some sets of proposed intentions to be mutually inconsistent. It does not thereby generally single out action on any one set of specific intentions as morally required. On the contrary, the ways in which maxims can be enacted or realized by means of acts performed on specific intentions must vary with situation, tradition and culture. The specific acts by which we can show or fail to show loyalty to a friend or respect to another or justice in our dealings with the world will always reflect specific ways of living and thinking and particular situations and relationships. What reason can provide is a way of discovering whether we are choosing to act in ways (however culturally specific) that we do not in principle preclude for others. The "formal" character of the Categorical Imperative does not entail either that it has no substantive ethical implications or that it can select a unique code of conduct as morally worthy for all times and places. Rather than presenting a dismal choice between triviality and implausible rigorism, a universality test can provide a rational foundation for ethics and maintain a serious respect for the diversity of content of distinct ethical practices and traditions.

6

Between consenting adults

Much of Kant's ethics is distant from the ordinary moral consciousness of our day. But one pair of Kantian notions is still widely current. Few moral criticisms strike deeper than the allegation that somebody has used another; and few ideals gain more praise than that of treating others as persons.

But this consensus is often shallow, since there is little agreement about what it takes to use others in morally problematic ways or to treat them as persons. I shall look here at three common conceptions of these ideals, which make little distinction between the two of them. I shall then outline interpretations of both that seem to me more convincing and richer than the commonly accepted ones. On the interpretations I offer the two ideals are distinct, though related. Merely not to be used is not enough for being treated as a person. Making another into a tool or instrument in my project is one way of failing to treat that other as a person; but only one way.

At a certain point I shall return to the Kantian texts to suggest that the sort of understanding of these ideals that I have outlined is at stake there. But the exegetical ambitions are limited. I shall say nothing about Kant's conception of a person and its supposed metaphysical background. I shall not spell out all the textual considerations that lie behind this reading of the Formula of the End-in-Itself. I merely state and will not try to show that one of these reasons is that this interpretation can make sense of Kant's puzzling claims about the equivalence of the various formulations of the Categorical Imperative. I shall not explore Kant's thoughts about using oneself and treating oneself as a person. I shall try only to make plausible a certain understanding of what it is to use others and to treat them as persons. I shall therefore use illustrations from areas of life where we often fear that human beings are used or not treated as persons, and in particular from presumed sexual and economic uses of others. I shall argue that an adequate understanding of what it is to treat others as persons must view them not abstractly as possibly consenting adults, but as particular men and women with limited and determinate capacities to understand or to consent to proposals for action. Unless we take one another's limitations seriously, we risk acting in ways

This chapter originally appeared in *Philosophy and Public Affairs* 14, No. 3 (Summer 1985), 252–77. Copyright © 1985 by Princeton University Press.

that would be enough to treat "ideal" rational beings as persons, but are not enough for treating finitely rational, human beings as persons.

A second aim is to provide a reading of some central claims of Kant's ethics that does not depend on an inflated view of human cognitive and volitional capacities, does not generate implications that are rigorously insensitive to variations of circumstances and is not tied to a strongly individualistic conception of agency.

The personal touch

One view of treating another as a person rather than using him or her is that it demands a certain tone and manner. If we show indifference to others, we do not treat them as persons; if our interactions are personal in tone, whether sympathetic or hostile, we treat them as persons. On this view employers who are cold or distant with their employees do not treat them as persons, but involved employers do so. A prostitute who does her or his job with uninvolved perfunctoriness is using the clients, and if their manner is similar, they use her or him; but if each had a personal manner the relationship would be personal and neither would use the other.

If this is what it is to treat others as persons and not to use them, neither notion can be fundamental for moral or political thought. We are familiar with uses of others that are cloaked by an involved and concerned manner. A planned seduction of someone less experienced treats him or her as means even when charmingly done. Employers who take paternalistic interest in employees' lives may yet both use them and fail to treat them as persons. Yet relationships without a personal tone may neither use others nor fail to treat them as persons. An impersonal relationship with a sales assistant may not use him or her in any morally objectionable way, nor fail in treating him or her as other than a person. A personal touch may, we shall see, be an important aspect of treating others as persons. But the notion entirely fails to capture the requirements for avoiding using others and provides a scanty account of treating others as persons.

Actual consent

A deeper and historically more important understanding of the idea of treating others as persons sees their consent to actions that affect them as morally significant. On this view it is morally objectionable to treat others in ways to which they do not consent. To do so treats another as a thing or tool, which cannot, so does not, consent to the ways in which it is used; such action fails to treat others as persons, who can choose, and may withhold consent from actions that affect them.

On this understanding of treating others as persons, rape and seduction are decisively unacceptable. The rapist's victim is coerced rather than consenting; and the seducer's victim lacks insight into what is proposed, and so neither can nor does consent to it. But many relationships between prostitutes and their clients are not, on this view, morally objectionable, since they are relationships between consenting adults. Similarly, slavery and forced labor and various forms of economic fraud use others and do not treat them as persons, but a contractual relationship like that between employer and employee does not use others or fail to treat them as persons.

This liberal understanding of avoiding using others and of treating them as persons encounters difficulties of various sorts when we consider what consent is.

An initial difficulty is that it is unclear what constitutes consent. In legal and institutional contexts the criteria are supposedly clearest. Here formal procedures supposedly show who consents to which actions by which others. But here too presumptions of consent are defeasible. Even the clearest formulae of consent, such as signatures and formal oaths, may not indicate consent when there is ignorance, duress, misrepresentation, pressure or the like.[1] Such circumstances may void contracts and even nullify marriages. Formal procedures for consenting may reveal only spurious consent, and so cannot guarantee that everyone is treated as a person in this second sense.

Where formal procedures are lacking, the problem of determining what has been consented to is greater. Various debates about express and tacit consent reflect these difficulties. But the real problem here is not that consent is sometimes given in ways that are implicit rather than explicit, but that it is standardly unclear where consent – even the most explicit consent – stops. A nod to the auctioneer, though "implicit", conveys a quite precise consent to offering a price increased by a specified amount for a particular lot. At other times the boundaries of explicit consent are unclear. Like other propositional attitudes, consent is opaque. Consent may not extend to the logical implicatons, the likely results, or the indispensable presuppositions of that which is explicitly consented to. A classical and instructive example of this range of difficulties occurs in liberal political debates over how far consent to a particular constitution (explicitly or implicitly given) constitutes consent to particular governments formed under that constitution, and how far consent to a particular government or party constitutes consent to various components of government or party policy. The notion of loyal opposition is never more than contextually determinate.

A second range of difficulties arises when the consent given does not match the activities it supposedly legitimates. Marxist critics of capitalist economic forms suggest that workers do not consent to their employment despite its outwardly contractual form. For workers, unlike capitalists, cannot (at least in "ideal" capitalism) choose to be without work, on pain of starvation. Hence the outward contrac-

---

1   Excessive reliance on formal indicators of "consent" suggests doubts whether the consent is genuine. Consider the widespread European use of "treaties" to "legitimize" acquisition of land or sovereignty by seeking the signature of barely literate native peoples with no understanding of European moral and legal traditions. See D. F. McKenzie's discussion of the treaty of Waitangi in "The Sociology of a Text: Orality, Print and Literacy in Early New Zealand."

tual form masks an underlying coercion. Workers choose between employers (in boom times) but cannot choose or consent to nonemployment. Analogously, women in most societies hitherto have not really consented to their restricted life possibilities. A choice between marriage partners does not show that the married life has been chosen. The outward forms of market economies and of unarranged marriages may mask how trivial the range of dissent and consent is. In a Marxist view bourgeois freedom is not the real thing, and men and women in bourgeois societies are still often treated as things rather than as persons. Bourgeois ideologies offer a fiction of freedom. They structure a false consciousness that obscures the extent to which human beings are used and not treated as persons.

A third range of difficulties with taking actual consent as pivotal for treating others as persons emerges when abilities to consent and dissent are impaired. Discussions in medical ethics show how hard it is to ensure that the consent that patients provide to their treatment is genuine. It is not genuine whenever they do not understand what they are supposedly consenting to or lack the independence to do anything other than "consent" to what they think the doctor wants or requires. Patients cannot easily understand complex medical procedures; yet if they consent only to a simplified account, they may not consent to the treatment proposed. And their peculiar dependence makes it hard even for those who are informed to make independent decisions about proposed treatment. Paradoxically, the case of severely impaired patients may seem easiest to handle. Patients too impaired to give any consent evidently cannot be treated as persons in this sense. Paternalism may then seem permissible, even required, for those who are, if temporarily, *only* patients. But with less impaired patients we are not so ready to set aside the ideal of treating others as persons. The difficult case is raised by those who are, as Mill would have put it, "in the maturity of their faculties". Even when we are mature we are seldom ideal rational patients! Here we confront the possibility that consent may be spurious even when based on average understanding and a standard ability to make decisions.

It is not only when we are subjects or employees or patients that we have only a partial understanding of ways in which others propose to act toward us and only an incomplete ability to make decisions for ourselves. Others' apparent consent, even their apparently informed consent, may *standardly* be insufficient to show that we treat them as persons when we interact with them. The problems of the defeasibility and indeterminacy of consent, of ideological distortions and self-deception, and of impaired capacities to consent are all forms of one underlying problem. The deeper problem in this area is simply a corollary of the opacity of intentionality. When we consent to another's proposals, we consent, even when "fully" informed, only to some specific formulation of what the other has it in mind to do. We may remain ignorant of further, perhaps equally pertinent, accounts of what is proposed, including some to which we would not consent. ("I didn't know I was letting myself in for that!" we may protest.) Even when further descriptions are inferable from the one consented to, the inference may not be made; and often we cannot infer which determinate action will enact some proposal. If we want to give an account of genuine, morally significant, consent, we need to explain *which* aspects of actions must be consented to if nobody is to be used or treated as less than a person. An account of genuine consent must then show how the morally significant aspects of plans, proposals and intentions are picked out as candidates for consent.

Hypothetical consent

Before considering how such an account might proceed, I shall look at an account of treating others as persons that does not require us to know what they consent to. This strategy explains treating others as persons not in terms of the consent actually given, but in terms of the hypothetical consent fully rational beings would give to the same proposal. The strategy has obvious merits.

One merit is that it suggests that at least sometimes actual consent is not morally decisive, even if well informed. Hence it allows for our strong intuitions that even a consensus may be iniquitous or irrelevant (perhaps it reflects false consciousness), and that not everything done between consenting adults treats the other as a person. This approach also deals readily with cases of impaired capacities to consent. Since it appeals to capacities that are standardly lacking, there is, in a way, no difference in its approach to those in "the maturity of their faculities" and to those more gravely impaired. By the standards of full rationality we are all impaired. But we can always ask whether the fully rational would consent.

But these merits are the acceptable face of a serious deficiency in this strategy. If treating others as persons requires only hypothetical rational consent, we may, as Berlin long ago pointed out, find ourselves overriding the actual dissent of others, coercing them in the name of higher and more rational selves who would consent to what is proposed. It seems implausible that treating others as persons should even sometimes be a matter of overriding what others as we know them actually choose.

Other difficulties with this strategy arise from the varied conceptions of rationality invoked. Many conceptions of rationality presuppose a given set of desires. If these are the actual desires of the consenter, appeal to hypothetical consent will not overcome the worry that a consensus may be iniquitous or reflect local ideology. Yet if there is no appeal to the consenter's actual desires, but only to some hypothetical set of rationally structured desires, then the theory may be too weak to determine what would rationally be consented to. Given that there are many rationally structured sets of hypothetical desires, rational structure alone cannot determine what would rationally be consented to. But there are difficulties in spelling out the content and grounds of a stronger (e.g., quasi-Platonic) account of rational desires that might determine hypothetical consent.

The appeal of hypothetical consent criteria of treating others as persons is that it overcomes the limitations of actual consent criteria by endowing hypothetical agents with cognitive capacities that extend their understanding of what is proposed. But it is just not clear how far the insight even of the ideally rational reaches. Do they, for example, have a more determinate insight into proposals addressed to them than do those who make the proposals? What do they make of internally incoherent proposals? Which aspects of others' proposals are pivotal for the consent or dissent of the fully rational? A convincing account of hypothetical rational consent has to explain *which* aspects of others' actions must be hypothetically consented to if those actions are not to use others or to fail to treat them as persons. This approach cannot exempt us from the need to discover the morally significant aspects of plans, proposals and actions that are candidates for consent.

Significant and spurious consent

If the notion of consent is to help explicate what it is to treat others as persons, we need an account of genuine, morally significant consent, and we need to distinguish it from spurious or morally trivial consent. Three preliminary points seem to me significant.

First, morally significant consent cannot be consent to all aspects of another's proposals that may affect me. Any complicated action will be performed under many descriptions; but most of them will be without moral significance. Morally significant consent will, I suggest, be consent to the deeper or more fundamental aspects of another's proposals. If I consent to be the subject for a medical experiment and the timing slips, I may have been inconvenienced, but not gravely misled. But my consent will have been spurious, and I will not have been treated as a person, but indeed used, if I consented to a seriously misleading account of the experiment and its risks.

Second, if another's consent is to be morally significant, it must indeed be his or her consent. To treat others as persons we must allow them the *possibility* either of consenting to or of dissenting from what is proposed. The initiator of action can ensure this possibility; but the consenting cannot be up to him or her. The morally significant aspect of treating others as persons may lie in making their consent or dissent *possible,* rather than in what they actually consent to or would hypothetically consent to if fully rational. A requirement that we ensure that others have this possibility cuts deep whenever they will be much affected by what we propose. There is not much difficulty in ensuring that those who will in any case be no more than spectators have a genuine possibility of dissent. They need only be allowed to absent themselves or to express disagreement, distaste or the like. But those closely involved in or affected by a proposal have no genuine possibility of dissent unless they can avert or modify the action by withholding consent and collaboration. If those closely affected have the possibility of dissent, they will be able to require an initiator of action either to modify the action or to desist or to override the dissent. But an initiator who presses on in the face of actively expressed dissent undercuts any genuine possibility of refusing the proposal and chooses rather to enforce it on others. Any "consent" the proposal receives will be spurious, and will not show that others have not been used, let alone that they have been treated as persons.

Third, we need to understand what makes genuine consent to the more fundamental aspects of action possible. But there is no guarantee that any one set of requirements makes genuine consent possible in all circumstances. There may be some necessary conditions, whose absence always makes genuine consent or dissent impossible, and other conditions that are needed to make consent possible only in some circumstances. It is plausible to think that when we act in ways that would *always* preclude genuine consent or dissent we will have used others. For example, if we coerce or deceive others, their dissent, and so their genuine consent, is in principle ruled out. Here we do indeed use others, treating them as mere props or tools in our own projects. Even the most rational and independent cannot genuinely consent to proposals about which they are deceived or with which they are compelled to comply. Even if a proposal would have been welcomed, and coercion or deception is otiose, its enforcement or surreptitious imposition precludes consent.

In other cases a proposal for action may not in principle preclude consent and dissent, but the particular others affected may be unable to dissent from it, or genuinely to consent to it. A full understanding of treating others as persons should, I suggest, take some account of the particularities of persons. It must allow that we take seriously the possiblity of dissent and consent for others who, far from being ideally rational and independent beings, have their particular limitations that affect their abilities to dissent and to consent variously in varying circumstances. We are concerned not only to be treated as a person – any person – but to some extent to be treated as the particular persons we are. We are not merely possibly consenting adults, but particular friends, colleagues, clients, rivals, relations, lovers, neighbors; we have each of us a particular history, character, set of abilities and weaknesses, interests and desires. Even when others do not deceive or coerce us, or treat us in any way as tools, we may yet feel that they do not treat us as persons either. There is some point to the thought that being treated as a person needs a personal touch. Not being used may be enough for being treated as a person when somebody's particular identity and specific character are irrelevant, for example in commercial or other transactions with anonymous members of the public. (Even here we may think standards of courtesy must be met.) Still, in public contexts not being used may be the major part of being treated as a person; for if consent and dissent are in principle possible, we can refuse the opportunities, offers or activities that do not suit us. But where we have specific relations with particular others, being treated as persons may require far more. It may demand that we treat others not impersonally, but rather as the persons they are.

Possible consent: a Kantian reading

A shift of focus to possible consent has deep implications. When we see morally required actions as those to which others either actually or hypothetically consent, we implicitly view morality as partly contingent on desires. Another's actual consent will usually reflect his or her wants or preferences; and standard modern views of hypothetical consent construe it in terms of actual preferences on which a rational ordering is hypothetically imposed. Yet it seems implausible that treating others as persons can be of *prime* moral importance if it amounts only to avoiding what they do not want or would not rationally want. In a moral theory in which wants are basic, the notion of treating others as persons carries no independent weight. In Kantian terms we might say that the notion of a person does not matter in a heteronomous moral theory. If wants or rationalized preferences are morally fundamental, consent is of derivative concern. It is only within moral theories for beings who can sometimes act independently of desires or preferences that the notion of consent carries independent weight. In such theories it is important that consent be possible for others, but of less concern whether what they consent to is what they want.

An account of using others and treating them as persons that starts from the notions of possible consent and dissent reveals the Kantian origins of these notions. The Kantian texts also provide suggestions for explicating, elaborating and differentiating the two notions.

Kant's theory of action sees each act as performed on a *maxim,* an underlying principle used to guide and orchestrate more specific, ancillary aspects of action.[2] The Formula of the End-in-Itself enjoins action on maxims that

---

2   For other discussions of Kant's maxims see also Rüdiger Bittner. "Maximen"; and Otfried Höffe, "Kants kategorischer Imperativ als Kriterium des Sittlichen". The most basic consideration is that maxims are underlying principles, by which subsidiary aspects of action are governed and orchestrated. They must often be inferred from these subsidiary aspects. Even when they are the maxims of individual action, they are not always accessible to consciousness. And some maxims are not maxims of individual agents, but the maxims of institutions or practices. Hence not all maxims are intentions. Nor are all intentions maxims, since trivial and superficial aspects of action are often intended. The Categorical Imperative provides only a test of maxims; but it does not follow that anything is permissible provided it is a nonfundamental aspect of action. Since maxims guide subsidiary aspects of action, the latter will be morally required (or forbidden) when they are indispensable (or incompatible) with what is needed to enact and embody a morally worthy maxim in a particular context. Only in drastic conditions will what would otherwise be deeply wrong be legitimated because needed to enact a morally worthy maxim. In wartime Poland Schindler could act on a maxim of protecting some Jews only by enslaving them and collaborating with the Nazis. See Thomas Keneally, *Schindler's Ark.* In prerevolutionary St. Petersburg Sonya Marmeladovna could support and sustain her family only by prostitution. It does not follow that such actions would be either permissible or required to enact fundamental principles of justice or of love outside very unusual circumstances.

treat humanity whether in your own person or in the person of any other, never simply as a means, but always at the same time as an end. (G, IV, 429)

Here there are two separate aspects to treating others as persons: The maxim must not use them (negatively) as mere means, but must also (positively) treat them as ends-in-themselves (cf. *G, IV, 430*).

Kant describes the first sort of failure as action on maxims to which no other could possibly consent, and the second as pursuit of ends another cannot share. He writes of such a case:

The man whom I seek to use for my own purposes by such a [false] promise cannot possibly agree with my way of behaving to him, and so cannot himself share the end of action. (*G, IV, 429*)

The failure is dual: The victim of deceit *cannot agree* to the initiator's maxim, so is used, and a fortiori *cannot share* the initiator's end, so is not treated as a person. Similarly with a maxim of coercion: Victims cannot agree with a coercer's fundamental principle or maxim, which denies them the choice between consent and dissent, and further cannot share a coercer's ends. (Victims may *want* the same ends as their coercers; but that is not the same as sharing those ends, for one who is coerced, even if pointlessly, is not pursuing, nor therefore sharing, ends at all.) Those who are either deceived or coerced are then *both* used *and* not treated as persons.

It does not follow that nothing done in acting on a maxim of deception or coercion can be agreed to or shared by those deceived or coerced. On the contrary, deception standardly works by revealing subsidiary aspects of action, which misleadingly point to some underlying maxim to which consent *can* be given. Deception works only when the underlying proposal is kept obscure. The deceiver's actual maxim therefore cannot be consented to. A maxim of coercion does not have to be obscure – it may be brutally plain – but it clearly denies victims the choice between consent and dissent.

Although the boundaries of coercive action are often unclear, we can agree on central cases involving physical force, dire and credible threats and institutionalized forms of domination such as slavery. But here too victims can and do consent to many of the coercer's subsidiary intentions or proposals. It is always hard to know when "going along with" what is coercively proposed becomes collaboration with the coercer. (Rape trials are instructive.)[3] And it is hard to tell just when an ostensibly deceived party becomes a conniving party. But though such complexities make judgment of actual cases hard, they do not alter the point that a maxim

3 In more than one way. In this area remarkably exacting, but varied, conceptions of what constitutes evidence of dissent are put forward. See Carole Pateman, "Women and Consent"; her discussion of some inadequacies of "consenting adult" accounts of prostitution, in "Defending Prostitution: Charges against Ericsson"; and her discussion of the contract of prostitution, in *The Sexual Contract*.

of deception or coercion treats another as mere means and not as a person, even if the victim becomes so involved in the initiator's action that we judge that he or she has become a collaborator or accessory.

The second part of Kant's account of treating others as persons urges us not merely not to use them as means, but to treat them as "ends-in-themselves". By this he does not mean that others should be our goals or purposes. Only what we aim for, including what we desire, can be a goal or purpose. This sort of subjective end depends on us for its existence. Others, who exist independently of our action, cannot be subjective ends, but only ends-in-themselves. Ends-in-themselves may provide us with grounds of action not by being the *aim* or *effect* of action but by constituting *limits* to our actions (*G*, IV, 428).[4] Others may limit my action by being agents whose maxims guide their projects and activities to their varied ends. To respect a limit of this sort cannot be thought of on a spatial analogy of avoiding certain areas; for the varying activities of others take place in the world that we share, and not in discrete spatial capsules (as libertarians might prefer). Not to treat others as mere means introduces minimal, but indispensable, requirements for coordinating action in a world shared by a plurality of agents, namely that nobody adopt fundamental principles to which others cannot possibly consent. To treat others as ends may require further action when dissent is in principle possible, but those who are actually involved have limited capacities to dissent.

If we knew *only* that others are rational and fully autonomous, all we could do to treat them as persons would be to meet the negative standard of not using them. But we know a great deal about the men and women with whom we live, and in particular about their varied desires and limited rationality and autonomy. However, we can give no single formula for additional maxims of action that go beyond not using others and also meet the positive criterion of treating others of limited rationality and autonomy as ends-in-themselves. The Formula of the End-in-Itself, Kant claims, provides a criterion for the "wide" duties of beneficence (and of self-cultivation) as well as for the "strict" duties of justice (and of self-preservation and respect). But whereas the negative requirement of not using others can be stated in some (no doubt incomplete) abstraction from the particular features of other rational beings ("the problem of justice can be solved even for a 'nation of devils'" [*PP*, VIII, 366; 112, trans. O. O'N.]), we can give only an indeterminate account of the "positive" requirements for treating others as ends-in-themselves. Where treating others as persons goes beyond not using them, we must take into account "humanity in their person", that is, their particular

---

4 See Thomas E. Hill, Jr., "Humanity as an End in Itself." Hill's analysis of the Formula of the End-in-Itself is acute and instructive. However, he suggests that it has the advantage that it depends less on interpretation of the notion of a maxim (p. 91). But the question whether we are using others, or treating them as persons, is as sensitive to how we describe what we are doing as the question whether what we propose could be universally done.

capacities for rational and independent action.[5] This condition can be met with vacuous ease for ideally rational beings. But human beings, though they are creatures of reason rather than instinct, are yet only limitedly rational beings, of whose capacities for action we can give no determinate account in the abstract. The only abstract accounts we can give of the "positive" maxims on which we must act in treating other men and women as persons are very general policies. But these "wide" or "imperfect" duties to share others' ends can have determinate implications in particular contexts.

The "positive" aspects of treating others as ends-in-themselves require action on maxims of sharing others' ends. It is not enough when we deal with other human beings (as opposed to ideally rational beings) to act on maxims with which they can possibly agree, whatever their ends. It is also necessary to adopt maxims that "endeavour to further the ends of others" (G, IV, 430). To treat human beings as persons, rather than as "ideal" rational beings, we not only must not use them, but also must take their particular capacities for agency and rationality into account. Since other humans have varied ends, are precariously independent and rational, and are far from self-sufficient in other ways, sharing even some of their ends may make varied demands. Kant claims that these demands can be grouped under the headings of respect and love (or beneficence). He repeatedly uses physical metaphors to express the ways in which these two sorts of demands differ:

The principle of *mutual love* admonishes men constantly to *come nearer* to each other; that of the *respect* which they owe each other, to keep themselves at a *distance* from one another. (DV, VI, 447)

Policies of respect must recognize that other's maxims and projects are *their* maxims and projects. They must avoid merely taking over or achieving the aims of these maxims and projects, and must allow others the "space" in which to pursue them for themselves. Respect for others requires, Kant thinks, that we avoid contempt, mockery, disdain, detraction and the like and that we show others recognition (DV, VI, 461–8). Policies of practical love or beneficence require us to recognize the needs particular others have for assistance in acting on their maxims and achieving their ends. Love requires us to adopt maxims of "active, practical benevolence (beneficence), which consists in making another's well being and happiness my end" (DV, VI, 451). To do this is to make the other's ends, which would constitute his or her happiness, in part my own. Such benefi-

---

5   Hill construes "'humanity' as including only those powers necessarily associated with rationality and the 'power to set ends'" (ibid, p. 86). The reading offered here takes this point of departure but also stresses, as we must for instructive consideration of "wide" duties, that human rationality and agency are quite limited. Only so can we understand why Kant thinks both that others are limits, ends that are to be "conceived only negatively – that is, as an end against which we should never act" (G, IV, 437), and that there are positive duties to such ends. Where rationality and agency are patently fragile or incomplete we act against them if we assume that they are not and fail to support them. See Chapters 10 and 12 in this volume.

cence includes assistance to others, generosity, active sympathy and conciliatoriness and the avoidance of envy and malicious joy (*DV,* VI, 451–60).

However, the Kantian conception of beneficence is from the start antipaternalistic. The duty to seek others' happiness is always a duty to promote and share others' ends *without* taking them over, rather than a duty to provide determinate goods and services or to meet others' needs, or to see that their ends are achieved. Beneficence of this sort presupposes others who are at least partly agents and have their own ends. The tension between beneficence and treating others as persons, which is central to many discussions of paternalism, is absent from Kant's account:

I cannot do good to anyone according to *my* concept of happiness (except to young children and the insane), but only according to that of the one I intend to benefit. (*DV,* VI, 453)

What remains is, as Kant indicates, the unavoidable tension between love and respect. We experience it every time we try to work out how to share others' ends without taking them over.[6] It is a tension that has no general solution, but can be resolved in particular contexts. Kant's wide or imperfect duties specify no rules of action for all rational beings, for the ways in which sharing others' ends can perhaps be exemplified would differ wholly for other sorts of rational beings (imagine beings who are psychologically impervious to one another, or less dependent on the physical world than we are), and will in any case differ greatly for human beings with varied ends.

The overall picture that this reading of the Formula of the End-in-Itself generates is that a morally worthy life must be based on maxims of justice (including the rejection of coercion and deceit), of respect and of love. Such a life neither uses others (by acting on maxims that preempt consent or dissent) nor fails to share others' ends (by acting on maxims that either disregard or take over those ends or lend them no support). In each case it is our fundamental proposals, principles or basic policies that must meet these conditions. We neither do nor can make it possible for others, even for others closely affected, to consent to or dissent from *every* aspect (or even every intentional aspect) of what we propose; nor can we lead lives in which we at all times help all others achieve all their ends. Justice and respect vary with circumstances, and beneficence is in addition unavoidably selective. Nevertheless, there are occasions when action of a specific sort is required: There are contexts and relationships to others in which to do nothing or to do the

---

6 But what will count as a good resolution? One guideline might be this: The underlying principle of action should be one that subordinates sharing ends to leaving another with ends that can be shared. Hence only nonfundamental failures of respect may be part of loving action (e.g., presuming to make a minor arrangement or commitment for another that he or she will likely want made; Sonya Marmeladovna's sacrifice of self-respect out of a more fundamental love for her brothers and sisters); but where lack of respect is fundamental, the supposedly loving action will not be so.

wrong thing would be sufficient evidence that the underlying maxim or principle is unjust or lacking in respect or rejects beneficence. Even the unavoidable selectivity of love and beneficence does not mean that when we act on these maxims we can neglect the central projects of lives with which ours are closely involved. The particular demands of beneficence are sufficiently determinate when our lives are interwoven with other lives.

Morally worthy maxims and consenting adults

If this reading of the Formula of the End-in-Itself is to be more than Kantian exegesis, it should help us to think about using others and failing to treat them as persons. The classical examples of presumed sexual and economic use of others, in particular, should be illuminated. But there is one further difficulty in pursuing this thought.

Kant's analysis of treating others as persons leads him, in the first instance, to claims about maxims of morally worthy action. His fundamental moral categories are those of moral worth and lack of moral worth rather than those of right and wrong. Right and wrong, the categories of "legality", are, in his eyes, derivative from those of morality (*G,* IV, 397ff.; *DV,* VI, 218–20). Permissible action conforms in outward respects, but perhaps only in outward respects, with what is morally worthy. Specifically obligatory action not merely conforms outwardly to what moral worth requires, but cannot be left unperformed (in those circumstances) by agents whose maxims are morally worthy.

Yet we have seen that no determinate outward performance is prescribed by maxims of sharing (some of) others' ends. Imperfect duties do not have determinate outward manifestations. Even perfect duties may be performed in outwardly varying ways. For any underlying principle or maxim will have to be enacted or embodied in different ancillary aspects of action in differing situations. How then can we get from a Kantian account of not using others and sharing (some of) their ends – of morally worthy action – to a view of what it is right or wrong to do? How, in particular, can a Kantian account help us to think about the rights and wrongs of particular sexual or economic problems? Is it not likely that there are no timeless sexual or economic obligations for arbitrary rational beings? (And no sex and no economics.)

Yet we may have got a great deal of what we are likely to need. For we need to understand what would be right or wrong in actual, determinate situations. Kantian maxims do not entail rules or prescriptions for all possible contexts. Since a maxim is the *maxima propositio* or major premise of a piece of practical reasoning, it is not there that we should look for details about determinate situations. But when a maxim is supplemented by an account of a particular situation – the minor premise of practical reasoning[7] – we may discover which sorts of outward performance are required, compatible or proscribed in that situation. We may, for example, find that in *these* circumstances there is no way in which *that* sort of action could be compatible with justice; or on the other hand, that in *this* situation we must, if fundamentally committed to a maxim of love or of respect, include something of *that* sort. The conclusions of such reasoning will not be unrestricted; they will hold good not for rational beings as such, nor even for the human condition, but for quite specific human conditions. But when we act this is just what we need to know. We do not need to know what it would be to refrain from detraction or to be generous in all possible worlds, but only how to discern what would be respectful or generous in particular situations. Casuistry is indispensable in all movements from major premise to decision, and all claims about what is obligatory, permissible and forbidden hold only for determinate contexts. Even when we have reasons for thinking that the maxim of some action was itself not morally worthy, judgments of what is obligatory (or merely permissible or forbidden) are made by reference to the outward aspects of action that would have been required (or compatible or ruled out) by acting on a morally worthy maxim in that situation.

Treating others as persons in sexual relationships

If this account of using others and treating them as persons is plausible, it should throw light on areas of life where such failures are thought common. One such area is sexual relationships and encounters. We might also hope to gain some understanding of *why* sexual relationships are thought peculiarly vulnerable to these sorts of failure.

Some sexual coercion is relatively straightforward. It is not hard to see why the victim of rape or of lesser sexual assault is used. However, rape differs from other forms of coercion in that, because of the implicit nature of much sexual communication and social traditions that encourage forms of sexual duplicity, it is unusually hard to be sure when there has been coercion. Also coercion of less straightforward sorts may occur in some sexual relationships and transactions, including relationships between prostitutes and their clients. Here the outward transaction may be an agreement between consenting adults. But when we remember the institutional context of much (at least contemporary, Western) prostitution, including the practice of pimping, brothel keeping and various forms of social ostracism and consequent dependence on a harsh subculture, we may come to

---

7   Contrary to a whole tradition of Kant commentary, Kant has a great deal to say about the minor premise in practical reasoning, especially in the *Critique of Judgment*. For recent discussions see Hannah Arendt, *Lectures on Kant's Political Philosophy;* and Ronald Beiner's interpretive essay in the same volume and his *Political Judgment:* as well as Barbara Herman. "Mutual Aid and Respect for Persons", and "The Practice of Moral Judgment".

think that not all transactions between prostitutes and clients are uncoerced; but it may not be the client who coerces.

Deception is a pervasive possibility in sexual encounters and relationships. There are not only well-known deceptions, such as seduction and breach of promise, but varied further possibilities as well. Many of these reflect the peculiarly implicit nature of sexual communication. Commercial and various distanced sexual encounters standardly use the very means of expression that deeper and longer-lasting attachments use. But when the endearments and gestures of intimacy are not used to convey what they standardly convey, miscommunication is peculiarly likely. Endearments standardly express not just momentary enthusiasm but affection; the contact of eyes, lips, skin, conveys some openness, acceptance and trust (often enough much more); embrace conveys a commitment that goes beyond a momentary clinging. These are potent gestures of human emotional life. If insufficient trust and commitment are present to warrant such expression, then those who use these endearments and gestures risk giving false messages about feelings, desires and even commitments. But perhaps, we may think, at least in sexual relationships that are commercial or very casual or largely formal, it is well understood by all concerned that these expressions have been decontextualized and no longer express the underlying intentions or attitudes or principles that they might express in a more wholehearted relationship. But if such expressions are fully decontextualized, what part are they playing in an entirely casual or commercial or formalized encounter? If the expressions are taken at face value, yet what they would standardly express is lacking, each is likely to deceive the other. Relationships of prostitution, casual sexual encounters and the sexual aspect of faded marriages are not invariably deceptive. Such sexual relations may be either too crudely mechanical to use or misuse expressions of intimacy, or sufficiently informed by trust and concern for the language of intimacy to be appropriate. But relationships and encounters that standardly combine superficial expression of commitment with its underlying absence are peculiarly vulnerable to deception. Where too much is unexpressed, or misleadingly expressed, each risks duping the other and using him or her as means.

Avoiding deceit and coercion is only the core of treating others as persons in sexual relationships. In avoiding these we avoid clear and obvious ways of using as (mere) means. But to treat another as a person in an intimate, and especially an intimate sexual, relationship requires far more. These further requirements reflect the intimacy rather than the specifically sexual character of a relationship. However, if sexual relationships cannot easily be merely relationships between consenting adults, further requirements for treating another as a person are likely to arise in any sexual relationship. Intimate bodies cannot easily have separate lives.

Intimacy, sexual or not, alters relationships in two ways that are relevant here. First, those who are intimate acquire deep and detailed (but incomplete) knowledge of one another's lives, characters and desires. Secondly, each forms some desires that incorporate or refer to the other's desires, and consequently finds his or her happiness in some ways contingent upon the fulfillment of the other's desires.[8] Intimacy is not a merely cognitive relationship, but one where special possibilities for respecting and sharing (alternatively for disrespecting and frustrating) others' ends and desires develop. It is in intimate relationships that we are most able to treat others as persons – and most able to fail to do so.

Intimacy makes failures of respect and of love more possible. Lack of respect in intimate relationships may, for example, take both manipulative and paternalistic forms. The manipulator trades on the fact that the other is not just a possibly consenting adult, but one whose particular desires are known and may depend in part on the manipulator's desires. One who succumbs to so-called moral blackmail could have refused without suffering coercion and was not deceived, but was confronted with the dilemma of sacrificing something central to his or her life – perhaps career or integrity or relationships with others, or perhaps mainly the desire to accommodate the manipulator's desires – unless willing to comply. In intimate relationships it is all too easy to make the other an offer he or she cannot refuse; when we are close to others we can undercut their pursuit of ends without coercion or deceit. Modes of bargaining and negotiating with others that do not make dissent impossible for consenting adults in the abstract, and might be acceptable in public contexts, may yet undercut others' pursuit of their ends in intimate relationships. Here a great deal is demanded if we are to leave the other "space" for his or her pursuit of ends. To do so, and so maintain respect for those with whom we are intimate, requires not only that we take account of the particular interlock of desires, dependences and vulnerabilities that have arisen in a given relationship, but also that we heed any wider social context whose modes of discourse and received opinions may systematically undermine or belittle the other's ends and capacities to pursue them. Respect for others – the most basic aspect of sharing their ends – requires the greatest tact and insight when we are most aware of ways in which others' capacities to pursue ends are vulnerable.

Contexts that make manipulation hard to avoid also offer opportunities for paternalistic failures of respect. Unlike the manipulator, the paternalist does not deploy knowledge of the other and the other's ends to reduce his or her "space" for pursuit of those ends. The paternalist rather begins from a failure to acknowledge either *what* the other's ends are or that they are the *other's* ends. This failure of respect entails failures to share those ends, for to the paternalist they are either invisible or else not the other's ends but rather the ends to be sought for the other.

---

8 By this I don't mean merely that sexual desire may include desires that refer to the other's sexual desires, but more broadly that at least some desires in intimate relationships are altruistic in the strict sense that they can be specified only by reference to the other's desires. This allows for nonsexual and even for hostile intimacy, where desire may be for the frustration rather than the fulfillment of the other's desires.

The paternalist tries to express beneficence or love by imposing a conception of others' ends or interests. Lack of respect is then compounded by lack of love. Those who try to remake or control the lives of others with whom they are intimate do not merely fail in respect, however sincerely they may claim to seek the other's good. Paternalism toward those who have their own ends is not a form of love. However, since it is only fundamental principles of action (whether plans, proposals, policies or intentions) that must meet these standards, superficial departure from them when acting on morally acceptable fundamental principles may be acceptable, or even required. The jokes and surprises in which friendship may be expressed do not count as deceptions: but if they were incident to action or other maxims, they might constitute fraud or serious disrespect or unacceptable paternalism.[9]

Even in intimate relationships not all failures of love are consequent upon failures of respect. It is not only in manipulative and paternalistic action, where others' ends are respectively used and overlooked, that we may fail to share the ends of those with whom we are intimate. Failures of love also occur when the other's ends are indeed respected, and he or she is left the "space" in which to pursue them, yet no positive encouragement, assistance or support for their pursuit is given. Vulnerable, finite beings do not treat one another as ends merely by leaving each other an appropriate "space". Here again detailed knowledge of others and their desires, strengths and weaknesses offers wider possibilities. The support, concern and generosity we need from particular others if our pursuit of ends is to be not merely unprevented, but sufficiently shared to be a genuine possibility, are quite specific. If we are to treat others with whom we are intimate with love as well as respect, we must both see and (to some extent) support their ends.

Avoiding using others and treating them as persons both demand a great deal in intimate relationships. Only the avoidance of coercion demands no more than usual here, perhaps because coercion tends to destroy intimacy. Deception remains a possibility in any relationship, and more so where much is conveyed elliptically or by gesture. In brief sexual encounters as well as in commercial and formalized sexual relations the discrepancy of expression and underlying attitude offers many footholds for deception; even in sustained intimate relationships underlying attitudes and outlook can become, as it were, decoupled from the expression and gesture that convey them to the other, so that the language of intimacy is used deceptively. Intimate relationships also provide appropriate set-

9   A sensitive element of the pattern of casuistry outlined here is determining which principles are the maxim(s) of a given action, and which ancillary. Here counterfactual considerations must always be introduced. We can rebut claims that some principle of action is the maxim of a given act if we have reason to believe that what was done would not have been done but for circumstances under which either maxim might have been expressed by that act. A claim to be acting out of friendship rather than disrespect in throwing a surprise party could be rebutted if the party would be thrown even when friendship would require other implementations (the friend is exhausted or ill or bereaved or shy).

tings for manipulative and paternalistic failures of respect and of love. But the other side of these gloomy thoughts is that intimacy also offers the best chances for treating others as the particular persons they are.

Treating others as persons in employment relationships

It is odd that working life is also often thought to involve uses of others and failures to treat them as persons. Here we do not find the features that open sexual and intimate relationships to these failures. In modern employment relations communication is usually explicit; employers and employees must have some coinciding desires, but need and often have no desires whose content is determined by the other's desires, and may be quite ignorant of one another's specific desires and capacities. Yet there are reasons why this area of life too makes it hard to ensure that nobody is either used or treated as less than a person.

To begin with there are straightforward ways in which we can be used by those for whom we work. Coercion is as vivid a possibility here as in sexual contexts. Sporadic forms include press-ganging and underpayment of wages; institutionalized forms evidently include slavery and forced labor. Straightforward deception is also well entrenched in many forms of employment, and includes fraud and trickery of enormous variety. Hence some ways of being used in working contexts are obvious enough. These, however, are the working relationships that are precluded by developed economic forms, including specifically capitalism. Yet it is widely claimed that capitalist and perhaps other modern economic forms not merely do not treat workers as persons but use them.

This claim can be sustained only if there are unstraightforward ways in which workers are used, in which no maxims of coercion or deception can be attributed to any individual. When individuals act on maxims of coercion or deception we have straightforward failures, with which the legal system of capitalist or other developed economic forms can deal, and which the Kantian perspective, even in its standard interpretations, is well designed to detect. But unobvious forms of coercion or deception are harder to grasp.

A principal source of this problem is that the Kantian approach, like the legal frameworks with which it tallies, is standardly interpreted as individualistic. The interpretation of maxims adopted here is, however, too broad to entail individualism; it does not require that maxims be consciously entertained, nor therefore see only the fundamental intentions of individuals as maxims. On this account the guiding principle of any endeavor or practice or institution is its maxim. In standard economic relations, including employment, all individual intentions may be morally acceptable. The capitalist employer may have fundamental conscious intentions to which employees can indeed consent or refuse to consent, and so may appear on this score not to treat them in any morally objectionable way. What could be more paradigmatic of an offer that can be refused than an offer of employment that is, as they say in wage negotiations, "on the table"? If we argue that such offers are either coercive or deceptive, we must take a broader view of maxims, and judge not the principles that particular would-be employers have in mind but the principles that guide the institution of employment in a capitalist system. The underlying principle of capitalist employment, whatever that may be, might be judged to use some as means or to fail to treat them as persons, even where individuals' intentions fail in neither way.

The extension of ethical reasoning beyond individual concerns must then use the results of social inquiry. If, for example, we accept a Marxist account of capitalist employment, the Kantian framework would generate clear ethical results. On that account capitalist employers, whatever their individual intentions, base their action on a maxim of extracting surplus value (if they did not, employing others would be pointless). Since capitalism aims at profit, it must pay workers less than the value they produce. But this essential feature of capitalism is obscured from workers, who accept deceptive accounts of the terms of their employment, to which consent and refusal to consent are possible. But if the principle to which consent is possible (and actually given) is not the underlying maxim of capitalist employment, then this consent cannot show that there has been no deception at a fundamental level. What it can, however, show is that if there has been such deception, then it is, as in the case of the institutionalized coercion of organized prostitution, a deception without an individual deceiver.

Whether the underlying principle of capitalist employment *in fact* makes consent impossible is a further question. Might there not be a nondeceptive form of capitalism, in which the possibility of dissent is ensured by formulating offers of employment in terms of the principles that really underlie capitalist employment relations? On this hypothesis workers with fully raised consciousness would have a genuine possibility to dissent from or consent to terms of employment that were not ideologically masked, and so would not be used. They would understand that profits would be made off their labor, but might still accept the terms offered. If deceptive forms were all that is wrong with capitalist employment, it might be remediable. But on a Marxist analysis coercion lurks behind the deception. When the underlying form of the capitalist maxim of employment is disclosed, we discover that the deception serves a purpose (or many purposes), and in particular that it makes an activity that workers (under "ideal" capitalism) cannot choose to avoid, except on pain of the coercion of starvation, appear to them as one that they could choose or refuse. Employees will then invariably be used, since they can only dissent from or consent to a principle that is not really the underlying principle of their employement at all. Either they will be both deceived and coerced, if they do not see through this offer, or if they see through it, they will not be deceived, but only coerced. In either case they will be used.

This argument, of course, depends on accepting a Marxist account of the fundamental maxim of capitalist employment and rejecting ideologically opposed accounts, such as those that view all maxims as specific to individual agents and deny that the market itself can be thought of as grounded in maxims. The argument neither supposes nor shows that the claims made about employment relations in "ideal" capitalism apply accurately to employment relations in actual capitalist economies, where, for example, welfare payments may mitigate or remove the coercive character of threatened unemployment. For present purposes the interest of the sketch is to show one way in which workers may be used in the Kantian sense even under systems of employment that ostensibly enshrine the principle of free, and hence of possible, consent, and more generally to show how Kantian ethical reasoning might be extended to the activities of institutions.

In employment, as in other activities, being used is only one way of being treated as less than a person. A great many complaints that workers are not being treated as persons can be traced not to the ways in which they may be straightforwardly or unstraightforwardly used, but to the degree to which contemporary employment practices make a point of treating workers uniformly, and so not as the particular persons that they are. In this respect modern employment practices are wholly different from intimate relationships. Workers in modern (not only capitalist) economies are treated in standard and uniform ways that take little account of differences in ends and capacities to seek them. Where work is "rationalized" and there is a "rate for the job", and hours and qualifications are standardized, there are few ways in which employees' particular ends and abilities to pursue them are taken into account on the job. If doing a job well amounts to doing it the way the robot who may replace you would do it, the maxim of such organization of work cannot go far to treat employees as the particular persons they are. In such employment it is not misuse of information about others' ends or capacities for action, nor intentional failure to share ends, but rather systematic disregard of all particular characteristics that lies behind failure to respect or to share ends. Rationalized work practices treat all workers as persons (qualms about exploitation of employees apart) but take little account of their specific characteristics. This practice may be partly remedied in some workplaces, or eased by management or work practices that allow more worker involvement or self-management. But if such arrangements are only a matter of introducing "a personal touch", they impose outward forms of respect and beneficence without underlying changes that would treat workers as the particular persons they are, and may only introduce paternalistic and manipulative practices into working life.

A larger question in this area is whether working life should be like this. Shouldn't working life be impersonal? Isn't this our guarantee against nepotism, favoritism and other types of personal bias and patronage? Are not justice and respect the sole relevant standards in employment relations? The career open to talents has to be based on maxims of impersonal fairness. But the career open to talents is also the career closed to lack of talent and conducted without concern for the fact that we are not abstract "consenting adults". Perhaps the underlying issue is whether the lives of those who work with or for one another can be sufficiently separate for justice and respect to be the only considerations. Mutual solidarity and assistance that goes beyond what the job requires may not be dispensable whenever work is collaborative. Our working relations too are relations with determinate others and not with ideally rational economic men and women.

Conclusions

The popular view that we can readily be used or treated as less than persons both in intimate relationships and at work can be sustained in a Kantian framework. In each context we may be faced with proposals to which we *cannot* possibly (whether because deceived or because coerced) give our consent. But the characteristic ways in which we may be treated as less than persons even when not used are quite different in the two contexts. In intimate relationships everything is there that would make it possible to treat the other as the particular person he or she is, by respecting and sharing his or her pursuit of ends. Here if we fail to respect or to share the other's ends, the failure is imputable to us. But contemporary employment relations are set up on impersonal principles. Employer and employee have only "relevant" information about one another, and need only slightly coinciding ends. Hence when employees are not treated as the particular persons they are, the failure does not standardly rest with a particular employer, who may correctly think that he or she has done all that an employer should. The demand that we be treated as the particular persons we are on the job is a *political* demand for a "maxim of employment" that acknowledges our desire and perhaps need to be treated more as the persons we are, and less impersonally. It is a demand that we must take seriously if we doubt that we are, even in the maturity of our faculties, merely consenting adults.

7

Universal laws and ends-in-themselves

Kant's *Groundwork* is the most read and surely the most exasperating of his works on practical philosophy. Both its structure and its arguments remain obscure and controversial. A quick list of unsettled questions reminds one how much is in doubt. The list might include the following:

Why does Kant shift the framework of his discussion three times in a short work?
Does he establish that there is a supreme principle of morality?
Does he show that the Categorical Imperative is that supreme principle?
Does he show that human beings are free agents for whom such principles of morality are important?
What is the relationship between the various apparently distinct formulations of the Categorical Imperative?
To what extent are any (or all) of them action-guiding?

This chapter concentrates on the last two of these questions.[1] It is mainly about the equivalence of the various formulations of the Categorical Imperative; it also sketches ways in which the Categorical Imperative can guide action. I shall comment only on three significantly different formulations, the Formula of Universal Law (FUL), the Formula of the End-in-Itself (FEI) and then (more briefly) the Formula of the Kingdom of Ends (FKE).

By way of reminder the three formulations may be stated:

FUL: *"Act only on that maxim through which you can at the same time will that it should become a universal law" (G, IV, 421).*
FEI: *"Act in such a way that you always treat humanity whether in your own person or in*

This chapter originally appeared in *Monist* (1989).

1 This chapter takes up themes covered in part in the two preceding ones, which were written much earlier. I have tried to make the discussion self-contained as well as complementary. The principal development in my understanding of the issues is that I now take more seriously Kant's comments on our uncertainty about our own and others' maxims, and so now entirely avoid notions such as "volition" or "intention" that might suggest that maxims must be present to consciousness. This change forms part of an increasingly "anti-Cartesian" reading of the larger Kantian enterprise and is reflected here also in showing how we can respect the status of maxims as the hinge of Kantian ethical reasoning without thinking that morality must be psychologically "inward".

the person of any other, never simply as a means, but always at the same time as an end" (*G*, IV, 429).

FKE: This is not initially stated as a single second-order practical principle. Kant writes that "morality consists in the relation of all action to the making of laws whereby alone a kingdom of ends is possible" (*G*, IV, 434), where a "kingdom of ends" is characterized as "a systematic union of rational beings under common objective laws" (*G*, IV, 433). A later version runs: "All maxims as proceeding from our own making of law ought to harmonize with a possible kingdom of ends as a kingdom of nature" (*G*, IV, 436).

Since these are the versions of the Categorical Imperative for which Kant himself claims equivalence, it seems reasonable to restrict an initial discussion to them. He asserts that these three formulations of the Categorical Imperative are

at bottom merely so many formulations of precisely the same law, one of them by itself containing a combination of the other two. (*G*, IV, 436)

This is a puzzling claim. For he promptly interprets FUL as specifying the *form* that maxims of duty must have and FEI as determining the *matter* or end that they must have, while asserting that FKE provides a *complete determination* of all morally worthy maxims. How can all three formulae be "so many formulations" of the same law if the first two are essentially incomplete and complementary, whereas the third combines the two incomplete formulae and is itself complete? How can he say this and then go on rather dismissively to assert that the significant difference is "subjectively rather than objectively practical" (*G*, IV, 436), and to suggest that it is just that FUL is best followed in moral judgment "in accordance with the strict method" (*G*, IV, 436), whereas FEI is useful when "we wish also to secure acceptance of the moral law" (*G*, IV, 436)? Surely Kant cannot have it both ways. If the three formulations are at bottom the same, then the first two are also complete, and contain all that the third contains, and any differences are indeed merely subjective; if the first two are incomplete and specify distinct aspects of the third, then none of them is at bottom the same as any other, and the difference between them is by no means merely subjective.

A surprising amount hinges on the resolution of this dilemma. If the claim of equivalence cannot be sustained, the argument of *Groundwork*, and more generally of Kant's ethics, is deeply unsatisfactory. Most of the arguments or argument sketches that he provides for the supreme principle of morality lead us to (at least toward) FUL; yet much that he and many of his admirers (and even of his critics) find attractive and significant in guiding moral reflection and action derives from FEI. It is the ideal of treating persons as ends and avoiding using them as means, not the ideal of acting on universalizable principles, that has become part of our culture. If the formulations are not equivalent, then the attractive idea of treating others as ends and never as means may not be groundable by Kantian arguments, and the charges of rigorism and formalism that are perennially leveled against FUL may lead us to conclude that even if Kantian arguments show that this is the supreme principle of morality, still we have not discovered a principle that can help us lead our lives.

A preliminary consideration of the three formulations suggests that they *must* be distinct, for two reasons. First, they rely on distinct sets of concepts. FUL invokes the notions of *action on a maxim* and of *universal law;* FEI those of *action, persons, means* and *ends* and *humanity;* FKE those of *action, law* and *kingdom of ends.* Second, FUL apparently proposes a single test of the morality of actions – that they be performed on universalizable maxims – whereas FEI apparently makes two demands – that others not be treated as mere means *and* that they be treated as ends-in-themselves. If these initial impressions are confirmed, Kant's practical philosophy is deeply flawed. We can make sense of the structure of *Groundwork* only if there is some reading of the formulations under which the claimed equivalences hold. The most demanding task for such a reading would be to connect FUL and FEI. If these two can be shown to be "at bottom the same", then so plausibly can FKE. Conversely, any otherwise plausible reading of FUL and FKE that sustains their equivalence gains some support from the fact that Kant claims that they are equivalent and that it is vital to his argument that they be so.

Agents and maxims: the common context of the formulae

The three formulations are all offered as tests that agents can apply to proposals for action. The Categorical Imperative is nowhere proposed as a principle that will by itself generate or entail a universal moral code. It is not a moral algorithm (unlike the Principle of Utility) but (supposedly) a criterion of moral action for agents who act freely, and so may start with various possible proposals for action. The common assumption of the three principles is that there is some way by which agents can filter these initial proposals to check whether they are morally acceptable. Each formulation of the Categorical Imperative is offered as an answer to the agent's question "What ought I to do?"[2] on the assumption that agents will have certain tentative plans, proposals and policies that they can consider, revise or reject – or endorse and pursue.

A first account of the difference between the three formulations might stress the differing perspectives from which this agent's question is taken up. FUL addresses the question from the perspective of agents who acknowledge that others too are agents, and enjoins them to shun principles that could not be

---

2   This is the second of the three questions that Kant formulates as the fundamental concerns of reasoning beings. The other two questions are "What can I know?" and "What may I hope?" In the *Logic* and the *Anthropology* all three are said to be aspects of the question "What is man?" For a line of thought that suggests that the fundamental question of practical thinking is better taken as "How ought I to live?" see Bernard Williams, *Ethics and the Limits of Philosophy.*

adopted by others, that is, that could not be universal laws. FEI addresses the agent's question from the perspective of agents who acknowledge that action affects others, and enjoins them to avoid damaging others' capacities to act. To settle whether or not FUL and FEI are equivalent, the answers the agent's question receives when explicated from these two perspectives must be compared. First, however, the two versions of the agent's question must be explicated.

Kant sees action as undertaken on certain principles, which he speaks of as determinations of the will or as agents' *maxims*. The interpretation of the notion of a maxim has been the scene of much argument. For present purposes five points are needed. I shall state them briefly without textual comment; these are points on which there is some agreement.[3]

First, a maxim is a *subjective* practical principle in the sense that it is a principle of action of a subject or agent at some time. This is no more than a restatement of the point that Kant's ethics presupposes agents with principles or policies of action, which are then to be tested, rejected or accepted, rather than offering a practical algorithm that prescribes a correct act for each situation.

Second, we can speak of *the maxim* of a given act. From this it follows that not every principle that an act exemplifies is its maxim, nor even every principle that embodies a description under which the agent acts. Maxims are not to be equated simply with intentions, which may be multiple, some of them profound and others superficial. Rather, a maxim is the *underlying* or *fundamental* principle of an action in the sense that any other principles to which the act conforms are selected and explicable because that is what it takes to act on a certain maxim in that situation (as perceived by the agent). The maxim of an act is the principle that *governs* the selection of *ancillary* principles of action that express or implement the maxim in a way that is adjusted to the agent's (perceived) circumstances. (The maxim is the *maxima propositio* or highest principle of some piece of practical reasoning.) This point is crucial for Kant: If acts could have multiple maxims, no test of the moral character of maxims could guide action. One of the commonest lines of criticism of Kant on this issue works by assuming that maxims are to be identified with agents' intentions (or perhaps simply with practical principles that an act exemplifies), infers that acts do not have unique maxims and concludes that the Categorical Imperative, *whatever its demands may be,* cannot in principle guide action.

Third, it does not follow from the claim that maxims are underlying principles that they must be the policies of a lifetime or even of a prolonged stretch of life, although they may be just that. Scrooge made miserlinesss his maxim, but was not doomed to perpetual miserliness. It is a corollary of taking the freedom of

---

3   For relevant discussions see Rüdiger Bittner, "Maximen"; and Otfried Höffe, "Kants kategor-ischer Imperative als Kriterium des Sittlichen". See also Chapter 5 in this volume; Onora O'Neill, "Agency and Anthropology in Kant's *Groundwork*"; and Barbara Herman, "Mutual Aid and Respect for Persons".

agents seriously that maxims are not unchangeable dispositions. Even uncharacter-istic action is performed on some maxim. However, many agents will in fact hold some maxims for long periods, using them repeatedly to guide their action in varying situations. The specific acts that express, say, loyalty in friendship or commitment to the profit motive will, of course, vary enormously depending on the contexts in which agents find themselves. (If this account of what a maxim is is correct, the long litany of claims about Kant's demand for rigid and insensitive uniformities of conduct may be misplaced.)

Fourth, the maxim of an act may be a principle that embodies *no* description under which an agent consciously acts. Kant takes it that agents' self-consciousness is fallible; we are opaque to ourselves (as also to others) and may be unsure which principle governs our actions in any situation. We may *hope* that we are fundamentally honest, but be well aware that situations we have faced have been ones in which, as luck would have it, honesty was the best policy, so that we were never put to the test. All that we can do to try to ensure that we are honest on principle rather than by luck is to align our outward actions with those that would express a maxim of honesty in ways appropriate to each situation we face. It remains possible that some new situation will disclose to us how limited and fragile our honesty is, leading us to doubt whether the stretch of life that con-formed so well to the outward demands of honesty was actually governed by a maxim of honesty.

Fifth, since the implementation of maxims will differ according to circum-stances, a test on maxims is not *and cannot be* enough to determine the rightness or wrongness of particular acts (their "legality"); it can only reveal the moral quality or worth of maxims (and so is in Kant's terms a test of "morality"). Kant defines duty not (as would be common today) as outward performance of a certain sort, but as action that embodies a good will, that is, action on a maxim of a certain sort (*G*, IV, 397). However, although moral worth is more fundamen-tal than rightness in Kant's theory, rightness and wrongness are more easily ascertainable. This is simply a corollary of the opacity of our self-knowledge. If we are unsure what the maxim of a given act is, we cannot be sure whether it is morally worthy. Despite their best efforts at principled and self-conscious action, agents are prey to self-deception and selective perception. This is not rare or exotic but commonplace – we are repeatedly tempted to ascribe maxims that place acts and agents in a more flattering or a more lurid light. By contrast, it would be relatively easy, *if we had a test to identify morally worthy maxims,* to determine whether an agent who acted on such a maxim would have acted in a specific way in those circumstances. In his most pessimistic moments Kant doubts whether we can ever know that a morally worthy action has been per-formed. If he is right we can never judge the morality of acts. This pessimism need not, however, stop us from judging whether acts that conform to such maxims have been performed – provided that we have a criterion for identifying morally worthy maxims.[4] The various formulations of the Categorical Imperative are supposed to provide this criterion.

This preliminary account of Kant's theory of action provides the common context for each formulation of the Categorical Imperative. It enables us to distinguish two views of what it might be for FUL and FEI to be "at bottom the same". The two formulations might be equivalent in that both classify maxims, and derivatively the acts that conform to or violate those maxims, in the same ways: They might be simply extensionally equivalent. Any maxim that would be rejected as morally unworthy by FUL would also be rejected as morally unworthy by FEI; the same maxims would be identified as maxims of duty by both tests; the same acts would be classified as right or wrong according to their conformity or nonconformity to those maxims of duty. Alternatively, FUL and FEI might be intensionally equivalent, if it could be shown not merely that they in fact yield the same results, but that this result follows from the nature of the formulations. If FUL and FEI can be shown intensionally equivalent, then extensional equivalence is also shown; but merely extensional equivalence would not guarantee that the formulations are "at bottom" the same. A merely extensional equivalence would have practical use, for it would show that either formulation could be used to identify maxims of duty. However, if we want insight into why these formulations are both versions of the supreme principle of morality, we will need to be shown not merely *that* they yield the same results, but *why* they do so.

The formula of universal law

FUL states that we should act only on those maxims through which we can will at the same time that they be universal laws. This is often misconstrued as a claim that morally worthy maxims must be ones that we are willing, that is, want, to see universally adopted (cf. Golden Rules, Universal Prescriptivism). This may not be such deeply dyed heteronomy as a utilitarian pursuit of maximal satisfaction of desires; but it is heteronomy nonetheless, and Kant rejects it decisively (e.g., *G,* IV, 430n).

Kant's understanding of FUL is uncompromisingly rationalist. He asks whether we can without contradiction will (not "want") a maxim (underlying

---

4 How then can the Categorical Imperative demand morality as well as legality? Presumably it demands that we *strive* to adopt morally worthy maxims; not that we know when or whether we or others have succeeded. The effort to be morally worthy is most plausibly thought of simply as the effort to align action with that which would be done on a principle of moral worth. Even those who succeed in this effort for a long stretch of life will have no guarantee that their maxims were morally worthy: A set of acts no more determines a unique maxim than a set of observations determines a unique natural law. If this conclusion is correct, persistent anxiety that action that accords with duty may yet not be done out of duty is neurotic. The point has a familiar theological analogue: If "by their fruits ye shall know them" is correct, then a persistent worry about the state of one's soul or salvation that is separated from the effort to do good works is neurotic. I am indebted to David Milligan for prompting on this point.

principle) to hold as a universal law. His explication of his idea reveals that FUL (like FEI) has two components. He writes:

We must be *able to will* that a maxim of our action should become a universal law – this is the general canon for all moral judgment of action. Some actions are so constituted that their maxim cannot even be *conceived* as a universal law of nature without contradiction, let alone be *willed* as what *ought* to become one. In the case of others we do not find this inner impossibility, but it is still impossible to *will* that their maxim should be raised to the universality of a law of nature, because such a will would contradict itself. (*G*, IV, 424)

These two distinct aspects of FUL are to serve as the criteria for maxims of strict (or perfect) and of wide (or imperfect) duties. Kant brings duties of justice and of respect for self and others under the first heading, and duties of beneficence and self-development under the second.[5]

Maxims that violate strict duties are said to yield *contradictions in conception* if we try to universalize them: The very attempt to think of the maxim as universally adopted breaks down owing to some incoherence in the way the world would have to be if it were universally acted on. For example, the means required for all to adopt and act on the maxim might be incompatible with the results of all adopting and acting on the maxim. A maxim of deceit can readily be seen as one that we cannot even conceive as univerally adopted. The project of deceit requires a world with sufficient trust for deceivers to get others to believe them; the results of universal deception would be a world in which such trust was lacking, and the deceiver's project was impossible. Of course, this is not to say that in the actual world there is some contradiction in the thinking of each deceiver. Far from it. Deceivers simply aim to use the trust that others have created to get their own deception believed. They rely, as Kant puts it, on substituting generality (and their own exemption) for universality (*G*, IV, 424). The Categorical Imperative is a thought experiment that we can reject: That is why Kant must *show* that it is the supreme principle of morality, and why we can defy it. It is only when we take up the thought experiment and try to universalize a nonuniversalizable maxim that a contradiction shows up in our thinking.

There is a fair amount of agreement on this type of account of contradictions in conception, but little on whether it provides a plausible criterion for the range of duties conventionally classified as perfect duties. Some commentators argue that contradictions in conception emerge only from attempts to universalize maxims whose universalization would destroy a *practice* on which any action on the maxim depends (as universalizing false promising undercuts the practice of promising on

5   The argument of this chapter does not rely on the notorious examples of *Groundwork*. Even if these are good illustrations of Kant's theory, they are only *illustrations*, unavoidably illustrations for a specific type of rational being and actually illustrations for human beings with quite determinate social relations. The question of the equivalence of the formulations of the Categorical Imperative cannot be resolved by inspecting the illustrations, or by comparing different uses of an individual illustration. On the status of Kant's illustrations see Chapter 9 in this volume.

which each proposed false promise depends). They suggest that other maxims, for example those of coercive and of brute violence, which aim to destroy or damage, respectively, agents' plans and their bodies, can sail past the contradiction in conception test. They suggest that there is no contradiction in universal coercion or in universal killing or murder or assault. However, both instrumental and brute violence undercut the agency of those whom they victimize. It is not merely that victims do not in fact will the maxims of their destroyers and coercers: They are deliberately made unable to do so, or unable to do so for some period of time. A test that demands action only on maxims that all can adopt will require that action not be based on maxims of victimizing.

It is unclear how the contradiction in conception test would deal with *self-inflicted violence,* such as suicide or self-mutilation, or with *violence to willing victims,* such as assisted suicide and sadism toward masochists. Kant thought such maxims violations of duty; but the Categorical Imperative may not show this. These cases are at least complex, and need to be discussed in their own right, rather then with the aim of "rescuing" or condemning the way Kant articulated them. I shall not do so here because the sorts of violence that most concern us are brute and coercive violence, and here the implications of FUL are definite. There is a palpable contradiction in the thinking of an agent who adopts a maxim of murder or assault, or of duress and intimidation, which aims to destroy or undercut at least some other's agency, yet (tries to) will the same maxim as a universal law. Agents cannot coherently (nor honestly) assume that the agency of those whom they *plan* to destroy or damage can *already* be discounted! It is only after a killing that its victims are no longer agents; before the killing they are agents and must fall within the scope of FUL; victims even of minor coercive violence are evidently agents before and after the violence, which cannot be willed as a universal law because it aims to undercut agency, at least for some time.[6]

Maxims that violate wide or imperfect duties are said to generate contradictions in the will when we try to universalize them. A contradiction in the will is not a contradiction in thinking, but a contradiction between the thought experiment of universalizing a maxim and the background conditions of the lives of specifically *finite* rational agents. Kant speaks of beings such as ourselves as *finite* rational beings not only because their rationality is limited, but because they are finite in many ways. They have limited capacities to act that can be destroyed or undercut in many ways. Self-sufficiency is an incoherent goal for finite rational beings; at most they can coherently aim to minimize their dependence on others. They cannot universalize maxims either of refusing to accept any help or of refusing to offer any help, since help may be needed for the survival of their agency. The thought experiment of willing a world of principled nonbeneficence is not one

---

6   For discussions of FEI and violence see Thomas E. Hill, Jr., "Humanity as an End in Itself": and Barbara Herman, "Murder and Mayhem".

that finite rational beings can make consistent with an awareness of the limitations of their own agency, on which all their plans for action (including the futile – or perhaps self-deceiving – plan of self-sufficiency) are premised. A duty of beneficence grounded in this way is only an imperfect duty: It demands only the rejection of a maxim of refusing (to give or receive) any help, and not the adoption of a maxim of providing or accepting all help (which would in any case be impossible). Which particular forms of help should be offered or accepted by finite rational beings must vary. The types of helping and being helped that are vital to sustain agency will vary in different situations and with different sorts of finitude.

These considerations show, if they are plausible, only that there is a reading of FUL that escapes the common charge that the formula identifies no maxims of duty, and the rather less frequent claim that there is no difference between the two aspects of the formula.[7] It is a further matter to show that Kant provides an account of practical reasoning that includes procedures of deliberation that lead from maxims to particular decisions. Although it is slightly tangential to the main point of this chapter I shall sketch an account of deliberation to which I believe Kant is committed; without this it is hard to set out the various moral distinctions that agents can draw using the Categorical Imperative.

In the first place the Categorical Imperative allows us to distinguish maxims of different sorts. Maxims that are not universalizable are contrary to duty; to act out of such maxims is morally unworthy. Maxims that are universalizable are not contrary to duty; to act out of them would not be morally unworthy. Where a maxim is universalizable but the maxim of rejecting it is not, the maxim is one of duty and to act out of it would be not merely not morally unworthy but morally worthy.

Most practical reasoning is not a matter of determining the moral status of maxims. We usually already have learned or worked out the moral standing of many common maxims of duty and of many "cautionary" maxims whose adoption would be contrary to duty. These standard maxims are the principles that we take care to inculcate and identify before we ever meet life's problems. They, rather than the second-order Categorical Imperative, constitute the almanac with which we commonly set sail on the sea of life. We have good reason to check the almanac we inherit; but fortunately it does need to be recalculated before every move.[8]

The almanac can be used to guide deliberation about specific proposed acts.

7 For the latter claim see recently Wolfgang Kersting, "Der kategorischer Imperativ, die vollkommenen und die unvollkommenen Pflichten", esp. p. 414.
8 The metaphor is lifted from Mill, because it is a good metaphor. It may seem plausible that there will be (incomplete) convergence between Kantian maxims of duty and the rules of thumb with which a utilitarian sets sail. I doubt whether the degree of convergence can be charted, in part because of the impressionistic quality of much utilitarian deliberation. Despite its calculating ambitions, utilitarian deliberation has to embark with data that are all too pliable.

Kant distinguishes duty from conformity to duty, and much practical reasoning remains to be done after an agent knows and seeks to observe (or flout) the standard maxims of duty. For example, a certain proposed act may be one that could not (in the actual circumstances) be performed by somebody whose maxim was a maxim of duty; such an act would be forbidden. Another act may be one whose omission would (in the actual circumstances) be incompatible with acting on a maxim of duty; such an act would be obligatory. Presumably most acts are neither forbidden nor required in most circumstances. If Kantian reasoning does not classify maxims exhaustively into maxims of duty and maxims that are contrary to duty, and Kantian deliberation reveals that the acts that express or that violate a maxim in particular circumstances vary, then there may be some acts that are forbidden or required in certain circumstances, and others that are forbidden or required in all circumstances. Kantian reasoning does not even aim to provide an algorithm for action; nor does it automatically generate an "overload" of obligations. On the other hand, the common claim that FUL is without practical import is apparently mistaken. FUL provides a way to discriminate maxims of duty, and the pattern of deliberation just sketched can link those maxims to particular contexts of action and decision.

The formula of the end-in-itself

Humanity and rational nature

FEI states that we should treat humanity, in ourselves and in others, "never simply as a means but always at the same time as an end". There are so many apparent discrepancies between this formula and FUL that it is worth beginning by reemphasizing a basic similarity. FEI too answers an agent's question. It purports to tell agents what they ought to do. Although the term *maxim* does not occur explicitly in the formulation of FEI, I shall take it that we must read it as a claim about the maxims that ought to guide action. The notion of a maxim plays the central role already explicated in Kant's theory of action; without it we can neither distinguish the types of actions that are to be prescribed or proscribed by duty, nor consequently work out which particular acts may be forbidden or obligatory in specific situations.

The most striking discrepancy between FUL and FEI is that FEI refers explicitly to *humanity*. This might suggest that the two formulations cannot be equivalent. Is not FUL formulated for rational beings as such, and FEI a much more restricted formulation that is relevant only to human beings? Does not this show that FEI can *at best* be a special case of FUL? If this is the whole story, we shall not be able to make much sense of Kant's subsequent claim that the formulae are "at bottom the same".

To see whether it is the whole story we need to consider the relationship between claims about rational beings as such and claims about human beings in *Groundwork*. Kant insists in the preface on the need for "pure moral philosophy completely cleansed of everything that can only be empirical and appropriate to anthropology" (*G*, IV, 389). As in other works, he proceeds on the assumption that there may be many species of rational beings, but that we are acquainted only with our own. Hence his illustrations of the Categorical Imperative are constrained to use instances drawn from human affairs, but they are intended to illustrate a theory that is not restricted to human beings. Given the structure of the work it *cannot* be shown in Chapters I and II that these are genuine illustrations, for it is not until the latter parts of Chapter III – after page 450 – that Kant gives reasons for thinking that human beings are indeed free and rational beings.

So long as the agent's question is taken to be "What ought I to do if my maxims are to be such that any other free and rational agent can adopt them?", this causes no problems. FUL can be stated without assuming even that there are any other agents: The boundaries of the class of free and rational beings can be left indeterminate. But if the agent's question is to be asked in a form that emphasizes the agency of whoever may be affected, something must be said about the scope of the formula. We can only answer "What ought I to do if my maxims are to leave intact the agency of those whom my action may affect?" if we take some view of who those other agents are. Yet the structure of *Groundwork* means that Kant is in no position in Chapter II to assert that or whether there are any free and rational agents. In particular he is in no position to assert human freedom or rationality. (He is, of course, well aware that it is part of our common understanding of morality that we are free and rational beings – but only the considerations of Chapter III could vindicate that assumption.)

Kant's move in this predicament is appropriate and quite explicit. He argues hypothetically, using an assumption that can only be vindicated at a later stage of the argument. He invites us to *suppose* that there are free and rational beings, for example ourselves:

Suppose, however, there were something *whose existence* has *in itself* an absolute value, something which as *an end in itself* could be a ground of determinate laws . . . (*G*, IV, 428)

He continues, in a mode he uses rarely but (I believe) quite deliberately, by signaling that what he says is (at this point in the argument) mere assertion:[9]

Now I say that man, and in general every rational being, *exists* as an end in himself, *not merely as a means* for arbitrary use by this or that will . . . (*G*, IV, 428)

9 See Kant's usage at p. 448: "Now I assert . . . And I maintain . . . " Here too he is explicitly introducing a claim about human freedom that he emphasizes has not yet been argued. The assertoric mode is used not to replace argument but to signal that what we can have *at this stage* is avowedly mere assertion. Cf. Chapter 3 in this volume.

He tells us quite explicitly that the principle *rational nature exists as an end in itself* is "put forward here as a postulate" and that the "grounds for it will be found in the final chapter" (*G*, IV, 429). At the moment we need not concern ourselves with the plausibility of the supposition. What we are given is a provisional means by which we can refer to a specific class of free and rational beings who can be thought of as on the receiving end of proposals for action. The actions of rational beings of a specific sort do not affect all other rational beings without restriction. They affect a restricted class of rational beings who are, to put the matter vaguely, part of the same world.

Hence for human beings the Categorical Imperative can be formulated as a principle constraining the maxims to be adopted by those whose action affects humanity. However, the term *humanity* is no more than a placeholder. Since it is "rational nature in general" of which Kant postulates that it exists as an end-in-itself, FEI could also be formulated, for example, as the requirement to treat Martianness or rational animality or rational extraterrestriality never as mere means but always as an end-in-itself. [10]

Ends-in-themselves and mere means

The reference to "humanity" in FEI is then, it seems to me, not a significant restriction of the scope of the principle. It is simply one way of reminding ourselves that we must take *some* view of the range of agents whom our action affects. It is obvious enough why *we* are interested in formulating the principle by reference to human beings; but in doing so we do not rule out the formulation of analogous principles of many other sorts, and we do not vindicate the claims that human beings are free and rational, nor that they are ends-in-themselves.

Whatever the specific nature of some type of rational being, Kant asserts at page 428 that it is an "absolute value" and an "end-in-itself". Why an *absolute* value? The obvious point to latch onto is the initial contrasting claim of Chapter I that all goods apart from a good will are conditional goods. Rational beings presumably must be nonconditional values because they alone can will anything; hence they alone can have a good will. As the presuppositions of nonconditional good, rational beings must then be of absolute value. Why *ends-in-themselves?* Beings that have nonconditional or absolute value cannot be subjective ends – for subjective ends are conditional on the subject whose ends they are. Yet if rational beings, who are the recipients of one another's actions, fail to orient their actions to respect or sustain one another's agency, they fail to treat one another as ends even in a "negative" sense. They may destroy or undercut one another's agency

10   An analogously determinate form of FUL could be read into the Formula of the Law of Nature: "*Act as if the maxim of your action were to become through your will a universal law of nature*" (*G*, IV, 421). Here too we are asked to consider whether a maxim could hold universally among the rational beings of some specific natural order.

and willing. Hence rational agents who treat one another as ends must act on maxims by which rational agency itself is subordinated to no other ends, but rather is made a constraint or limit on all pursuit of ends: They must treat one another as ends-in-themselves.

If we are to go any further toward showing whether FUL and FEI can be equivalent, we need to see more specifically what it would be to treat certain beings, say human beings, as ends-in-themselves. Kant's account of the matter is most readily developed by considering the contrast he draws between treating something as a mere means and treating it as an end-in-itself; so I shall first sketch what it is to treat another as mere means.

To treat something as a mere means is to treat it in ways that are appropriate to things. Things, unlike persons, are neither free nor rational; they lack the capacities required for agency. They can only be props or implements, never sharers or collaborators, in any project. Things cannot act, so can have no maxims, so cannot consent to or dissent from the ways in which they are used. Nothing we can do disables things from acting on the very maxims we ourselves adopt – for that is something from which they are in any case wholly disabled. When we impose our wills on things we do not prevent, restrict or damage their agency – for they have none. The parallel to FUL is clear. FUL, in requiring that we act only on maxims through which we can also at the same time will that they be universal laws, places no restriction on our treatment of things. All that counts is that the maxim be adoptable by others, and our treatment of things is to be constrained only insofar as needed to secure that possibility.[11]

By contrast, if we treat other agents as mere means, we do prevent, damage or restrict their agency. We use them as props or implements in our own projects, in ways that preempt their willing and deny them the *possibility* of collaboration or consent – or dissent. It is not merely that we may act in ways to which they *do not* consent; we act on maxims to which they *could not* consent. Kant offers a good example of the way in which deceit precludes the *possibility* of the other's acting on the maxim on which the duper acts:

The man whom I seek to use for my own purposes by such a [false] promise cannot possibly agree with my way of behaving to him and so cannot himself share the end of the action. (*G*, IV, 429)

The modalities are important here. To use another as mere means, as Kant sees it, is to act on a maxim that the other *cannot* also adopt. This amounts to acting on a maxim that one *cannot* at the same time will as universal law. The false promiser,

---

11   The sharp distinction Kant draws between persons and things is not convincing. The intermediate possibilities often perplex us. Are infants and animals, the senile and the comatose, things or persons? Provided that we respect other persons, may we use all inanimate objects as mere means – including works of art, deserts and wildernesses, the earth itself? Despite his insistence that ethics is for *finite* rational beings, Kant fails to address the full implications of finitude.

the deceiver, the coercer, the rapist – all of them *guarantee* that their victims cannot act on the maxims they act on. (If erstwhile victims adopt the maxims of those who victimized them, they have regained some agency and become collaborators and colluders, not victims, and the initiator's maxim must be reconstrued.) Maxims by which we treat another as mere means are maxims that lead us to contradictions in conception when we try to universalize them.[12]

This, I think, shows partial equivalence between FUL and FEI. The contradiction in conception version of FUL is intensionally equivalent to the aspect of FEI that requires action only on maxims that do not treat humanity, or more generally rational nature, as mere means. In using FUL to test our maxims we check that those maxims could be acted on by all other agents; in using FEI to test our maxims we check that action on them disables no other agents from adopting them. The two checks must yield the same results.

It remains to consider more closely what it is to treat others as ends-in-themselves and whether doing so is equivalent to acting on maxims that survive the "contradiction in the will" version of FUL. How does treating others as ends-in-themselves go beyond refraining from using them as mere means?

Ends-in-themselves (if there are any) must, unlike subjective ends, hold equally for all agents. They cannot be agents' goals, but only universal constraints on the pursuit of goals. A necessary and hence universal constraint or limit on the pursuit of goals is constituted by the need to maintain the conditions of the pursuit of goals, that is, the need to maintain agency throughout the universe of agents under consideration. A major part of what is required to maintain agency consists in not undercutting or destroying it by using any agent as mere means. However, the agency of finite rational beings is too vulnerable for us to be able to secure it merely by guaranteeing that it is not undercut or destroyed. We cannot adequately protect it merely by rejecting maxims that make others' agency logically impossible. Finite rational beings also need positive support from others if they are to remain agents.[13] Kant thinks that

12   This account of FEI may seem implausibly weak. Surely, one may think, what is reprehensible is proceeding without others' *actual* consent – it is not enough to make sure they have the possibility of consent. This is, I believe, an illusion. We do no wrong if we proceed without any actual consent from others who are wholly unaffected by our actions. If we proceed without the actual consent of those who are involved in some way, we do it by bypassing their wills, and so making both consent and dissent not merely absent but *impossible* for them. There are good reasons to prefer a formulation of the principle that looks at possible rather than actual consent to others' maxims. First, it avoids the unclarities and inadequacies of actual consent criteria; second, it provides a way of covering under a single principle the cases of those whom an action affects and those whom it does not.

13   Different forms of finitude would presumably require differing maxims of imperfect obligation. Human beings are sociable beings who form close bonds, reproduce sexually and have a long infancy; they suffer pain, illness, old age and death. They are highly vulnerable, both physically and psychologically. They depend enormously on others for large parts of their lives, and are partly dependent on others throughout their lives. When things go badly their very capacity for agency fails. They clearly have reason to take imperfect obligations most seriously. For other

humanity could no doubt subsist if everybody contributed nothing to the happiness of others but at the same time refrained from deliberately impairing their happiness. This is, however, merely to agree negatively and not positively with *humanity as an end in itself* unless everyone endeavours also, so far as in him lies, to further the ends of others. (*G*, IV, 430)

Simple restraint from using other finite beings as mere means may not be enough to secure their agency. If vulnerable sorts of agency are to be developed and kept intact, the bearers of such fragile capacities for action may also need help in achieving certain subjective ends. The sorts of help they may need are unpredictable. Kant thinks that among human beings two principles of imperfect obligation are important. One demands that we not show principled indifference, let alone hostility, to the subjective goals of others: that we not make nonbeneficence into a principle. The other demands that we not neglect to develop some talents or abilities that may be useful in pursuing our own or others' ends.

These limited maxims of beneficence and of developing talents are maxims of imperfect obligation. Nobody could act on a maxim of securing all the ends of all others, or of developing all possible talents. On Kant's account, to make the happiness of others a matter of imperfect obligation is to help others in achieving ends that they cannot achieve unaided, but that are both permissible and important to their survival as agents. Only by making the ends of others to some extent our own do we recognize others' agency fully, and acknowledge that they are initiators of their own projects as well as responders to our projects, and moreover vulnerable and non-self-sufficient initiators of projects. That (I think) is the point of the idea that we should agree "positively" with humanity as an end-in-itself. We ought to act on maxims of supporting others in ways that secure their agency. Support for others' projects is owed not because their individual ends are objective, but because they are *their* ends, and some success in acting is vital to their remaining setters of ends. Equally, some success in acting is vital to secure our own capacities to act, and if we have wholly neglected the means to such success, our own (and perhaps others') agency may be endangered. Agency must be not merely (negatively) respected but (positively) fostered if beings like ourselves, who are precariously able to act and never self-sufficient, are to interact in ways that do not suppress but secure agency. The equivalence of treating others as ends-in-themselves and of acting on maxims that can pass the contradiction in the will test is based on the fact that both principles express the idea that agency be secured for all. Among vulnerable beings agency can be secure for all only when agents act to support as well as to respect one another's agency.

---

sorts of finite rational beings there might be little to duty beyond justice and respect. Kant's famous comment in *Perpetual Peace* that the problem of justice can be solved even for a nation of devils perhaps suggests that matters other than justice cannot be solved, and sometimes are not significant, for rational beings of other sorts.

The question of equivalence

The readings of FUL and FEI sketched in the preceding sections have been informed by two fundamental concerns.

First, each has been based on a certain understanding of Kant's theory of action, and in particular of the crucial role of maxims as the point of application of the Categorical Imperative. Maxims, I have claimed, are *underlying* principles of action, which govern the choice of surface principles, but may well be inaccessible to consciousness. This interpretation has the corollary that the fundamental notion of Kant's ethical theory, that of *duty,* cannot (contrary to the assumption of many interpreters) be equated with the notion of obligatory action. Kant defines duty as involving good will (*G,* IV, 397); the basic relation of action to duty is that of action "out of" duty. Since he also holds that maxims, the underlying principles of actions, may be imperfectly known to agents and to others, he neither does nor can equate right action, which it is constantly our business to judge, with action out of duty. Either right action is permissible action, that is, action that in the actual circumstances does not indicate a maxim that is contrary to duty; or it is obligatory action, that is, action that in the actual circumstances cannot be omitted if maxims of duty are to be observed. Right action of either sort may *in fact* be governed by – done out of – quite varied maxims. Finite agents cannot be sure that their maxims are untainted by self-interest; they can make sure that their actions conform to untainted maxims.

In the second place both readings have taken Kant's rationalism seriously. Neither reading has referred to desires or to inclination. I have interpreted FUL as a criterion for picking out maxims that *could* be universally adopted by finite beings capable of agency; and I have understood FEI as a criterion for picking out maxims that beings capable of agency *could* survive and accept being adopted by others whose action affects them. The difference between the two formulae is indeed one of perspective. Any set of maxims that could be universally adopted among a set of interacting finite beings who are capable of agency is a set of maxims that secures and does not destroy the agency of those whose interaction it constrains.

The Categorical Imperative in the FUL and FEI formulations asks us to solve a certain sort of simultaneous equation: to determine a set of maxims that could be adopted simultaneously by all members of a possible world of interacting and non-self-sufficient beings. To do this we may adopt either the perspective of one who checks whether all others can follow certain proposed guidelines for action, or the perspective of one who asks whether all who are acted upon will retain the capacities for agency that would permit action on the proposed guidelines. The two perspectives can be combined, as they are in FKE, when we ask whether the maxim(s) in question can be adopted in a "systematic union of rational beings under common objective laws – that is, a kingdom" (*G,* IV, 433). The thought experiment of the kingdom of ends is one where we consider ourselves both as acting (as hypothetical universal legislators) and as acted upon (as hypothetical subjects to those laws, whose agency would be destroyed by a law that made others into mere means or failed to treat them as ends-in-themselves). Each formulation of the Categorical Imperative is then a way of testing maxims for their conformity to the basic requirements of a possible community of beings who are and remain capable of action, despite the vulnerability to one another's action of their capacities to act.

The equivalence between FUL and FEI can be thought of as an equivalence between an agent's and a recipient's perspective on the possibility of action of a certain sort. However, care is needed here. Contemporary deontological ethics discusses ethical relations both in terms of obligations (what ought to be done) and in terms of rights (what ought to be received). But the perspective of obligations and the perspective of rights are not even extensionally equivalent. Specifically, if there are any imperfect obligations, then there are at least some obligations whose performance is not allocated to specified others, to which no rights correspond. FEI is not just a criterion for a set of rights; like FUL it includes a criterion for picking out principles of imperfect duty. FEI remains a response to an agent's question, with the specific twist that the agent asks: "What ought I to do, given that my action impinges on others, and may destroy or erode their capacities for action?" Looking at principles of action in terms of their impact on agents, and the possibility of the principles being consented to by those on whom they impinge, is a different matter from looking only at principles of recipience. Kant's question is always fundamentally the agent's question, "What ought I to do?", not the recipient's question, "What am I owed?"[14]

Matter, form and symbol

Even if these readings of FUL and FEI are accepted, and the claimed equivalence is found convincing, we still have no insight into Kant's claim that FUL gives the form and FEI the matter of maxims of duty (G, IV, 436). Indeed, in a way the puzzle is increased. If the formulae are equivalent, then surely if either gives the form, so must the other, and if either gives the matter, so must the other.

Kant's use of distinctions between matter and form is an intricate matter; I offer only brief comments. We might ask how we can think of the difference of perspective between FUL and FEI as a difference between giving the form and giving the matter of the Categorical Imperative. FUL focuses on maxims agents can universally act on, that is, on the possible "form" of universal agency; FEI focuses on the maxims according to which agents can treat others, who are in a

---

14 For exploration of asymmetries between theories of rights and of obligations see Chapter 10 in this volume and Onora O'Neill, *Faces of Hunger: An Essay on Poverty, Development and Justice*, esp. Chaps. 6–8.

sense the recipients or "matter" of their action, if those others' agency, that is, ability to adopt maxims, is not to be impaired. FUL emphasizes the form that action must take if action of the same form is to be possible for all; FEI emphasizes the constraints that preserve the "matter" that makes agency possible. Just as the figure and the ground of a pattern may be mutually determining, and yet leave us in no doubt which we call the figure and which the ground, so the universalizable form of maxims of duty and the agency-respecting content of maxims of duty may be mutually determining without being indistinguishable. Indeed, only if the relation between the form and matter of the Categorical Imperative is mutually determining in this way can Kant's claim that the formulae are at bottom the same and yet distinguishable make sense.

If the form and matter of maxims of duty are in this way mutually determining, Kant's other claims about the relation betwen the formulations of the Categorical Imperative are more readily understood. The "incompleteness" of FUL and FEI is not a matter of their needing to be supplemented if they are to be applied; the point is rather that neither is fully *explicit,* and that they are inexplicit in complementary ways. FUL emphasizes not making impossible like action by others, rather than the constraints on action that preserving others' agency imposes; FEI emphasizes the constraints on action that preserving others' agency imposes, rather than the like action whose possibility for others is thereby left open. Whether we start moral reasoning from one perspective or from the other, we can use the criterion to consider both which sorts of action are possible for all members of a possible world of agents, and which sorts of mutual treatment and restraint remain available in a possible world of agents who can adopt the same maxims.

And so we are led to FKE. Kant tells us that this is a "very fruitful concept" (*G,* IV, 433). Yet it does not add to the content of FUL and FEI. Its "fruitfulness" lies rather in two facets. First, it acknowledges both the figure and the ground of the moral pattern. Second, the visual metaphor of form and matter, figure and ground, is mapped onto the heritage of religious and political metaphors in which an ideal "kingdom" or "realm" is the symbol of dreamed-of but unachieved community. The ideals of morality can be imaged as the communion of saints and as the social contract. Kant's use of the metaphors of "kingdom" or "realm" in *Groundwork* is austere; yet it is the potent symbol of ideal community that points us to later works where he links his answers to the questions "What ought I to do?" and "What may I hope?" The embodiment of the Categorical Imperative in human life is no doubt incompletable: It points us toward hoped-for possibilities, toward this-worldly as well as other-worldly eschatologies, toward political as well as religious futures in which an "ethical commonwealth" or "church invisible" is seen as a path toward unflawed community.[15]

---

15 Cf. Paul Ricoeur, "Freedom in the Light of Hope", and other essays in his *The Conflict of Interpretations.*

If these considerations are plausible, Kant can coherently claim that the various formulations of the Categorical Imperative are all "at bottom the same", although FUL and FEI are complementary and FKE combines both. If they are not plausible, there is a hiatus in the center of Kant's ethics. We would have reason to judge that his arguments led toward a formal supreme moral principle of indeterminate scope, but not toward the resonant principle that most draws our admiration.

8

Kant after virtue

Intelligibility and rationality

It is always fun to see somebody saw off the branch on which he is sitting; but if we are on the same branch, we may worry about where the landing will be. Alasdair MacIntyre's *After Virtue*[1] is gripping reading for anybody interested in the prospects for an objective ethics. MacIntyre appears almost to sever the possibility of such an enterprise. He diagnoses modern moral discourse as deeply fragmented, condemning us to "interminability of public argument" and "disquieting private arbitrariness" (p. 8). Liberal pluralism, with its agnosticism about the good for man, is only a genteel and halfhearted expression of a Nietzschean position (pp. 112 and 240). The crucial *intellectual* move by which this predicament – the unexpectedly sour fruit of the Enlightenment project – was reached was the rejection of "a moral tradition of which Aristotle's thought was the intellectual core" (p. 110). But the transition has not been merely intellectual: The fragmentation of modernity is patent in innumerable aspects of our social and cultural lives.

Yet MacIntyre does not intend to undercut the possibility of practical reasoning. He holds that the Nietzschean view that "all rational vindications of morality manifestly fail" (p. 111; cf. p. 107) is (despite its "terrible plausibility" [p. 238]) necessarily inconclusive (Chap. 9 and pp. 239–41). The targets of Nietzsche's destructive arguments are those very thinkers of the Enlightenment whose writings are based on a rejection of Aristotelianism. Hence "Nietzsche does not win the argument by default against the Aristotelian tradition" (p. 240), and "the key question does indeed become: can Aristotle's ethics, or something very like it, after all be vindicated?" (p. 111). MacIntyre's central positive claim is that "the Aristotelian tradition can be restated in a way that restores intelligibility and rationality to our moral and social attitudes and commitments" (p. 241). His aim in cutting back the pretensions of modern moral thought is not to fall into any sort of moral relativism but to make room for the regrowth of Aristotelian ethics.

MacIntyre's restatement of the Aristotelian tradition in *After Virtue* concen-

This chapter originally appeared in *Inquiry*, 26 (1984), 387–405.

1 Alasdair MacIntyre, *After Virtue: A Study in Moral Theory.* Parenthetical references in this chapter, if not to Kant's works, are to this book.

145

trates on the restoration of *intelligibility*. He takes to task various modern conceptions of human action and self-identity that undermine intelligibility (Chaps. 14 and 15). Human activity is not composed of basic actions, each intelligible in isolation (p. 190); human actors are not composed of sets of roles, each with its separate goals and standards (p. 190 and Chap. 3). Intelligible action requires a setting of practices and institutions. Such settings themselves have histories without which agents' various intentions are unintelligible; "behaviour is only characterised adequately when we know what the longer and longest-term intentions invoked are and how the shorter-term intentions are related to the longer" (p. 193). And once we are concerned with "longer and longest-term intentions" we cannot accept any "liquidation of the self" (p. 191); rather we need a "narrative concept of selfhood" (p. 202), a

concept of a self whose unity resides in the unity of a narrative which links birth to life to death as narrative beginning to middle to end. (p. 191)

When we live the narrative of our lives many different continuations of the story are possible at a given juncture:

If the narrative of our individual and social lives is to continue intelligibly . . . it is always both the case that there are constraints on how the story can continue *and* that within those constraints there are indefinitely many ways that it can continue. (p. 201)

As agents we seek intelligible continuations of our narratives, continuations that will give unity to individual lives and to traditions. MacIntyre interprets this quest for unity in human lives and traditions as a reconstrual of the Aristotelian good for man. For Aristotle the good for man, human flourishing, consisted in living a reason-guided life within the practices and institutions of the *polis*. In MacIntyre's reconstrual of the Aristotelian tradition the good for man does not presuppose a determinate social and political context, and we therefore cannot form a determinate concept of the good for man. But we can seek to move toward such a conception, whatever inherited context of practices and institutions forms the setting of our lives. This position commits MacIntyre to an open-ended, almost procedural vision of the human telos: "the good life for man is the life spent in seeking for the good life for man" (p. 204). In many ways this is closer to post-Enlightenment conceptions of human nature as inherently intelligent and rational, yet otherwise open, than it is to Aristotle's more determinate conception of human nature.

Such a quest for the good is not merely an endeavor to live with the tradition we inherit, and in so doing to exemplify whatever specific virtues the practices of this tradition require. It is also an attempt to order these goods, to move from an inherited and historically determinate "moral starting point" (p. 205) toward lives and ways of life in which what is inherited from a tradition is developed and extended and changed. The restored objectivity of moral claims is to be understood by reference to the particular sort of unity and coherence toward which a tradition and the lives embedded in it may develop (p. 209). This development will be mediated by the continuing embodied debate that is internal to any live tradition.

But if traditions embody such "continuities of conflict" (p. 206), then there will always be (as MacIntyre points out) many ways in which to develop a tradition and many ways in which the lives led within a developing tradition may acquire narrative unity. The choices that individuals confront, and that they may collectively make for the traditions they inhabit, are often choices between equally intelligible continuations. Hence we cannot avoid the question whether one intelligible continuation of a life or tradition might be better or worse than another. It is therefore vital to know what "sustains and strengthens traditions? What weakens and destroys them?" (p. 207), and also whether some traditions are themselves evil and others not.

If there are many ways in which a life or tradition might acquire narrative unity, then we must, it seems, be concerned with more than the intelligibility of lives and traditions. In particular it would seem that we might want to know what reasons there are to pursue one rather than another intelligible continuation of our lives and traditions, and therefore that we should be concerned with *rationality,* and in particular with practical reason. Yet in *After Virtue* MacIntyre says surprisingly little about practical reason. He hints that there is one virtue over and beyond those needed to maintain existing practices and the individual lives set within them, namely "the virtue of having an adequate sense of the traditions to which one belongs or which confront one" (p. 207). This virtue is needed to "grasp . . . those future possibilities which the past has made available to the present" (p. 207). Yet MacIntyre's account of this virtue is disappointingly sketchy:

its presence or absence rather appears [in] the kind of capacity for judgment which the agent possesses in knowing how to select among the relevant stack of maxims and how to apply them in particular situations. (pp. 207–8)

As historical counterparts to Aristotle's *phronimos* MacIntyre instances Cardinal Pole and Montrose, whose practical reasoning manifested "those virtues which enable their possessors to pursue both their own good and the good of the tradition of which they are the bearers" (p. 208). Not only does this formulation seem to presuppose a determinate conception of the good for traditions and lives led within traditions; it leaves us with a vague understanding of the capacities for practical reasoning that Montrose and Pole had.

MacIntyre's conception of the good for man is less determinate than Aristotle's, and a great deal of our understanding of his position must therefore hinge on his account of the other pivot of Aristotelian ethical thought, the theory of practical reasoning. Since this account is not fully developed in *After Virtue,* but is promised us in a future book (p. 242),[2] it may seem premature to focus on the account of practical reasoning that MacIntyre's project requires. But just because practical reasoning seems to me to be central to MacIntyre's enterprise, though, so far, its least clearly mapped region, it also seems very much worth exploring. My aim in this exploration is constructive; in particular I hope to suggest that, despite MacIntyre's decisive rejection of Kantian ethics, Kant's account of practical reasoning has much to offer MacIntyre's project.

In MacIntyre's critique of modernity criticisms of Kant's ethics play a central part. In consequence he draws no help from the greatest theory of practical reasoning of modernity. Yet modern ethical thinking itself constitutes – as MacIntyre has amply shown – a tradition of debate: a tradition whose intelligible continuation might take a number of forms. In joining this debate I hope to show that Kant's ethics can be differently construed, and that, so construed, it includes an account of practical reasoning that is highly relevant to MacIntyre's project. There are, I think, also features of MacIntyre's account of the intelligibility of action that are notably, and damagingly, lacking in Kant's ethics. However, this is an occasion not for seeing what MacIntyre's work might contribute to the refurbishing of Kantian ethics, but for seeing what Kant's ethics can offer to MacIntyre's refurbishing of Aristotelian ethics.

I shall not, however, spend any time showing that MacIntyre's reading of Kant is a misreading. His understanding and criticism of Kant is venerable enough; in many respects it dates back to Hegel. A rebuttal of this reading would therefore demand a confrontation with a long and continuing tradition of commentary on Kantian ethics. This tradition rests a great deal on Kant's illustrations of this ethical theory; the reading of the Kantian enterprise on which I shall draw is based more on Kant's account of the structure and capacities of his theory. My concern here is not to argue that this procedure yields a superior reading of Kant's ethical writings, but rather to emphasize elements that may be valuable for MacIntyre's enterprise. I shall begin by pointing to four aspects of MacIntyre's reading of Kant that seem to me to stand in the way of a positive use of Kant's work in completing the enterprise of *After Virtue*.

Four venerable Kant criticisms

Perhaps the most fundamental of MacIntyre's criticisms of Kant is that he thinks Kant is paradigmatic of modern moral philosophers in that he has tried to write an ethic of rules rather than ethic of virtues. "In Kant's moral writings . . . we have reached a point at which the notion that morality is anything other than obedience to rules has almost, if not quite, disappeared from sight" (p. 219; cf. pp. 42 and 112).

2   Since published: Alasdair MacIntyre, *Whose Justice, Which Rationality?*

Secondly, by trying to fit an ethic of rules into a universal conception of human nature Kant is led, in MacIntyre's view, to the implausibilities of contending that there is a unique set of moral rules for all men and all time. The traditional charge of *rigorism* against Kant is that he misguidedly holds that

reason . . . lays down principles which are universal, categorical and internally consistent. Hence a rational morality will lay down principles which both can and ought to be held by *all* men, independent of circumstances and conditions, and which could consistently be obeyed by every rational agent on every occasion. (p. 43)

The difficulty of rigorism can best be indicated by pointing to any plausible moral rule that cannot be universally acted on, or to any morally trivial or pernicious rule that can be universally acted on (p. 44). Notoriously, "Do not steal" can be acted on only where the institution of property has arisen, but everyone can obey an injunction to face north at noon. Universality does not seem to yield plausible necessary or sufficient conditions for rules to be moral rules.

It is easy to move from the problem of rigorism to a third of the traditional difficulties of Kant's ethics, *formalism*. This is the claim that Kant's theory lacks substantive moral implications. It is awkward to maintain the charges of rigorism and formalism simultaneously, but they form a natural sequence. If the only plausible moral rules must take account of varied circumstances, they must have determinate content, and so cannot be derived from or discriminated by purely rational or formal considerations. MacIntyre joins those who see Kant's ethics as merely formal and not action-guiding:

The project of providing a rational vindication of morality had decisively failed; and from henceforward the morality of our predecessor culture — and subsequently of our own — lacked any public, shared rationale or justification. (p. 48)

The source of Kant's formalism lies in his repudiation of an adequate, substantive conception of human nature. In MacIntyre's view, Kant correctly saw the futility of the heteronomous project of seeking to derive morality from an account of human nature as it actually exists, and in particular from human wants as they actually are. MacIntyre also takes it that Kant has a conception of human nature: Kant's strictures on a morality that is based on "human nature" are in fact criticisms of attempts to ground morality on the nonrational aspects of human nature (p. 50). Kant's problems, according to MacIntyre, arose from a fourth inadequacy in his and other modern theories, namely a misguided attempt to base ethics on an impoverished conception of human reason. Modern thought in general mistakenly sees reason as only calculative and so unable to deliberate about ends. It therefore precludes the possibility of an ethic that is both universal and substantive. If there is any ethical theory that suffers neither from rigorism nor from formalism, Kant has missed the mark. According to MacIntyre, Kant has a defective conception of rationality and more generally of practical intelligence: "For Kant one can be both good and stupid" (p. 145).

Reasoning and acting

This coherent set of objections of Kant's ethics is both formidable and venerable, and I hope to show that it should be rejected. Even if this point is convincing, it will not amount to any vindication of Kant's ethics. But it will at least show that his enterprise deserves serious attention from anyone who wants to work out an ethical position that is grounded on a conception of practical reasoning but lacks Aristotle's certainties about the good for man.

The nub of MacIntyre's criticisms is the contention that rationalism in ethics would have failed if it could not at least discriminate (even if not generate) a unique moral code for all times and places. He holds that Kant must be seeking an ethical position whose *content* is universal. This is far from many of Kant's claims – if not always from the spirit of his examples. Kant's notion is that the content of our maxims of action does not derive from reason at all. What reason supplies is a test of the morality of acts we propose. If reason is to be practical, that is, to guide action, it has to be connected in some way to the particularities of persons, situations and lives. What we do, in the end, is always a quite particular act, and one bound to reflect the conceptual, and probably the institutional, resources of the setting in which the act is performed. Given this point, the likelihood of universal moral rules that reason supplies or discriminates would depend on there being universal, conceptual and probably institutional resources. Kant may have been more optimistic than many of our contemporaries on this point. But his claim that reason can be practical does not hinge on this optimism. On the contrary, the possibility of *practical* reason hinges for Kant on the possibility of bringing reason to bear on what is most evidently particular and local about proposals for action. Reason, in the form of the Categorical Imperative, is to be brought to bear on the *maxim* on which an agent proposes to act. A maxim, Kant states, is "a subjective principle of action" (*G*, IV, 421n; cf. 401n). By this he means that it is the principle of action adopted by some agent at a particular time. (It may, but need not, be subjective in the other sense of aiming at what that agent wants.) Maxims, being principles of action, are potential candidates for formal distinctions: They (unlike mere reflexes and reactions) have the syntactic structure that would be necessary for formal distinctions to be applied. For example, maxims might be divided into the consistent and the inconsistent.

It is tempting, given this standard information, to construe maxims as agents' intentions. However, there are a number of reasons for thinking that this is too hasty, and that at least not all of an agent's intentions are maxims. In the first place, Kant habitually speaks of "the maxim" of an agent in a given context; but in acting there is often much that is intentional, some of it relatively specific and some of it quite indeterminate. As MacIntyre insists, "shorter-term intentions . . . can only be made . . . intelligible by reference to some longer-term intentions" (p. 193). Maxims, one might then think, would have to be those principles embodying intentional descriptions of what agents propose that have the prominence of decisions, or of intentions for the future. This is certainly a common understanding of what Kantian maxims are, but not, I now think, an adequate one.

In the first place, intentions for the future are (among all the descriptions of what we do intentionally) the most likely to be transparent to consciousness. Indeed, many would hold that intentions for the future *must* be something that an agent is aware of or avows. But Kant insists that agents are not always aware of, nor ever infallible about, what their maxims are (*G*, IV, 398–9; *DV*, VI, 446). The human heart is opaque and self-knowledge is not reliable. We cannot even know whether there has ever been a truly moral act. We cannot even be sure about our own maxims. And the source of the obscurity is not the difficulty of the rational test that maxims of moral action must meet, but our uncertainty about the maxims that lie behind our own and others' acts.

A second reason why maxims cannot be understood as conscious decisions or intentions for the future is that not every act is preceded by any such intention. Yet Kant holds that (mere reflex action apart) we always act on some maxim. Even unplanned and negligent action, for example, is performed on some maxim and so open to moral assessment. Negligent failure to develop any talents is one of Kant's standard examples of morally unworthy action.

But if an agent's maxim is not an intention for the future, a consciously formulated decision, what is it? We know at least that Kant thinks that the maxims that we should act on are ones that could be universally acted on. Hence it is unlikely that those intentional accounts of what an agent is doing that incorporate reference to the particular features of the agent's context or situation could be the agent's maxim. Further, there are many such specific intentions in most sequences of action, but there is supposedly a single maxim.

For these and further reasons it seems most convincing to understand by an agent's maxim the *underlying* principle by which the agent orchestrates numerous more specific intentions. For example, in making a visitor welcome I may make a cup of tea. In so doing there are numerous specific intentions: the warming of the pot, the offer of sugar and the like. But what guides and makes sense of these specific ancillary intentions is the underlying principle. Had that underlying principle differed, then I would not have performed just those acts, or not just in those ways. Had I perhaps wanted to make the visitor unwelcome, there would have to be at least some variation in the outward performance. In a different social setting – for example among the Athenians, who had no tea – the same underlying principle would have had to be expressed by way of a different set of specific intentions: wine or conversation, perhaps. It is also possible that the specific intentions with which a given underlying principle might appropriately be implemented in one context could be used to enact a different underlying principle in another context. Our specific intentions can all too easily be "taken the wrong way". Underlying principles, however, need not be longer-term princples, for we remain free to change them. It does not, however, follow that we are free to adopt just any underlying principle – for example, one formulated in terms of the concepts of an alien tradition.

If maxims are underlying principles in this sense, it is clear enough why Kant should have thought it difficult to tell on what maxim a given act is performed. For a given outward performance might be ancillary to more than one underlying maxim. The action that seems disinterestedly helpful may be performed for the sake of a good reputation (*G,* IV, 398–9; 407). Kant often proposes that isolation tests – such as asking, "Would I have done it if nobody had known?" – can help us to know what the maxim of an act is. But such tests are not decisive when they appeal to counterfactual possibilities, given that the consciousness of agents is not transparent.

This construal of what maxims are has very definite implications for the venerable criticisms of Kant's ethics that MacIntyre renews. In the course of examining these we can also find multiple corroborations of the proposed understanding of what a maxim is.

Moral rules and rigorism

If maxims are underlying principles that make sense of an agent's varied specific intentions, then it seems that it may be quite misleading to think of them as adoptions of moral rules, in the sense of rules that prescribe or proscribe specific actions. Maxims will rather be indeterminate guidelines that can be acted on *only* when *supplemented* by more specific intentions. For example, if a maxim were as indeterminate as "don't deceive others", then in a certain (modern) context it might be reflected in matters such as not writing false checks or becoming a spy or manipulating public opinion, but in other (traditional) contexts these actions might be unavailable, indeed incomprehensible. In such contexts we might think that specific intentions such as not concealing weapons or food supplies from others might be important in implementing a maxim of no deception.

But if this is the case, then maxims can have little to do with the rightness or wrongness of acts of specific types, and much more to do with the underlying moral quality of a life, or aspects of a life. In adopting maxims of a morally appropriate sort we will not be adopting a set of moral rules at all, but rather some much more general guidelines for living. To have maxims of a morally appropriate sort would then be a matter of leading a certain sort of life, or being a certain sort of person. The core of morality would lie in having appropriate underlying principles rather than in comforming one's actions to specific standards.

These inferences about what it would be to have morally appropriate maxims are entirely borne out by Kant's views on morality. He distinguishes at all times between acting out of morally appropriate maxims, which is the heart of morality, and merely acting in accordance with such maxims, an outward conformity that is important for the "legality" rather than the morality of action. Action that meets the inner standard is on Kant's account morally worthy or virtuous; action that meets the latter standard is morally right. However, he classifies only those maxims to which no single more specific outward performance is indispensable as *maxims of virtue*. For such maxims the notion of outward conformity is indeterminate. It is clear enough that for Kant the categories of virtue (the morally worthy or virtuous, the morally indifferent and the morally unworthy or vicious) are more fundamental than the categories of right (the obligatory, the [merely] permissible and the forbidden). For his definition of right action is that it conforms in (at least) outward respects to action that is done out of a morally worthy maxim (*G*, IV, 398ff.; *MM*, VI, 218–20).

In spite of the strikingly clear textual evidence that Kant sees moral worth or virtue as more fundamental than mere rightness, there is a great weight of Kant commentary in which, as in *After Virtue*, it is claimed that Kant is in the first place a thinker who gives to the notions of right and wrong a central place. Perhaps a source of this reading is that Kant asserts that he is concerned above all with *duty* – and duty for modern thinkers is concerned with the external aspects of action. It is common to think of Kant as having wrought a change in our understanding of duty by thinking of duties as attaching not to particular roles and positions but to rational beings as such, but there is another equally major difference between his and most modern conceptions of duty. Kant writes *explicitly* at the beginning of his most read work on ethics that "the concept of duty . . . includes that of a good will (*G*, IV, 397) and, it seems, sees our duties as in the first place duties to act out of certain maxims – that is, to structure our moral lives along certain fundamental lines, or to have certain virtues. Kantian moral duties cannot be exacted. Kant's conception of duty is Christian or Stoic rather than that of an ethic of rules of action; this has been said before, but (I think) more often rejected in favor of a pharisaical reading. As works are the fruit of faith in a particular context, so right action can be seen as outward reflections of particular underlying maxims in a particular situation. Since maxims have to be diversely implemented in diverse situations, it may be that even if we can establish which maxims a person of virtue must adopt, we will still not be able to establish that action of any specific sort is morally obligatory.

Indeed, thinking further along these lines, it seems unclear whether one can expect to derive *any* account of right and wrong action from an account of moral worth or virtue. For the very fact that underlying principles must be acted on in ways that reflect specific situations and institutions suggests that we may not be able to generate any rules of action that are morally required regardless of context.

Kant accepts this point with respect to the duties that he calls imperfect duties. In the case of maxims such as those of beneficence or self-improvement there may be no determinate action that is invariably required. Yet he holds that other maxims of morally worthy action − those that formulate maxims of strict duty − do include or generate some rules of action that are morally required in all contexts. However, one may well think that Kant was mistaken in holding that there were any rules of action required for the implementation of underlying moral maxims in all contexts. His examples of right action, as MacIntyre and others have repeatedly pointed out, refer to particular social institutions. But the implications of this fact are unclear. Does it suggest that Kant cannot successfully claim that he has *any* theory of right? Or does it suggest that a theory of right *must* be to some extent context-specific, whereas a theory of virtue can and need not be?

There is also a range of further unclarities in Kant's position here. For example, he says nothing about the possibility of action on a morally worthy maxim that is supported by inappropriate or ill-chosen specific intentions (care for others manifested in a policy of attentive criticism) or about avowed maxims of action that do not appear to be supported by any specific intentions. He consequently assumes too readily that it is possible to determine what actions, considered apart from whatever underlying maxim they may implement, will be ascertainably actions that are determinately obligatory, permissible or forbidden. But what is not in doubt, I suggest, is that Kant offers primarily an ethic of virtue rather than an ethic of rules.

The Kantian virtues, however, are not fixed states of character whose outward expression forms readily identifiable and generally recognized patterns. In hard times, in Roman and in modern empires, the virtues are not *and cannot be* exemplified in the standard "lives" of communities. The very fragmentation of modern life, which MacIntyre repeatedly stresses, requires that the maxims of virtuous men and women be supported and expressed in particular situations by specific intentions that reflect very varied possibilities and predicaments. There are no *stock* ways in which the Kantian virtues of respect and justice, beneficence and self-development can be enacted. Today just men and women may find that they must either get their hands dirty or refuse involvement, rather than share in the political life of their communities. The same considerations that cast doubt on the possibility of *Rechtslehre* for human beings as such make of the Kantian virtues matters in the first place of constant inward morality but variable outward expression. The Kantian virtues are indeed not the Aristotelian virtues; but if MacIntyre's own analysis of modernity is correct, they are as close as we can get in modern conditions, and MacIntyre's account of a way forward into new communities sketches a counterpart to Kant's discussions of human moral progress in his later writings. The very conditions that render *Rechtslehre* for men as such unattainable require Kant to separate the moral life into principles and outward observance.

Indeed, it is not implausible to suggest that Kant's ethics is *already* a response to the fragmentation of modernity that MacIntyre laments. The Kantian "opposition" of (human) nature and morality is the fundamental alienation that underlies the fragmentation of the moral life. This is not something that we can simply "overcome", but rather the historical reality that requires all modern ethical thinking to focus on ethics for those living in defective communities, where there may be no standard ways to map inward virtue onto outward requirements. Kant is deeply pessimistic in his perception of the predicament, and offers no reasons for thinking that, as things now are, a life guided by maxims of virtue will be a flourishing or happy one. Although we may rationally *hope* for the long-term coordination of virtue and happiness, as things now are, and in particular as we now are, the virtuous life may cost us rather than constitute our happiness.

If Kant does offer both a morality of virtue and a separate account of right action, the charge of rigorism falls. For this is the claim that Kant's moral theory proposes, as the principles of morals, rules that are clearly not universal rules. But if his theory is not in the first place one that yields rules of action at all, it is also not a theory that proposes universal rules of action. At most the charge of rigorism might be leveled at Kant's theory of right, when and insofar as he claims that certain maxims of morally worthy action can be acted on only in ways that are implausibly narrow, and so seeks to identify unlikely universally binding outward duties.

Formalism, teleology and practical reasoning

By establishing that Kant's ethic is not (primarily) an ethic of rules, and so not (centrally) vulnerable to the charge of rigorism, we have shown only where practical reasoning is to be applied. We have done no more than outline the target for practical reasoning. It remains to be seen whether reason can indeed discriminate among possible maxims and in so doing provide any sort of criterion of virtue, let alone whether practical reason can establish anything about what is outwardly right in particular situations.

The charge of formalism, which MacIntyre reiterates, is the claim that Kant has quite failed in his aim of showing how reason can be practical. The Categorical Imperative, supposedly the supreme principle of practical reason, is alleged to bear no fruit. To show that this is not the case it is necessary to offer a reading of the Categorical Imperative that does yield conclusions, and also to give some reasons for thinking both that the Categorical Imperative is a purely rational principle and that the distinctions it draws are indeed morally significant. At this point, and in the face of many shipwrecks, I can offer no more than a sketch of how this might be done.

To make it plausible that the Categorical Imperative is a rational principle, I intend here to focus initially on the Formula of Universal Law, leaving aside all mention of ends-in-themselves and all discussions of the equivalence or nonequivalence of distinct formulations of the Categorical Imperative. The Formula of Universal Law runs: "*Act only on that maxim through which you can at the same time will that it should become universal law*" (*G*, IV, 421). The test proposed is that we ask whether the maxim by which we propose to guide our acting be one that we *can* simultaneously will that all others should act on. There is no mention here of what we would want all others to do, or of what everybody might want done. The point is to consider what we *can* consistently will be done, not only by ourselves but also by all others. In restricting our maxims to those that meet the test of the Categorical Imperative we refuse to base our lives on maxims that necessarily make of our own case an exception. The reason why a universalizability criterion is morally significant is that it makes of our own case no special exception (*G*, IV, 404). In accepting the Categorical Imperative we accept the moral reality of other selves, and hence the possibility (not, note, the reality) of a moral commuunity. The Formula of Universal Law enjoins no more than that we act only on maxims that are open to others also. Here once again we find corroboration of the reasons for regarding maxims as underlying guidelines rather than as specific principles of action. For clearly countless trivial and morally indifferent rules of action cannot be universally acted on; yet the fact that not everyone can live in the same manner or place does not suggest that there cannot be moral principles.

The maxims that cannot consistently be willed as universal laws are, it seems, those that if acted on by some cannot then be acted on by others. If, for example, successful action on a maxim will *in principle* preclude others from successfully making that maxim the basis of their action, then the maxim is not universalizable. Intuitively, Kant's claim is that the underlying principles of a life (and perhaps of a tradition) are morally unworthy if they cannot be shared. Surface intentions, by contrast, may be unsharable without threatening the possibility of community. The demand for universalizability is a demand that the deepest principles of our lives not preclude the possibility of community.

To show that this understanding of Kant's universalizability principle does have substantive implications, and that the charge of formalism fails, it is necessary to sketch some sample derivations. One group of plausible examples of maxims that cannot be universally shared would be maxims whose central aim would, if realized, defeat the very possibility of action: A maxim of coercion, a maxim of deception and a maxim of controlling or enslaving others are all maxims that in this sense cannot be willed as universal laws. Anyone who makes such maxims the guidelines or underlying principles of a life must, if consistent, assume that not all others can do the same. For those who are coerced or deceived, or enslaved or controlled by others, cannot guide their lives by maxims at all, and hence also cannot adopt a maxim of coercion or deception or enslavement. The maxim of abrogating one's own capacity for autonomy – of choosing not to choose – is a somewhat special case: Such a maxim of deference cannot be universalized because it is in the first place self-defeating; a life in which the capacity for autonomy is successfully abrogated is no longer a life led on any maxims, and hence no longer a life in which morally worthy maxims can be adopted.

The pattern of practical reasoning by which such arguments proceed requires consideration not only of the princples whose universalizability is in question, but also of the indispensable means and standard results of action on such principles.[3] Deception cannot be universally successfully practiced because an indispensable means to deception is trust, whereas a standard result of deception is mistrust. Hence the patterns of argument that may show a principle to be one that cannot be univerally shared must rely in part on means—ends reasoning. However, this does not mean that Kant has a merely instrumental conception of rationality, but only that his account of rationality includes an account of instrumental reasoning. Instrumental reasoning in Kant's theory is concerned not with reckoning efficient means to morally arbitrary ends, but with showing how virtuous underlying intentions can and must be supplemented by specific intentions that take account of the natural and human world in which action takes place. Instrumental reasoning provides *one* of the ways in which MacIntyre's "shorter-term intentions" can be intelligibly related to "longer-term intentions" (p. 193). (The difference between Kant's and MacIntyre's formulations at this point seems to be only that Kant is concerned with the *depth* of intentions and MacIntyre with their *duration*.) It is plausible that our deepest principles – those that govern most of our activity – will be long-term intentions, but the two are not coextensive. There seem to be reasons for preferring a focus on underlying rather than on long-term principles in an account of moral life. Long-term principles may sometimes be trivial, and the most significant principle of a life may change – for example in conversions, or just in growing up. In either Kant's or MacIntyre's theory an account of instrumental reasoning is indispensable; without it maxims of virtue are inert, mere expressions of good will rather than actual good willing.

A further group of maxims can be shown to be nonuniversalizable by arguments that rely not only on the Formula of Universal Law but also on the fact that human beings are agents, so have some projects, yet are limited and so cannot guarantee the success of their projects. For example, a maxim of persistent refusal of help to others has as its universalized counterpart a maxim enjoining all to make the refusal of help a guideline of their lives. But to will this is to will a world in which a necessary means for nonomnipotent beings to achieve their ends has been rejected. Nonomnipotent beings must, if they will consistently, will that some help be sometimes given. Hence formal considerations alone can show a maxim of refusal of help to be morally unworthy for finite but free and rational beings. (This argument, incidentally and interestingly, goes through whether refusal of help is understood as "refusal to give help" or "refusal to accept help".)

---

3   Cf. Kant's discussion of the Principle of Hypothetical Imperatives as a principle of instrumental rationality at *G*, IV, 417, and comments in Chapter 5 in this volume.

A maxim of refusal to develop any abilities can be shown to be nonuniversalizable by a similar argument. To adopt a maxim of nondevelopment of abilities is not in itself nonuniversalizable. For it is *possible* that others will have abilities and lend them to one where one's own abilities fail. But to will the universalized counterpart of this maxim is to will a world where everybody has neglected to develop talents, and so a world in which one does not will at least some means that are necessary for nonomnipotent beings to achieve whatever ends they may have. Hence such a maxim can be universalized by beings who have projects yet are finite only if they reject any principle of instrumental rationality. Neither of these arguments shows that any specific act of help or development of specific talents is morally required.

These arguments to show that some maxims cannot consistently be universalized are sufficient to show that the charge of empty formalism, which has so often been made against Kant, does not hold. The nonuniversalizability of fundamental principles is clearly of deep moral significance. In general, claims about the moral status of more specific intentions and acts holds only for determinate contexts. Only if some more specific principles enjoin actions that are *indispensable in all circumstances* for action on a morally worthy maxim can specific principles of action themselves be shown to be morally worthy. But such is the variety of human ways of life that few actions can be held indispensable in this way. Even the avoidance of lying (at least in a narrow verbal sense) may be dispensable in a nondeceiving Trappist community. The avoidance of theft and fraud may be dispensable means to avoiding deception in a society in which property institutions are still lacking. There are no specific intentions that are indispensable for all who adopt a maxim of not always refusing help or the development of abilities. This suggests again that moral rules, because they prescribe and proscribe specific types of action, can indeed not be derived without substantive premises about specific sorts of social arrangements: Since the means that are indispensable for action on a morally worthy maxim are typically contingent on social arrangements, Kant's picture of right action is inadequate. For in abstraction from context it is indeterminate what the outward aspects of morally worthy action are, and hence indeterminate to what (merely) right action should conform. *Rechtslehre* not merely cannot be part of a critique of practical reason, it cannot be part of a metaphysic of morals that establishes "legal" duties for the human condition. It can be part only of more local determinations of rules that must be followed within particular social and cultural settings. This does not, however, require us to adopt a relativist account of right action, since the moral worthiness of particular institutional settings and social practices, in terms of which judgments of right and wrong may be established, is itself open to judgment in terms of the underlying maxims by which a life shaped by such institutions and practices is informed. Traditions too may be judged morally, as indeed MacIntyre judges the liberal tradition, by their deepest principles.

If these arguments are plausible, we have found at least one possibility for developing a theory of practical reasoning that does not rely on teleological claims. Kant's critique of teleology in ethics in the second *Critique* is in part the rejection of a project that MacIntyre too condemns. The project of constructing a heteronomous ethic, which derives moral rules from the actual wants of human beings, though of perennial appeal, is rejected by Kant and MacIntyre alike. Ostensibly Kant rejects the possibility of a teleological ethic of the other, perfectionist type, whereas MacIntyre adopts an (indeterminate) form of perfectionism. But in fact Kant's conception of human rationality commits him also to an indeterminate conception of the good for man. The conception of the good for man that can be read out of Kant's account of human nature in the abstract is no more determinate than the leading of a life that is guided by universalizable, and rationally implemented maxims. The good life for man is one of projects that invite and never preclude the collaboration of others. In the context of a particular life led in a certain context, we may of course be able to say some much more determinate things about what is needed if the indeterminate end of actions and the possibility of moral community are to be maintained.

MacIntyre claims to want to keep closer to Aristotle and to reconstruct a conception of the good for man, and of the virtues that will constitute this good at a given time. But the distance between Kant and MacIntyre is less than this claim suggests. MacIntyre too offers no determinate conception of the good for man. He takes it that our moral starting point must be given, but not that there is any universal moral starting point. The practices in which our lives are set are given but varied, just as Kantian maxims may be given yet varied. But how we develop our quests for the good beyond the given starting point depends upon *which* development of a tradition we pursue, and this depends in large measure on the way in which the "internal debate" of that tradition is conducted. Hence a great deal needs to be said about how that debate is conducted. Otherwise we may not be able to distinguish changes that develop and expand a tradition from changes that corrupt it. An explicit account of the standards such embodied debates should meet would constitute a theory of practical reasoning. It would enable us to distinguish, among the intelligible continuations of the narratives of our lives and traditions, those continuations that we have reasons to seek. Plausibly the two central components of Kant's theory of practical reasoning – universalizability and instrumental rationality – must constitute parts of any theory of practical reasoning. Traditions ossify if they become esoteric or elitist, as traditions whose fundamental principles cannot be universally shared must do. (I take it that the fundamental principle even of some sorts of aristocratic tradition can, though it need not, be shared by nonaristocrats.) Traditions fade if their fundamental principles are no longer appropriately expressed in ancillary intentions (as it seems the Tory tradition has faded, despite surviving rhetoric, after a century of living in clothing stolen from Whigs, monetarists and other liberals).

Universalizability and instrumental rationality are the features of Kant's theory of practical reasoning that might most evidently be of use to MacIntyre; but other features might also be worth consideration in developing the theory of practical reasoning that *After Virtue* demands. Although MacIntyre is surely right in claiming that Kant says too little about the requirements for intelligible action, he is, I believe, mistaken in his criticisms of Kant's claim that judgment cannot be taught and is a peculiar talent (p. 145). It does not follow from these claims that Kant holds that goodness does not require reason or intelligence – as we have just seen, Kant's theory of practical reason is arduous. Kant's grounds for thinking that judgment cannot be taught is a *rejection* of purely calculative conceptions of practical reasoning: There are and can be no algorithms for applying rules or principles in particular situations. (If there were, we would have to apply an infinity of rules for applying rules for applying rules . . .) [*CPR,* A133/B172]). The judgment that MacIntyre imputes to Cardinal Pole and to Montrose cannot be reduced to any set of algorithms, but is nevertheless a crucial aspect of practical reasoning that we need to understand. And Kant does offer us a variety of explorations of the structure of judgment, both in the *Critique of Pure Reason* and, in particular, in his discussion of the differences between determinant and reflective judging in the *Critique of Judgment,* and especially in the *First Introduction to the Critique of Judgment.* In focusing on "reflective" judging Kant took up the problem of the way in which we can move to the universal when "only the particular is given". A central feature of a moral tradition lies in the characteristic ways in which such moves are made – the ways in which certain particular situations are construed as morally salient and others as morally insignificant. In the embodied debate within any tradition the modes of reflective judging that determine what will be experienced as moral problems and issues are as significant as the resources that are deployed to resolve these issues and predicaments.

The Kantian picture of practical reasoning requires the coordination of a number of elements. It requires capacities for reflective judging, for the critical deployment of concepts that articulate our moral situation. It requires the capacity to universalize, which is needed if the fundamental intentions of our lives are not to be ones that others cannot share. It requires also capacities for reasoning about means and results that will relate our fundamental principles to the situations in which we actually find ourselves, and lead us to contextually appropriate ancillary intentions. This is hardly an impoverished conception of practical reasoning.

Conclusions

What I have suggested here is no challenge to most of MacIntyre's critique of modernity. The disarray and bickering in ethics; the prevalence of attempts to ground ethics on what people actually want and the predilection for merely "calculative" conceptions of human reason seem also to me to be both common and disastrous features of modern ethical thinking. What I am, however, proposing is that Kant lies further away from us than his conventional status as arch-Enlightener suggests. For Kant offers us primarily an ethic of virtue rather than of rules, and he does not see human reason as merely calculative. His modernity lies in his rejection of a conception of human nature and its telos that is sufficiently determinate to yield an entire ethic. But just on this point MacIntyre too is modern. Further, the less determinate, but formal and rational, conception of human nature on which Kant relies is sufficient for the grounding of at least some fundamental maxims of virtue. Kant offers us a form of rationalism in ethics that (despite the unfortunate suggestions of some of his examples) does not generate a unique moral code, but still both provides fundamental guidelines and suggests the types of reasoning by which we might see how to introduce these guidelines into the lives we actually lead.

I have said nothing here about a number of difficulties that may afflict Kant's ethics – nothing, for example, about his individualism or about whether his theory can handle cases of false consciousness or about his conception of human autonomy. I am suggesting only that if we are on a quest for the good for man, and so in the process of debating, weighing and considering the constituent practices and virtues of our own traditions, it would be a good idea to set aside some of the most venerable criticisms made of Kant's ethics and to look at his actual account of reason in action. The regrowth of Aristotelian ethics needs more than a severe pruning of the Enlightenment enterprise and a renewed focus on the conditions for intelligible lives and traditions. It also requires that we graft onto this account of intelligible action a theory of practical reason that can be used to guide lives and traditions among their possible futures.

Postscript

This chapter was the earliest of the essays in this volume, and I would not now hold to all its conclusions. In particular I now think that characterizing Kant as offering an ethic of virtue because he insists on the priority of principles over their outward expression is misleading. The point about moral principles on Kant's account is not that they are psychologically inward – to think of it in that way, even if one allows for the opacity of maxims, is to adopt a "Cartesian" view of maxims as agents' mental states. Maxims may be inferences from action; they may be imputed to practices or to institutions rather than to individuals (though Kant rarely does so – only in the later essays and in the *Religion* does he speak of duties that are not individual). The sense in which maxims are inward is only that they are not outward – they are not inscribed on the surface of action. It would be better to describe them as *underlying* rather than as psychologically inward principles, and therefore the comparison between Kantian and Christian or Stoic virtue made here can mislead. I now think that it would be more apt to say that Kant offers an ethic of principles, rather than one specifically of virtues, and that principles can be variously embodied – both as virtues of individual characters or of institutions and also in practices and even in decision procedures. In short, although Kant constantly distinguishes "inner" and "outer" aspects of duty (*MM,* VI, 218–20; *G,* IV, 397–8), "inwardness" needs to be taken with caution. Kant's fundamental notion is that of the morally worthy principle that provides guidelines not only for matters of outward right and obligation, but for good characters and institutions as well. His position is action-centered and can allow for agent-centered ways of thinking; but its basic framework is not specifically agent-centered.

I have not tried to alter the essay substantially, both because the connection with MacIntyre's project would be obscured, and because others have taken it as exemplifying a particular possibility in debates about Aristotelian and Kantian ethics.[4]

4   See, e.g., Robert Louden, "Kant's Virtue Ethics"; and George R. Lucas, "Agency after Virtue".

PART III

Kant's ethics and Kantian ethics

9

The power of example

Less than twenty years ago Peter Winch complained of the

fairly well established, but no less debilitating tradition in recent Anglo-Saxon moral philosophy, according to which it is not merely permissible, but desirable to take *trivial* examples.[1]

The examples of which he complained were trivial in either or both of two ways. Some were examples of the minor perplexities of life, such as returning library books or annoying the neighbors with one's music; some were examples described only in outline rather than in depth; and some examples were both minor and schematic.

Since Winch wrote these words the climate of Anglo-Saxon moral philosophy has changed. The wintry ethics of logical positivism and the cold spring of metaethical inquiry have supposedly been supplanted by a new flourishing of substantive ethical writing. This new concern has developed in two quite distinct genres of writing on ethics. In Britian the change is apparent in the writings of Winch and of others working in a Wittgensteinian vein.[2] Throughout the English-speaking philosophical world, and especially in the United States, it shows in "philosophical discussions of substantive legal, social and political problems" that apparently confront us.[3] In writing both of the Wittgensteinian and of the "problem-centered" variety we find no attempt to spare the reader from

This chapter originally appeared in *Philosophy*, 61 (1986), 5–29, published by Cambridge University Press.

1 Peter Winch, "The Universalizability of Moral Judgements", pp. 154–5.
2 A basic source for this writing is Wittgenstein's 1929 "Lecture on Ethics", which was published together with reports of conversations that Wittgenstein later had with F. Waismann and Rush Rhees. Wittgenstein's discussion of examples in nonethical contexts is also influential. In addition to the essays in Peter Winch's *Ethics and Action*, Wittgensteinian approaches to ethics include Rush Rhees, *Without Answers;* D. Z. Phillips and H. O. Mounce, *Moral Practices;* R. Beardsmore, *Moral Reasoning;* Rodger Beehler, *Moral Life;* various articles in *Philosophical Investigations*, including Cora Diamond, "Anything but Argument?"; some essays in R. F. Holland, *Against Empiricism;* and some in D. Z. Phillips, *Through a Darkening Glass.*
3 William Ruddick, "Philosophy and Public Affairs". This article surveys the movement in applied ethics in the United States up to 1980. It lists the main journals, charts institutional bases and affiliations and identifies both some successes and some dangers of the movement. Since the literature is vast, no complete list of sources can be offered. Ruddick's article provides a sketch at a moment when the movement could still be surveyed in a short article. For more recent discussions see David M. Rosenthal and Fadlou Shehadi, *Applied Ethics and Ethical Theory.*

considering either the most tragic or the most lurid examples, both public and intimate. Indeed, some writers now apologize not for the trivial but for the sensational nature of their examples.[4]

Yet there are great differences between the ways in which these two genres of ethical writing have tried to replenish Anglo-Saxon moral reflection with substantive examples. I shall try here to show how these differences reflect distinctive conceptions of practical reasoning, and in particular of the prospects for resolving ethical problems. Both Wittgensteinian and problem-centered writing in ethics differ from much earlier writing in that (for quite different reasons) they view the examples they discuss as relatively independent of ethical theory. But in most other respects the differences between the approaches are enormous. Wittgensteinian writing, I shall argue, has tended to be more reflective, but, despite some claims to the contrary, it has also been more remote from moral life and in particular from the practical resolution of moral problems. Problem-centered writing, by contrast, aims above all to be practical, in the sense of resolving moral problems. But at times it risks being too unreflective in its construal of what these problems are. To provide an appropriate context for these discussions I shall first sketch an older view of the role of examples in ethical thinking. Finally, in the last section of the essay I shall try to sketch an account of the application of practical reasoning that is both reflective and practical.

Older views of examples in ethics

The use of trivial, schematic examples in writing on ethics was prevalent during and after the period of Logical Positivism, but is compatible with many older views of the point of examples in ethical writing. Kant's comments on examples form a well-known and well-developed instance of a traditional view; they will also serve as background to some less familiar Kantian themes on which I shall draw at a later stage.

On Kant's view actual cases of moral deliberation do not use examples at all. When we have to decide what to do we are required to test the principle on which we propose to act according to the Categorical Imperative. It is only at a prior stage of assimilation of the Categorical Imperative and its more central implications that examples may be useful as illustrations of moral action rather than as applications of moral theory. Some examples are *hypothetical:* They consist of more or less specific principles of possible action (e.g., the principles of cheating a

---

4 A sample of lurid examples includes abortion by craniotomy; drowning a child in a bath; organizing judicial murder; adjudicating mutiny; having a child to grow a kidney transplant for the father. Although Phillipa Foot apologized when she introduced sensational examples in "The Problem of Abortion and the Doctrine of Double Effect", p. 31, many writers now seem quite at home with harrowing examples.

gullible customer, or of systematic refusal of help to others)[5] whose moral significance can be determined (at least illuminated) by application of the Categorical Imperative. Other examples are *ostensive:* They point out acts or persons or lives some of whose features are held to be morally significant (e.g., taking the life of Christ as a model for imitation, or the action of some others as a warning or cautionary tale) (*DV,* VI, 476–85; *R,* VI, 54–60).[6] .

When we come to apply the Categorical Imperative (or any derivative moral principles) to *actual* cases – where we have to act or decide – we face the difficulty that, however detailed the subordinate principles previously worked out, however diverse the examples of action that have been pointed out, these can at most help us to discern the moral status of a maxim of proposed action, but can never determine fully just what sort of act should be performed. Hypothetical examples, being themselves principles of action, must evidently remain indeterminate even when relatively specific, and so cannot fully determine any act. The acts or persons or lives that are pointed to in ostensive examples may, in themselves, be fully determinate. But their relevance to a case in hand must (since there is never total correspondence of features) be guided by some (necessarily indeterminate) understanding of the morally significant aspects of the example. Ostension, as is well known, is always equivocal and requires interpretation. *Judgment* is therefore always needed when principles are applied to particular cases or when ostensive examples are adduced as relevant guides. Neither principles nor examples alone can guide action.

Kant insists that there can be no complete rules for judging particular cases. In the first *Critique* he writes:

Judgment will be the faculty of subsuming under rules; that is, of distinguishing whether something does or does not stand under a given rule . . . General logic contains, and can contain no rules for judgment . . . If it sought to give general instructions how we are to subsume under these rules, that is, to distinguish whether something does or does not come under them, that could only be by means of another rule. This in turn, for the very reason that it is a rule, again demands guidance from judgment . . . judgment is a peculiar talent which can be practised only, and cannot be taught. (*CPR,* A132–3/B171–2; cf. A199)

He goes on to liken judgment to "mother wit [*Mutterwitz*]" and insist that "its lack no school can make good". However, he presumably means only that there can be no *algorithms* for judging and no formal instruction, for he allows that "sharpening of the judgment is indeed the one great benefit of examples" (*CPR,* A133–134/B173–4).

---

5   These are two of the well-known four examples of which Kant makes repeated use in *Grundlegung.*
6   Kant draws, but does not always observe, the distinction made here between hypothetical examples and ostensive examples (*Beispiel, Exempel*); see *DV,* VI, 479n.

In particular he favors the use of examples in educating the power of *moral* judgment:

it would be most helpful to the pupil's moral development to raise some casuistical questions in the analysis of every duty and to let the assembled children put their reason to the test of how each would go about resolving the tricky problem put before him . . . casuistry is most suitable to the capacity of the undeveloped and so is the most appropriate way to sharpen the reason of young people in general . . . (*DV*, VI, 482–3)

The primary use of hypothetical and ostensive examples is then educational. By considering examples we become better able to judge cases requiring decision and action. Kant summarizes the point in a much-quoted metaphor whose sense has, perhaps, become obscure in the usual translation: "examples are thus the go-cart [*Gängelwagen* – a child's "walker", formerly known as a go-cart] of judgment" (*CPR*, A134/B173–4).

Examples provide us with support at the stage when our (moral) judgment is faltering. The famous four (hypothetical) examples of the *Groundwork* help us to see what might be involved in applying the Categorical Imperative; so does the less famous but more traditional ostensive example of the *Religion,* where Christ is construed as the archetype (*Urbild*) of moral perfection. They are indeed highly schematic examples. However, no addition of detail could make them fully determinate, and if they were cluttered with detail they would lose their pedagogic usefulness. Good illustrations need to be clear and simplified, even caricatures, if they are to get their point across. They need not, however, be trivial in the other sense. Good examples need not draw on life's minor dilemmas, and Kant's examples generally do not; on the other hand it may not matter if they are examples of minor dilemmas, provided that they are appropriate illustrations of principle. If ethical examples are seen as illustrations they may (but needn't) be trivial; but they must present sparse sketches rather than deep or nuanced pictures.

In viewing examples of moral (or immoral) action as schematic illustrations of moral theory or outlook, which help to develop powers of judgment, Kant joins a long tradition that sees attending both to hypothetical cases and to the deeds and lives of others as ways in which to develop powers of discrimination about cases requiring action. From the New Testament parables and Aesop's fables through morality plays, histories and stories of heroes and cautionary tales, to contemporary work on moral education, examples have been used to make points that are independent of any specific example and might equally well have been conveyed and illustrated by other examples. In this tradition, however, Kant is distinctive for his articulation of the relationships between moral theory or principles, illustrative examples and the judgment that is involved in actual moral decisions, none of which he thinks a dispensable part of the moral life.

Examples viewed as illustrative are theory-dependent. Far from being independent of moral principles, they are themselves more narrowly specified, but unavoidably still indeterminate principles. Such examples can have a point only if they illustrate a principle; illustrations must be illustrations of something. But the conception of examples as dependent on theory and principles does not preclude all critical use of examples to cast doubt on moral principles. Sartre's famous example of the young man who is torn between caring for his mother and joining the Free French is a case in point.[7] Here the example is purportedly used not to illustrate a moral principle but to show that moral principles and codes cannot make our decisions for us. However, the entire force of the example – the reason that it so evidently casts decision back on the agent – depends on the fact that the young man (and Sartre's readers) can see the situation as a conflict of moral principles or ideals. Only those who see relevance both in personal devotion and in a certain conception of public duty can appreciate this dilemma. Sartre works to leave his readers on the cusp: Both loyalties are vividly characterized. Hence this example, while theory-dependent, cannot be set out schematically. Its power depends on making it difficult for us to think that giving precedence to either loyalty would be right. But turning example against theory in *this* way does not require us to see such examples as independent of theory: On the contrary, the principle of construction of the example is entirely theory-led. The anguish that Sartre sees in moral responsibility reflects a conception of principles as still having a central part in the moral life. We find ourselves confronted with problems and dilemmas whose force derives from certain moral positions and principles that, tragically, lack the resources to resolve the problems they generate.

A Wittgensteinian view of examples

An entirely different view of the use of examples is found in contemporary Wittgensteinian writing in ethics. In his "Lecture on Ethics" Wittgenstein said little about examples, and was still largely concerned with the Tractarian view of ethics as lying outside the world and hence not expressible in propositions. Rush Rhees records that in later conversations Wittgenstein thought "it was strange that you could find books on ethics in which there was no mention of a genuine ethical or moral problem," refused to discuss a highly schematic historical example (Brutus's killing of Caesar), but enlarged and elaborated on a contemporary (hypothetical) example of conflict between the demands of work and of marriage.[8]

Since then insistence on a fastidious respect for the detail and nuance of examples has become a hallmark of Wittgensteinian writing in ethics. Examples are conceived neither as incidental, let alone sketchy, illustrations of moral theory and principles, nor as models for moral action, nor just as morally educative.

7 J.-P. Sartre, "Existentialism Is a Humanism".
8 Rush Rhees, "Some Developments in Wittgenstein's View of Ethics".

Rather, the claim made very clearly by Winch, and supported by other Wittgensteinian writers (often with the very same emphasis), is that

> what we can do, I am arguing, is to look at particular examples and see what we *do* want to say about them: there are no general rules which can determine in advance what we *must* say about them.[9]

Examples are here neither merely illustrative nor primarily educational. They are not theory-led but are themselves the pivot of moral thought; hence the importance of considering serious rather than trivial examples. Instead of schematic, possibly unimportant illustrations of principle and theory, Wittgensteinian writers provide elaborate and extended discussions of serious moral vicissitudes.

The Wittgensteinian focus on examples rather than moral theory and principles has a number of distinctive features. Typically, the focus is on examples of completed action in a context that invites moral consideration or assessment, rather than on less complete examples of a situation that raises moral problems or dilemmas, as though the primary exercise of moral judgment were to *reflect* or *pass judgment* on what has been done rather than to decide among possible actions. Given this emphasis on examples of completed action, one might perhaps expect such writing to draw heavily on actual (perhaps including historical or legal) cases and case histories, that is, on ostensive examples of a publicly accessible sort. But in fact Wittgensteinian writing draws predominantly on literary examples of action in a context that has moral aspects, as well as on hypothetical examples constructed on similar lines.[10]

As we shall see, this preference for literary examples, chosen almost entirely from novels, has important implications. This is not because the literary situations discussed are bizarre or difficult to understand; on the contrary it is a corollary of being committed to discover "what we *do* want to say" that we must start with mutually comprehensible examples, and not, say, with examples drawn from science fiction or from alien traditions of letters. The examples shown are counterfactual, but they are not counternomic or even remote from us; rather, care is taken to present examples that are plausible or at least comprehensible, or become so when scrutinized. The importance of depending on literary examples is rather a matter first of the *authority* of the literary text in the presentation and construal of each example, and secondly of the *type of example* to be found in works of literature.

The literary examples discussed by Wittgensteinian writers on ethics are dis-

---

9 Peter Winch, "Moral Integrity".
10 Literary works can provide ostensive examples of a sort, for a literary figure may be presented or taken as a model or exemplar of certain virtues or failings. Such figures may be important in moral education. Some are discussed in J. B. Schneewind, "Moral Problems and Moral Philosophy in the Victorian Period". There are interesting parallels between the contrasts Schneewind finds between intuitionist and utilitarian writing in the nineteenth century and some of the contrasts between Wittgensteinian and problem-centered writing discussed here.

tinctive, nuanced and well articulated by the authors of the literary works from which they are drawn. It is hard to challenge the articulation of such examples and all too easy to agree with Winch of such examples that each is sui generis and in itself a complete example of moral thinking that can provide no basis for prescribing for others,[11] and so, more generally, that moral theories are redundant, since no task remains to be done once examples have been fully articulated. On the other hand, the fact that works of literature (and especially novels) tend to be preoccupied with private rather than public crises has produced in Wittgensteinian ethical writing a focus on inwardness and personal relations and a lack of attention to the dilemmas of public and working life.[12]

The Wittgensteinian approach to ethics by examples depends on the possibility of arriving at "what we *do* want to say" in the course of reflecting on the example. This method must presuppose sufficient community of moral views – an ethical tradition, perhaps, or a shared ideology – for there to be something that "we" (whoever "we" may be; and this is a large question) do want to say about a given example. Where that shared tradition is lacking, some Wittgensteinian writers claim, we find ourselves confronting not moral disagreement but a breakdown in moral communication – an impasse of incommensurable moral frameworks. For example, Phillips and Mounce claim in *Moral Practices* that in our society certain fundamental phrases [*sic*] such as "honesty is good," "lying is bad" or "generosity is right" are not genuine expressions of a position (pp. 7–9). These are not matters over which we might either agree or disagree and reflect and argue, but are "taken as a matter of course" (p. 8). They are parts of the framework that makes moral judgment intelligible. According to Phillips and Mounce, "we do not *decide* that lying is bad, because the alternative, that it is good, is not something we can bring before our minds" (pp. 8–9).

Beehler, by contrast, holds in *Moral Life* that it is the practice of caring that provides the fundamental framework that makes moral discussion possible but is itself beyond discussion. He claims that "you cannot decide to care about others" and that "Caring about others is integral to the 'moral point of view' " (p. 155). Any attempt to provide reasons for caring involves a *petitio principii* (p. 160), and moral discourse is therefore confined to those who already care. Beardsmore in *Moral Reasoning* makes remarks in a similar vein about different practices: "there is a range of concepts (murder, adultery, suicide, truth-telling) which are in some sense constitutive of morality" (p. 44; cf. pp. 160ff.). He asks rhetorically:

would it . . . make sense to suppose that a man brought up to regard suicide, murder and adultery as evils might somehow get outside these values and ask himself whether they

11 Winch, "The Universalizability of Moral Judgments".
12 Writing that discusses Wittgensteinian approaches to moral philosophy seems more concerned with how such approaches might change one's conception of politics than with questions of *Rechtslehre*. See Hannah Pitkin, *Wittgenstein and Justice;* John Danford, *Wittgenstein and Political Philosophy;* and Alan Wertheimer, "Is Ordinary Language Analysis Conservative?".

were not perhaps virtues? It should be quite clear that on my account such a question would be incoherent. (p. 79)

Clearly these and similar claims about the practices that underlie the moral life are taken as instancing Wittgenstein's insistence that "in the end there must be agreement in judgment."[13] Traditions and practices, it is held, must be shared if there is to be any moral discourse; and if they are shared we can conduct discussion of particular ethical cases and what "we" might agree to say about them without invoking any principles or theories that are not implicit in those practices. But the framework on which agreement rests must lie beyond possible discussion or dispute: It is not "a matter for decision".

On the Wittgensteinian account as developed by these writers, moral reasoning presupposes shared moral traditions and practices. Only within such a context can moral discourse about examples take place, and questioning of the shared framework of moral practices is not possible. In this picture genuine moral disagreement is taken to be preliminary and dispellable; if it persists, what we really have is a case of noncommunication. The only permanent possibilities are moral agreement and lack of moral communication. In a way this approach has dissolved the area of primary moral concern for problem-centered approaches to moral reasoning, which is the range of moral problems about which we can communicate but about whose solution we cannot readily agree.

This dissolution of what the other type of contemporary Anglo-Saxon writing in ethics takes as most problematic depends heavily on the reliance on literary examples. For it is the authority of the text that imposes a largely shared interpretation of examples. The only acceptable disagreements about the construal of literary examples are those for which there is warrant within the text. Nobody can reasonably speculate whether the interpretation of such examples hinges entirely on factors of which the author has neither told nor hinted. (It is hardly open to a Wittgensteinian to adopt principles of interpretation – whether radically subjectivist or deconstructive – that call in question the possibility of a shared, open reading of the text). Consider how impertinent it would be to construe *Macbeth* as a murder mystery[14] by adducing extratextual hunches, or to wonder whether Raskolnikov was not perhaps mistaken in thinking that he had murdered Alyona Ivanovna, who survived his assault and was finished off by someone else, so that his entire experience of agitation, guilt and remorse is just misplaced. Even in a poor whodunnit, extratextual importations are suspect; they are totally destructive of the literary examples on which Wittgensteinian ethical reflection builds. But in respecting the integrity of literary examples, the depth and ubiquity of

13 Ludwig Wittgenstein, *Philosophical Investigations,* nos. 241–2. This passage is much discussed by the writers referred to in footnote 2 above: Phillips and Mounce, *Moral Practices,* pp. 62–72; Beehler, *Moral Life,* pp. 92–7; Beardsmore, *Moral Reasoning,* pp. 120ff.
14 Impertinent and hilarious. See James Thurber, "The Macbeth Murder Mystery".

moral disagreement are obscured. Yet without a focus on literary examples, with their artificial exclusion of many types of moral disagreement, it is hard not to be skeptical of many Wittgensteinian accounts of moral deliberation. For these accounts suggest that we can deliberate only insofar as we share the practices of those with or about whom we deliberate.

This position leads readily both to moral conservatism and to moral relativism. Wittgensteinian methods of moral reflection practiced among the like-minded will yield a local consensus of views; Wittgensteinian methods practiced by those of disparate moral traditions will lead to no shared conclusions, but to a realization that moral communication has broken down at some points. The perspective is at once disquieting and comforting. It is disquieting because we sense that we *can* communicate many of our disagreements to those of different traditions; we cannot easily believe that those with whom we persistently disagree over, say, the eating of animals, the nature of property or the limits of favoring our own families and friends are beyond the pale of moral communication on these topics. On the other hand the Wittgensteinian vision of moral communication and justification as essentially local[15] is comforting because persisting disagreement is seen as something we could not have hoped to resolve by reasoning, but may nevertheless be able to deal with by educating or converting those of alien moral outlook and bringing them within our own pale.[16] If conversion succeeds, moral practices will be shared and moral communication possible. Faced with breakdowns of moral communication we can seek to enlarge (or perhaps shrink or restructure) the moral outlook and imagination of the other.

It is notable, however, that Wittgensteinian discussions of moral "conversions", of coming to see the sense or point of a mode of life in a different way, tend to see such conversions as an "education of the heart" toward enlarged and deepened moral sympathies. This seems empirically dubious – plenty of people have been converted (or corrupted) to mean or violent or racist moral practices and outlook – and in any case assumes a standpoint from which distinct moral traditions can be compared, which is not obviously available within the Wittgensteinian approach. We have to remember that within a position that sees all justification as relative to locally accepted practice, any reason for converting those beyond the pale of one's own current practices would be matched by others' reasons for undertaking a counterconversion. There is no neutral standpoint from

15 See, for example, Rush Rhees, "Natural Law and Reasons in Ethics", and "Knowing the Difference between Right and Wrong", both in his *Without Answers*, pp. 94–6, 101.

16 Wittgensteinian proposals for dealing with apparent disagreements that reflect incommensurable practices can be found in Beehler, *Moral Life*, esp. pp. 162–74; Diamond, "Anything but Argument?", 27ff.; D. Z. Phillips, "In Search of the Moral 'Must': Mrs Foot's Fugitive Thought", esp. pp. 152–3; and Stephen Clark, *The Moral Status of Animals*, pp. 186–7. The latter work is only selectively Wittgensteinian, but is so on the matter of resolving obstinate disagreement.

which to discern who is the missionary and who is seducing missionaries into "going native".

Much of our difficulty in this area is due to a feeling that we don't know how much to read into Wittgenstein's claim that "in the end there must be agreement in judgment". For even if we accept that communication requires *some* agreement in judgment, we are quite unsure *how much* disagreement there can be before communication breaks. Do "we" share the traditional Sicilian practices and form of life sufficiently to be able to communicate, and so after sufficient reflection to agree, with traditional Sicilians about when revenge killings are and are not required? Or do "we" share too few of their traditions and practices even to communicate with them on the topic of revenge killings? A revealing – and literary – example for Wittgensteinian ethical reflection might be the predicament of Burgess's Victor Crabbe,[17] caught and drowned in the ethical babel of nearly postcolonial Malaya, who can understand and even appreciate alien moral practices, but is powerless to resolve the dilemmas with which he is faced. Ethical writing that has nothing to propose for Crabbe's situation (except "conversions": but whose?) has little appeal for those whose lives confront them continually with heterogeneous practices. Traditional ethnocentrism was prepared to override the practices of those beyond its pale; it preached and practiced a colonialist ethic, offering to "natives" at most the opportunity for "them" to assimilate to "us". Wittgensteinian ethnocentrism, it appears, has nothing to say to those who live beyond "our" local pale; in the face of a world in which adherents of distinct practices meet increasingly it proposes a retreat to the cosiness of "our" shared world and tradition. Perhaps it is not surprising that such a conception of ethics should flourish mainly in the academies of a formerly imperial power, and that it should focus predominantly on judging what has been done. Precisely because of the variety and transience of ethical practices, to which Wittgensteinian writers draw our attention, we cannot easily lead our lives without raising questions that are not just internal to but about local practices. In doing so, however, we can still leave open the question whether there is a rational or neutral standpoint from which all moral problems can be resolved.[18]

Wittgenstein himself appears to leave opening enough for such inquiry, for he asserts only that communication requires agreement in *judgment,* and that this does not preclude disagreement over opinions.[19] A number of Wittgensteinian writers, in particular Winch himself and R. F. Holland, have moved Wittgensteinian ethical writing in this direction. They have sought to interpret Wittgen-

---

17 Anthony Burgess, *The Long Day Wanes: A Malayan Trilogy.*
18 Many Wittgensteinian writers insist that deep moral conflicts cannot be resolved, so that there are ineliminable and tragic conflicts of moral outlook. See Beardsmore, *Moral Reasoning,* Chaps. 9 and 10; and Phillips, *Through a Darkening Glass,* esp. the first three essays. Even if some disputes are irresolvable, and in some of these cases tragedy is unavoidable, there may still be more than local justification by which other disputes can be resolved.
19 Wittgenstein, *Philosophical Investigations,* nos. 241–2.

stein's comments on absolute value, and to show the possibility (indeed importance) of coming to see the sense of different ways of construing one's life. Winch, for example, allows that "it is important for philosophers to see that there are other possible [moral] outlooks[20] and that "certain moral conceptions . . . must be recognized in any human society."[21] But these moves away from the predicament of relativism are matched by increased insistence that the primary task of ethics is reflection rather than the resolution of problems. The moral life is seen as consisting in coming to understand things in a certain light, in seeing the sense of one's life as a whole. Winch is at pains to emphasize that such understanding is itself a form of activity. But seen in the context of many more traditional conceptions of ethics, it is only one sort of activity and perhaps not the most significant. Indeed, if examples *are* the pivot of moral thought, this is not only because there is no acceptable theory, but also because they are instances of problems in human lives that stand in need of resolution. Reflection and even understanding are not enough to bring to human difficulties – unless, of course, these difficulties are merely imagined, as they are in works of literature.

Literary examples impose a spectator perspective; and in context the imposition is without costs. For just as we cannot challenge the interpretation of a literary example beyond appropriate bounds of literary interpretation, so we do not have to do anything, beyond "deciding what we do want to say" about the example and making sense of it. We do not have to decide whether to turn Raskolnikov in or whether to find Billy Budd guilty. The concern shown by Wittgensteinian writers on ethics for detailed examples understood in their context conveys an atmosphere of moral seriousness and closeness to moral life. But this is in some ways illusory. For those Wittgensteinian writers who reject relativist readings of Wittgenstein do not offer an account of moral practice and decision that goes beyond the practice-based conception of ethical decision offered by relativist writers. Winch maintains that "a decision can be made only within the context of a meaningful way of life,"[22] and Holland suggests that "politics", by which he clearly understands all compromising intervention in an evil world, is ethically impossible.[23] But if much of lives are, like Victor Crabbe's, surrounded by discrepant practices and set in the interstices of "meaningful ways of life", then a Quietist or Stoic ethic will be at most of inward help.

Winch claims that moral reflection can guide our acting as well as our passing judgment, for he describes reflection on examples as "making a hypothetical agent's judgment" and as "reflecting on what I would think it right to do in such

---

20 Peter Winch, "Can a Good Man Be Harmed?", p. 200.
21 Peter Winch, "Nature and Convention", p. 58.   22 Ibid., p. 55.
23 R. F. Holland, "Absolute Ethics", in his *Against Empiricism*, pp. 135–42. Holland draws a stark dichotomy between "absolute ethics", which must be an ethic of forgoing and nonintervention, and "consequentialist ethics", which is prepared to do evil for the sake of greater good, and so to engage in "politics". "Politics", he claims, "belongs for overdetermined reasons to the pursuits that have to be forgone" (p. 137). Mere forgoing is not likely to leave us uncompromised.

a situation".[24] He holds that such judgments do not commit us to judgments about what others in a like situation should do, and so that in that context "the universalizability principle is idle" (a claim that has been considerably disputed,[25] but which I will not discuss). But it is clear that in making a transition from "hypothetical agent's judgments" to any actual moral judgments, Winch does, as he explicitly states,[26] rely on a weak universalizability principle. For if he did not, there would be no reason for thinking that any literary example or any hypothetical agent's judgment has *any* implication for action. The move from an example and the judgment reached by reflecting on the example in the light of our shared practices to a decision about an actual case, which is unlikely to match the example in all respects, is far from obvious. Somehow we have to decide whether *this* very situation that we confront is one for which *that* example is relevant. Precisely because the examples are elaborate there is less chance of a clear match between example and actual situation that there would be in a pattern of moral thought that relied on "stock", schematic examples. It is difficult to see how the transition from articulated and intelligible literary or hypothetical examples to moral decisions is to be made without the mediation either of principles or of theory that indicates or suggests which *sorts* of correspondence between example and actual case are important and which trivial. Without such principles the spectator perspective from which Wittgensteinian moral reflection begins dooms it to a "moral connoisseurship" that fails to resolve the problems we actually face. It is perhaps, then, not surprising that Wittgensteinian writing in ethics has produced no wider or more popular ethical movement. Literary examples (and perhaps particularly ostensive examples drawn from literature) may be of the greatest importance in moral development and education;[27] but the Wittgensteinian claim that moral thought can be reduced to "looking at particular examples and seeing what we do want to say about them" excludes elements that are indispensable if moral thought is to be not just a spectator sport but a guide to action.

Examples in problem-centered ethics

Problem-centered writing in ethics is based on a conception of moral thought and inquiry quite different from that of Wittgensteinian ethics. As in some more

24 Winch, "The Universalizability of Moral Judgements", p. 154.
25 See, for example, Roger Straughan, "Hypothetical Moral Situations": Roger Montague, "Winch on Agents"; and Michael Levin, "The Universalizability of Moral Judgements Revisited".
26 Winch, "The Universalizability of Moral Judgements", p. 154.
27 This point is quite independent of Wittgensteinian considerations. See, for example, Christopher Butler, "Literature and Moral Education"; A. D. C. Petersen, "A Vanishing Tradition in Moral Education"; T. Beardsworth, "The Place of Literature in Moral Education"; L. O. Ward, "History – Humanity's Teacher"; and Clive Jones, "The Contribution of History and Literature to Moral Education".

traditional ethical writing, a central task of ethical theory is seen as the resolution of moral problems and disagreements by the application of principles to cases that can themselves be picked out and identified independently of the theory or principles that are to be brought to bear on their resolution. So central is this commitment to making ethics practical that mere illustration of principles by hypothetical and theory-led examples has tended to take second place to (sample) applications of principles to supposedly independently arising moral problems. The examples mostly discussed are therefore in one respect like Wittgensteinian examples, in that their force is not thought to depend on any ethical theory or principle. But this is not because examples and the practices they embody are taken as constitutive of moral thought, but rather because examples are taken to be there in the world, candidates for investigation and resolution by any of a variety of possibly adequate moral theories.

An apparent exception to this view of the relation of theory to examples in problem-centered writing is Rawls's method of reflective equilibrium. The moral judgments with which (tentative) moral theories are to be equilibrated are not independent examples or problems, but simply more determinate moral principles. In seeking a reflective equilibrium we are only constructing, and not applying, a moral theory containing both more and less general principles. Once a theory has been built and tested by this method, it is available for application to further problems, which may be thought quite independent of theory. Problem-centered ethical writing aims at far more than the articulation of examples in terms that are implicit in those examples or their context. It aims to justify certain principles that are then to be applied to examples. The goal of ethical thinking is a reasoned decision that can be defended in terms that appeal beyond local practice. Ethics, as in many traditional conceptions, is to be both reasoned and practical.

The moral problems with which this genre of ethical writing has been most concerned are disagreements and dilemmas of public and professional life, rather than those of intimacy and inwardness. Matters such as civil disobedience and conscientious objection, the justice of education or welfare or tax policy, the acceptability of affirmative action and reverse discrimination and of new applications of biotechnology, have all been much discussed in problem-centered writing. This focus on *Rechtsphilosophie* means that many problems discussed are described in terms used by the relevant professionals and specialists, such as lawyers, administrators, educators and doctors. This link with certain sorts of professional discourse is further emphasized when writers in problem-centered ethics seek to get involved with "practitioners" and help in making difficult decisions.[28]

Problem-centered ethical writing relies, of course, on hypothetical as well as on

28   Ruddick, "Philosophy and Public Affairs", p. 734.

actual cases. These hypothetical examples are generally quite similar to actual cases. There are, however, two exceptions. Writers who are heavily influenced by rational choice theory are willing to discuss hypothetical examples whose mathematical articulation makes them remote from actual human choosing. However, such examples are generally intended as illustrations of theory rather than as sample applications. In spite of the much-favored analogies with betting behavior, it is generally acknowledged that such approaches "idealize" human choosing and that various assumptions about the structuring of preferences, the availability of mathematically detailed information and the various principles of rational choice explored, are few of them likely to be realized. Human life mercifully affords few prisoner's dilemmas or chances to be a rational economic man. Insofar as such approaches present examples as illustrations rather than as applications, it is not the examples but the principles they are intended to illustrate that raise questions.

The second use of implausible examples is in discussions of medical and population ethics. In these areas we can often form no firm conception of human relationships, and may be unclear over human identities, so that some examples have a science fiction aspect. Choosing between population policies with varied utility implications is remote from the actual considerations (or lack of consideration) of those who procreate; choosing to have a child for purposes of kidney transplantation is even more remote. In large part, however, the more bizarre examples in bioethics reflect the revolution in biotechnology, which has so rapidly brought New (not always Brave) Worlds partly into our horizons. Genetic engineering and screening are, after all, now real possibilities, and the extensive debates over the definition of death have been triggered by real changes in medical technologies.

Beyond these two areas, there is little reliance on examples that are either counternomic or even socially decontextualized. J. J. Thomson (following a suggestion of Nozick's that perhaps has Humean ancestry) imagines at one point that by being pinched one could save thousands of cows from horrible suffering;[29] in another much-commented-on passage she elucidates a discussion of abortion with the example of a patient who finds herself the unconsenting other end of a violinist's life-support system.[30] Bernard Williams's discussion of an invitation to be a guest executioner[31] and Nozick's examples of innocent threats and innocent shields[32] lack social context. However, in the main, if less self-consciously than in Wittgensteinian writing, the examples discussed in problem-centered writing do

29 Judith Jarvis Thomson, "Some Ruminations on Rights".
30 Judith Jarvis Thomson, "A Defense of Abortion".
31 J. J. C. Smart and Bernard Williams, *Utilitarianism: For and Against*. Williams uses the example only to raise doubts about Utilitarianism – a fair-enough move since the theory is claimed to be competent for any case. The implausibility of the example is well brought out in Holland, "Absolute Ethics", in his *Against Empiricism*.
32 Robert Nozick, *Anarchy, State and Utopia*, pp. 34–5.

not lack social context. The fact that so many examples are drawn from public and professional life ensures that this will be the case and also that contexts can easily be supplied by the reader for examples that are only briefly characterized.

The fact that the individuation and specification of both actual and hypothetical examples are often derivative from the standard categories of various professions has considerable implications. It means that the greater hesitancy and psychological depth to be found in many of the literary examples discussed by Wittgensteinian writers are lacking, as is perhaps only appropriate in examples whose provenance is the discourse of public life. But it means also that much problem-centered writing risks proceeding with unreflective acceptance of established categories and labels. This danger is perhaps less in writing on new problems that the revolution in biotechnology has produced. Here we find reflection on fundamental notions such as those of health, illness, disease and life and death themselves. But the grip of established conceptions of what problems there are is quite evident in areas with a staider tradition of public discourse. In his recent survey of the U.S. movement in applied ethics, William Ruddick identifies "the 'legalization' of philosophy" as a principal danger and states that for some, "public issues are tied to current court concerns".[33] Legalization may be matched by other forms of officialization. This sort of consensus about the specification of problems is quite compatible with disagreement about their solution. Unlike Wittgensteinian writers, problem-centered writers take disagreement about solutions seriously, as something to be rationally resolved rather than assumed away as a presupposition of moral discourse.

Writing in ethics that accepts without thought too much that is the traditional or current outlook and discourse of the staff of policy-making institutions and of other professions is, however, in danger of providing no more than a limited critique of institutional and social arrangements. The worldly success of problem-centered writing in ethics (which contrasts vividly with Wittgensteinian insularity) is in part achieved by willingness to accept established and establishment views of what moral problems there are. It is a partial, but only a partial, vindication of this acceptance to observe that many moral decisions must address moral problems as conventionally defined, because most decisions cannot wait on any revolution, inward or outward. For at least some (perhaps the most serious) moral problems, public as well as private, concern the ways in which we should construe and specify the problems we face. The reflective activity that is needed if moral problems are to be specified in a serious and non-question-begging way is no more dispensable than a theory of practical reasoning.

Both in its conception of the task of ethics as practical and in its insistence on the need for principles (and for attempts to justify them) problem-centered ethical writing has been more ambitious than Wittgensteinian ethical writing. But on a

33   Ruddick, "Philosophy and Public Affairs", pp. 744ff.

third matter of equal importance, the process by which examples and cases are generated, it is the Wittgensteinian approach that is the more demanding. Wittgensteinian writers have insisted that examples be fully articulated and understood, that we work toward an awareness of the practices they embody and even that we seek to find further ways of making sense of the examples. But problem-centered writers have said remarkably little about the process of individuating and specifying actual problems, or of the approach to be taken when there is difficulty or disagreement over the articulation or specification of a problem. And yet the very conception of practical reasoning as applying principles to cases requires that reflection precede reasoning.

Appraisals and principles: Can ethics be reflective as well as practical?

The problem of applying practical reasoning to actual cases arises in the first place from the difficulty of individuating cases. Our lives are not prepackaged into cases of moral dilemmas, each appropriately labeled for handy subsumption under a relevant principle. Even a highly reflective person may find it hard to recognize significant problems that come his or her way, or may fail to perceive morally significant characterizations of his or her own acts. Before we can decide what to do about an actual case, whether by reference to our shared practices or our reasoned principles, we must recognize the case as being of a sort that we can or should handle by reference to a specific practice or principle.

It does not follow that practical reasoning requires an algorithm by which to decide upon the (only or best) morally relevant description of a situation or problem. The possibility of applying a theory or principle, at least in some cases, requires only that we have at least some strategies for selecting among the many true descriptions of a situation ones that are significant for moral decision. What we need, minimally, if there is to be some possibility of a more than locally comprehensible applied ethics, are some ways of appraising or judging the sorts of cases with which we have to deal.

In Kant's earlier ethical writing the starting point of moral deliberation is the agent's maxim: a principle of action by which the agent proposes to guide his life, or some aspect of his life. Maxims clearly must use the conceptual resources available to the particular agent. For this reason one might suspect (with Hegel) that the vaunted universality of Kantian ethics is spurious. Kant presumably would have held that the shared human capacities to reason and understand preclude radical incommensurability. But the comprehensibility of alternative descriptions of a situation and of proposed lines of action is an insufficient guarantee of a way by which agreement on one rather than another equally comprehensible set of descriptions is to be the basis for action. If we have no way in which to reason over the formulation of descriptions of situations and (proposals for) actions, practical reasoning must remain local. In his later writings Kant turns to this issue, and discusses strategies by which we might arbitrate between competing construals of a situation, so engaging in reflective judging.

I have already noted some of Kant's remarks about the indeterminacy of rules or principles, and the need for judgment if we are to select a (determinate) act from the possible actions specified by a given rule or principle. In other places, especially in the *Critique of Judgment,* he suggests how we can judge which rules or principles may fit a given case. The passages are notoriously hard to interpret, and I shall gather together only some of the points that they suggest.

Kant now divides the faculty of judgment into two:

If the universal (the rule, principle, or law,) is given, then the judgment which subsumes the particular under it *is determinant* . . . If, however, only the particular is given and the universal has to be found for it, then the judgment is simply *reflective* (*CF,* V, 179).

The situation of agents is *in the first place* one that requires reflective judgment: Only when an account or description of a particular case has been given − only when a process of reflection has produced an appraisal of the case − can principles be applied and a solution sought. It is only then, at the point of action, that the problem of the indeterminacy of judgment arises. Unlike those who discuss prepackaged examples drawn either from literary texts or from the outlook of some group of specialists, agents must first come to an appreciation or appraisal of actual situations and possibilities for action. To suppose that they can instantly recognize their situation as having a certain specification simplifies, indeed falsifies, the predicament agents face. An agent may initially not even realize that this is a situation that requires or permits action. Even one who sees this much may be at a loss as to how the situation should be described or construed. Yet this construal or appraisal is a prerequisite for the application of principles, and, indeed, for evaluation in the light of accepted practices. Without minor premises reasoning cannot be practical.

The problem of reflective judging is that any actual example may fall under many descriptions and so exemplify numerous principles or practices, many of them prima facie of moral significance. The most significant single element in moral deliberation may well be coming to appreciate the actual case in a specific way, as falling under one rather than another set of descriptions and hence judgeable in the light of some rather than other practices or principles. We are so familiar with the degree to which different persons may make something different of closely similar situations (one sees challenge in a life situation another sees as humdrum; one is anxious or threatened where the other is relaxed and flourishes) that it can readily be seen why the appraisal of actual situations is crucial. Wittgensteinian writers are surely correct when they insist that focus on cases is crucial; but they fail to give a convincing account of how we can achieve this focus because of their concentration on literary examples where the problem of rival appraisals is greatly reduced. Problem-centered writing, I have argued, has generally been more cavalier still in its assumptions about the construal of actual moral problems. Even if we are convinced that we have grasped and justified the major premises required in moral deliberation (certain moral principles), we will not develop a practical ethics if we fail to formulate minor premises appropriate to the situations we actually face.

Kant remarks of reflective judging that "it stands . . . in need of a principle"; (*CJ*, V, 180; cf. *FI*, XX, 211). It is this claim and the suggestions he offers for meeting it that makes what he has to say important. Other philosophers have stressed the importance of appraisals for good decisions. Aristotle remarks that in the end decision lies with perception;[34] Simone Weil has emphasized the need for attending to what actually happens.[35] But Kant's claim is that appraisal itself can be guided in accordance with a set of strategies. When we judge or appraise a particular case reflectively we compare or combine it "either with other representations or with one's cognitive powers, with respect to a concept that is thereby made possible" (*FI*, XX, 211). This formulation offers no algorithm of reflective judging; indeed, there can be none. But it does suggest some overall strategies. We cannot merely judge whether or not a given case falls under any of a set list of concepts (that would be determinant judgment), but can search for concepts under which it might be placed, so locating it in a larger coherent and systematic whole. The strategies by which we reach such "situational appraisals" (the phrase is from Wiggins)[36] are relevant to all human endeavors including scientific inquiry and practical reasoning of all sorts, including specifically ethical reasoning.

Strategies that are particularly important in guiding scientific inquiry (and so indirectly important for action) include following certain well-known "maxims of judgment" (*CF*, V, 182) such as "nature takes the shortest path" and "nature does nothing in vain" and other canons of parsimony and simplicity. Such principles cannot guide determinant judging, but can regulate our search for scientific laws. These maxims or regulative ideas can guide us when "the particular is certain, but the universality of the rule of which it is a consequence is still a problem" (*CPR* A646/B674). The regulative use of these principles or ideas of reason provides ways for interrogating, but not determining, nature. More generally, they are ways of interrogating the actual situations in which we find ourselves, and so they are of more than theoretical importance.

The secound group of strategies for appraising a given particular are strategies for discovering the "coherence of experience with our own and others' cognitive capacities" (*FI*, XX, 220). What is at stake, it seems, are strategies by which we may move toward overcoming discrepancies between disparate appraisals of one situation. They are strategies, one might suggest, not for finding that one shares a

---

34 Aristotle, *Nichomachean Ethics*, 1142–3.
35 Simone Weil, "Attention and Will", and "Reflections on the Right Use of School Studies", pp. 44–5. Several Wittgensteinian writers comment on this point.
36 David Wiggins, "Deliberation and Practical Reason".

view with others but for seeking to share one. They can be thought of as strategies by which we seek to escape our private horizons by following the maxim "always to try to expand rather than to narrow one's horizon" (*L*, VII, 43; 48). When we adopt such strategies our "reflective act takes account . . . of the mode of representation of everyone else, in order, *as it were*, to weigh its judgment with the collective reason of mankind" (*CF*, V, 293).

By following both types of strategy of reflection we may hope to move from fragmentary and partial perceptions of actual situations and problems toward ones that are more complete and coherent and appropriately integrated both with our understanding of the natural world and with others' possible cognition. Such strategies are not relevant only to aesthetic judgment, but essential whenever we have to select among ways of grasping particular situations. They are indispensable when there is disagreement, and so the need to apprehend and appreciate others' appraisals and connect them to our own. Even when there is agreement in appraisal, complacency is misplaced, for a consensus may be unwarrranted: Hence all practical reasoning requires reflective strategies.

The strategies of appraisal that may be most important for practical reasoning *in general* will include ways of connecting our (initial, unreflective) construals of situations with possibly divergent construals. They might include a large range of "maxims of practical judgment in general", such as "take account of differences of information" or "listen to the other's reasons" or "consider *cui bono*" or "remember differences between intention and achievement". Even if we aim at manipulative or hostile rather than morally acceptable interaction with others, we will be thwarted if we do not regulate our activity by such maxims. The worldly-wise need good judgment.

Additional strategies may be important for making situational appraisals that become the minor premises of ethical reasoning. Here we may need not only to see what other views of a situation are and how they differ from our own, but also to arbitrate discrepancies. One maxim that may guide us here is the so-called maxim of enlarged thought, which enjoins us to think from the standpoint of everyone else (*CJ*, V, 294). Once we seek to share others' standpoints, and so become aware of incompatibilities between standpoints, further reflection may lead us toward reappraisals in which coherence is restored.

Since reflective judging follows strategies rather than algorithms, it cannot be shown to yield uniquely appropriate appraisals that form the only relevant basis for moral (or other) judgment. Strategies of reflection can, however, provide "guidance of the empirical employment of reason" (*CPR* A663/B691), can help us to detach ourselves from "subjective and personal conditions" of judgment (*CJ*, V, 293) and reach toward appraisals that would cohere with "the collective reason of mankind" (*CJ*, V, 293). They are strategies both for discerning the unity and systematicity of the natural world and for achieving connectedness and *rapprochement* between different possible perceptions of human situations. No doubt such strategies would — like other human activities — be pointless if we were isolated in mutually impenetrable and incommensurate conceptual schemes. But if we are not, these strategies may provide ways in which parochialism and ethical and other relativisms may in principle be eliminated from our appraisals of situations and so from the minor premises of ethical reasoning.

Kant's account of reflective judging offers suggestions for strategies by which we can appraise actual situations and problems. These strategies are quite different both from Wittgensteinian reliance on shared appraisals, and from problem-centered acceptance of established and "professional" appraisals of situations. The mere fact that an appraisal is shared or established does not show that it should be accepted. For its establishment may merely reflect shared culture or ideology. When we judge reflectively, rather than relying on literary or professional appraisals of cases, we may not be able to reach *any* shared appraisal of the actual situation. However, we will have some reasons to think that others who share few practices with us (though no doubt agree with us in judgment sufficiently for communication) may at least be able to see why we hold to one rather than another appraisal of the situation, and that it will be possible to discuss alternative appraisals, for our strategies of appraisal will require us to *listen* to others' appraisals and to reflect on and perhaps modify our own. We do not have to imagine that moral communication will break down whenever ways of life and social practices differ, nor that the effort to make sense of things is the whole of the moral life. Rather, the attempt to make sense of the nuances and complexities of situations, which is one of the most attractive features of Wittgensteinian ethical writing, might be incorporated in a more systematic form within an account of practical reasoning. If our search for appraisals of actual situations is guided by considerations of coherence and interpretability to all parties (and indeed to "the collective reason of mankind"), then an articulation of a case that arises out of appeals to shared practices is only *one* of the articulations that might be brought under consideration. Other, perhaps farther-reaching, types of appraisal might set a particular case in the context of different, perhaps conflicting, sets of practices, or in the context of a larger understanding of the natural and historical setting of diverse ways of life. Reflective judgment so understood is an indispensable preliminary or background to ethical decision about any actual case. Without it we can at best run through a set of fixed moral categories — whether we think of this as a list of accepted moral practices or as a sort of moral catechism — and posit that they provide an adequate basis for (determinant) judgments about actual moral situations.

Reflecting on examples, whether literary or hypothetical or ostensive, may educate us so that we become skilled at reaching situational appraisals. But appraisals alone cannot carry the burden of ethical decision. Indeed, it should be clear from the fact that situational appraisals are also indispensable for other modes of practical reasoning that they cannot provide any *sufficient* basis for ethics. If we are to be shrewd or worldly-wise or popular, or if we are to be good farmers or drivers or carpenters, situational appraisals, at least of a limited sort, will be indispensable. But activities of these sorts may often avoid rather than lead to ethical decisions. Specifically ethical decision, then, requires more than skill at appraising situations.

It is, however, easy to construct cases where it *seems* that appraisal is all that is needed, because the appraisal itself appears to show an example in such a decisively (!) good or poor light. So, for example, if we come to see the situation of a compliant but burdened member of a family as akin to slavery, or the religious conversion of a young person as a case of brainwashing, these jolting perceptions may seem to leave nothing further to be decided. Yet further consideration shows how open the disposition of such cases remains even after appraisal is completed. For it is not simply obvious what to do about such cases once they have been so construed, however complete and detailed and satisfactory and uncontested the appraisal. The practice of Wittgensteinian writers of focusing on literary examples of action already performed obscures both the fact that actual construals or appraisals of situations remain open to challenge, at least until action is undertaken (there are after all strategies and not algorithms of appraising), and the fundamental point that appraisals do not constitute decisions.

Because the most that we need to do about a literary example is to pass judgment, the gap between appraisal and a decision to act can be obscured. But appraisals can lead to decisions only when conjoined with principles. In actual cases of action we cannot elide *either* appraisals *or* the application of principles. For we must work out whether we are considering a case of family unity and filial devotion or of exploitation, of spiritual transformation or psychic coercion, and then, having reached an appraisal, must decide whether and how to act in the light of it and of principles. There may, after all, be decisive reasons against intervening or altering course even in situations we have come to see as lamentable, and many ways in which to intervene or change course if we decide to do so.

In saying that principles are indispensable we don't have to imagine that they make our decisions for us. We have rather to consider what is going on when we decide. Are we just picking one option for dealing with the situation as appraised? Or are we affirming where we stand and what we are? If the latter, then principles – even if discovered to us only when we act – are indeed indispensable to decision. To have reached the same "decision" by the toss of a coin or by mere whim would be something entirely different.

Principles, then, are not dispensable in practical reasoning. But in addition to their crucial role in moving from reflective appraisals to decisions, they may perhaps help us in reaching appraisals themselves. Ethical principles themselves can be used to augment our strategies for seeking coherent appraisals of situations, for we can use principles as *one* set of ways of interrogating a situation. We can ask, for example, "Has there been an injustice?" or "Has anyone been harmed?" or "If I do this, will it harm others or hurt their feelings?" However, if we once decided to settle for a finite and ordered list of principles as providing complete rules for the ethical appraisal of situations, the open-ended character of reflective appraisals would be lost: We would be left with a moral catechism that specified the types of determinant judgments that were taken as constitutive of the moral life.

Concluding remarks

We are now perhaps in a position to see why neither of the new waves of writing on ethics has given us a sense of how to solve moral problems, despite their evident eagerness to consider examples. Wittgensteinian writing has focused so exclusively on the discussion of specific (but usually literary and hence closed) situations in terms of shared practices or shared modes of understanding, on coming to see the sense of what has been done, rather than on deciding what is to be done, that it has said too little either about the difficulties of appraisal where practices are not shared, or are not morally acceptable, or about the move from appraisal to decision. Problem-centered writing also has paid too little attention to the difficulties of appraising actual situations, and has too readily accepted the standard descriptions of professionals and other specialists who have to attend to these situations as providing canonical appraisals, though it does not deny the need for principles. But even impeccable and subtle principles cannot lead to good decisions without appropriate minor premises. Principles without appraisals are empty; appraisals without principles are impotent.

10

Children's rights and children's lives

A friend who lived in New York could not see the sky from her windows. To discover the day's weather she had to peer at a glass-fronted building opposite, which offered a blurred reflection of part of the sky above her own building. I shall argue that when we take rights as fundamental in looking at ethical issues in children's lives we also get an indirect, partial and blurred picture. If no more direct, clearer and fuller account can be had, we will have to rely on any oblique and partial light that a theory of children's fundamental rights provides. If a clearer, more direct and more complete view of ethical aspects of children's lives is available, we have good reason to prefer it.

We may begin with a reminder of the appeal and importance of thinking in terms of children's rights. Children easily become victims. If they had rights, redress would be possible. Rather than being powerless in the face of neglect, abuse, molestation and mere ignorance, they (like other oppressed groups) would have legitimate and (in principle) enforceable claims against others. Although they (unlike many other oppressed groups) cannot claim their rights for themselves, this is no reason for denying them rights. Rather, it is reason for setting up institutions that can monitor those who have children in their charge and intervene to enforce rights. The Aristotelian thought that justice is a relation between equals, so inappropriate in dealings with children, is to be rejected. The lives of children are no private matter, but a public concern that can be met by fostering children's rights.

Many aspects of this view seem to me plausible. I shall not query the thought that children's lives are a public concern, nor the aim of securing *positive* (legal, institutional, customary) rights for children. I shall, however, query whether children's positive rights are best grounded by appeals to fundamental (moral, natural, human) rights. This conclusion does not threaten children's positive rights, which may have other grounds; nor does it deny that children have fundamental rights. Rather, I shall claim that children's fundamental rights are best grounded by being embedded in a wider account of fundamental obligations, which can also be used to justify positive rights and obligations. We can perhaps go *further* to secure the ethical basis of children's positive rights if we do *not* try to base them on claims about fundamental rights.

Theories of fundamental rights are most frequently queried from one or another consequentialist perspective. In those perspectives rights cannot be fundamental; if they were, they would sometimes obstruct goals of maximizing benefit or of minimizing harm. Since the whole point of appeals to fundamental rights is to "trump" appeals to other considerations (e.g., welfare, convenience, happiness), there is no denying that insistence on respect for fundamental rights is only contingently and at times not closely connected to good results. This is as true of adult as of children's rights, and is independent of any particular account of fundamental rights. The only view of rights that can be assimilated into consequentialist thinking takes them not as ethically fundamental "trumps" (as appeal to statutory rights is in legal thought) but as "rules of thumb" for maximizing good results. All of this is well known.

The arguments against theories of fundamental rights offered here neither depend on nor support any form of consequentialism. The perspective from which I shall argue, like that chosen by some writers on rights, is *constructivist*.[1] It differs from those approaches because it offers (in the first instance) an account of the construction not of *rights* but of *obligations*. I shall develop a view of obligation that is (broadly) Kantian, indeed more strictly so than numerous accounts of rights that are labeled Kantian. This account of obligations offers, I believe, a fruitful alternative to theories of fundamental rights in all contexts. In the last section of the chapter I hope to show that there are particularly strong reasons for adopting it in our thinking about children.

The strategy of argument will be simple. I shall first argue that theories that take rights as fundamental and those that take obligations as fundamental are not equivalent. The scope of the two sorts of theory differs, and does so in ways that matter particularly for children. Then I shall argue that a constructivist account of obligations has *theoretical* advantages that constructivist accounts of rights lack, although rights-based approaches sometimes have *political* advantages that obligation-based approaches do not. Finally I shall argue that in the specific case of children, taking rights as fundamental has political costs rather than advantages. I conclude that taking rights as fundamental in ethical delibera-

---

1   The term *constructivist* is particularly associated with Rawls's project of giving an account of justice whose justification is neither foundationalist nor subjective nor merely stipulative. In this chapter I use the term to cover approaches that seek to justify ethical principles by reference to an account of agency and rationality, without relying on claims about desires or preferences. Cf. John Rawls, *A Theory of Justice,* and "Kantian Constructivism and Moral Theory"; as well as, for example, Ronald Dworkin, "Justice and Rights", in his *Taking Rights Seriously,* pp. 150–83; Alan Gewirth, *Human Rights: Essays on Justification and Applications;* and Henry Shue, *Basic Rights: Subsistence, Affluence and U.S. Foreign Policy.* For further discussion see Chapter 11 in this volume. This paper does not presuppose, although it follows from, the constructivist account of reason developed in Chapters 1 and 2.

tion about children has neither theoretical nor political advantages, and suggest how we could obtain a more direct, perspicuous and complete view of ethical aspects of children's lives by taking obligations as fundamental.

Scope: the problem of imperfect obligations

When we have an obligation we are required to perform or omit some type of action. Sometimes we are required to perform or omit this type of action for *all* others. Sometimes we are required to perform or omit an act for *specified* others. Sometimes we are required to perform or omit an act for *unspecified* others, but not for *all* others. Obligations of the first two sorts may be thought of as having corresponding rights. Obligations of the third sort cannot plausibly be thought of as having corresponding rights.

It may help to fix ideas if we have in mind examples of obligations of each sort; however, these examples are no more than provisional illustrations. If a fully developed theory of obligations suggested that any of these illustrations was spurious, the illustration could be replaced with an example of a genuine obligation.

First, we are obliged to refrain from abuse and molestation of children, whether or not they are specifically in our charge. This obligation is owed by all agents to *all* children: The right-holders – all children – are specified. *Universal* obligations may be said to be *perfect* or complete obligations: They specify completely or perfectly not merely who is bound by the obligation but to whom the obligation is owed.[2] Universal obligations may also be *fundamental,* in the sense that they are not derived from any more basic ethical claim or relationship, and do not depend on specific social or political arrangements or on prior acts of commitment. If a universal perfect obligation is fundamental, then the rights that correspond to it are also fundamental rights.

Second, those who have undertaken to care for specific children will have obligations to them, and those specific children will have a right to care of an appropriate standard. Here too the obligation specifies completely or perfectly from whom performance is due and to whom performance is owed, and the obligation is a *perfect* obligation. However, it is not a universal obligation but one owed by *specified* agents to *specified* children, whose counterpart rights are *special* rights. *Special rights* depend on *special* relationships. Hence special obligations and rights are not fundamental; rather they are positive obligations and rights whose

---

2 They are not and cannot be completely specific about the act or forbearance that is owed: No act description can be fully determinate. Some accounts of the distinction between perfect and imperfect obligations suggest that the difference is only or mainly that the latter leave more "latitude" to act in various ways. Although it is plausible that imperfect obligations leave *more* latitude, I shall rest nothing on this difference, since it does not provide a clear demarcation between perfect and imperfect obligations. *Any* principle of obligation must leave action underdetermined: Deliberation and adjudication are indispensable in the application of principles of perfect as well as of imperfect obligation. See Chapter 12 in this volume.

specific content depends on the specific social and political arrangements and the roles and commitments agents undertake. For example, the specific acts required to fulfill the obligations that teachers or parents may have to children in their charge depend on the specific definitions of these roles in a given society. Such roles and practices and their component obligations and rights are open to ethical criticism and justification in terms of fundamental obligations and rights.[3]

Third, we may have a fundamental obligation to be kind and considerate in dealing with children – to care for them – and to put ourselves out in ways that differ from those in which we must put ourselves out for adults. This obligation may bind all agents, but is not one that we owe either to all children (such an "obligation" could not be discharged) or merely to antecedently specified children. What it will take to discharge this fundamental obligation will differ with circumstances; these circumstances will in part be constituted by social and institutional arrangements that connect specific children to specific others. Fundamental obligations that are not universal (owed to all others) are, when considered in abstraction from social and institutional context, *incomplete* or *imperfect*. This is a matter not just of the indeterminacy of the act or omission enjoined by the principle of obligation, but more fundamentally of the fact that so long as the recipients of the obligation are neither all others nor specified others, there are no right-holders, and nobody can either claim or waive performance of any rights. If there are any fundamental obligations that are imperfect in this sense, then there are some fundamental obligations to which no fundamental rights correspond.[4]

Once imperfect obligations are institutionalized, certain positive special obligations are established to which certain positive rights correspond. For example, one aspect of institutionalizing a fundamental obligation to care for children in particular social circumstances might be to assign social workers a positive obligation to monitor specific children at risk. The children so at risk would then acquire a corresponding positive right to be monitored by those social workers. However, the rights so institutionalized would not exhaust the content of a fundamental imperfect obligation. The obligations of roles such as parent or teacher or social worker are commonly taken to require more than meeting those rights that are institutionalized with the role.[5]

---

3 H. L. A. Hart, "Are There any Natural Rights?".
4 Although fundamental perfect obligations, like fundamental imperfect obligations, often need institutional embodiment (cf. Shue, *Basic Rights*), this does not obliterate the difference between them. It is only in the case of perfect obligations that right-holders are identifiable prior to institutionalization.
5 There are various reasons for thinking that the content of fundamental obligations cannot be completely institutionalized. First, the positive obligations of institutions are specified not only by the positive rights they create or confer, but also by their mandates, goals and purposes. (We understand well enough that institutions, like individuals, can fail in their obligations without violating any rights, that there can be positive as well as fundamental imperfect obligations.) Second, and more specifically, the obligations of institutions charged with securing public goods, or averting public harms, cannot be exhaustively decomposed into obligations to respect individ-

Although *imperfect* fundamental obligations lack corresponding rights, their fulfillment has not traditionally been thought optional: The very term *imperfect obligation* tells us that. What is left optional by a fundamental imperfect obligation is selection not merely of a specific way of enacting the obligation but of those for whom the obligation is to be performed. Those who do only what the children they interact with have a (universal or special) right to will do less than they ought. They will fulfill their *perfect* but not their *imperfect* obligations. In particular, parents or teachers who met only their perfect obligations would fail as parents or teachers. They would not merely fail to be saintly or heroic parents or teachers, that is, omit supererogatory action. They would fail in much that we take to be straightforwardly obligatory for parents and teachers.

Provided the distinction drawn here between perfect and imperfect obligations is retained, various other distinctions are easily accommodated. Because perfect obligations require action for all or for specified others, they have correlative definite, assigned rights, which can be claimed or waived and are in principle enforceable — even in a state of nature. Imperfect fundamental obligations, whose performance is not owed to all or to specified others, do not entail assigned rights and so are not claimable or waivable by right-holders or enforceable in abstraction from an institutional context that allocates recipients to agents. Imperfect obligations can be enforced only when they are institutionalized in ways that specify *for whom* the obligation is to be performed, that is, that define who holds the counterpart rights and can claim or waive them.

Contemporary ethical writing that is rights-based has difficulty in capturing these distinctions. If rights are taken as the starting point of ethical debate, imperfect obligations will drop out of the picture because they lack corresponding rights. The omission would be unworrying if advocates of rights also provided a broader ethical theory that could ground imperfect obligations. Unfortunately, a broader approach to the grounding of obligations is impossible within certain approaches to fundamental rights, and repudiated within others. Those who argue that there is an open-ended "right to liberty", so that any act that violates no other's right is permissible, clearly leave no room for any obligations other than perfect obligations to respect others' rights. What they leave room for is in fact nothing more than the pursuit of individual preference, even if it is given a dignified gloss by being classified as an "exercise of the right to liberty" or as "pursuit of a conception of the good".

Those who repudiate an open-ended "right to liberty", and so could allow for imperfect obligations, also surprisingly often deny that the space so provided is

---

ual rights. Third, certain obligations may be premised on the discretion of the obligation-bearer to allocate the performance of the obligation; those who see charitable giving as obligatory commonly think that there are no corresponding rights, since the allocation of such giving is at the discretion of the one who gives. I am indebted to Sheldon Leader for clarification of these points.

governed by any obligations.[6] Modern "deontological liberals" take pride in being agnostic about the good for man, and argue that insofar as action is not required by respect for others' rights, it is legitimately devoted to pursuit of our varied subjective conceptions of the good, that is, to action that reflects individual preferences. Liberal theorists who allow space for imperfect obligations, but then allocate that space to the pursuit of personal preferences, do not offer *any* account of imperfect obligations. It is no wonder that some of them characterize action that might traditionally have been thought a matter of (imperfect) obligation in jocularly trivializing terms, for example as "frightfully nice", a matter of "decency" or of being "morally splendid".[7] Sometimes such action is seen as a matter of individual preference, or style; sometimes it is promoted as supererogatory and so (once again) not obligatory. Recent rights-based thinking, whether libertarian or nonlibertarian, obscures the differences between mere expressions of individual style or preference, ordinary acts of kindness and consideration, which may (in a given context) be matters of imperfect obligation, and truly saintly or heroic action. Without an account of imperfect obligations all of these may seem no more than ways in which we have a right to act, since others' rights are no constraint.[8]

This narrowing of ethical vision makes it hard for rights-based approaches to provide a full account of ways in which children's lives are particularly vulnerable to unkindness, to lack of involvement, cheerfulness or good feeling. These lacks may be invisible from the perspective of rights. This may not seem significant if we think only of children in danger, but is vital if our concern is the quality of the lives children lead. Cold, distant or fanatical parents and teachers, even if they violate no rights, deny children "the genial play of life"; they can wither children's lives.[9]

6 Ronald Dworkin, "What Rights Do We Have?", in his *Taking Rights Seriously*, pp. 266–78, specifically denies that there is an open-ended "right to liberty"; yet he also insists that liberalism is agnostic about the good for man. See also his "Liberalism".

7 These phrases are taken from Judith Jarvis Thomson, *Rights, Restitution, and Risk: Essays in Moral Theory;* see esp. pp. 13–18, 58, and 64. Similar turns of phrase are used by many other writers.

8 Cf. further arguments to some of these conclusions in Joseph Raz, "Right-Based Moralities", esp. pp. 185–6.

9 See Edmund Gosse, *Father and Son.* For variations on the theme of withering parenting see F. M. Mayor, *The Rector's Daughter;* and Molly Keane, *Good Behaviour.* Recent philosophical writing on ethical issues affecting children often stresses the danger of relying too much on *positive* rights, which typically come into play in adversarial contexts and so are destructive of intimate and family life. See, for example, O. O'Neill and W. Ruddick, eds., *Having Children: Legal and Philosophical Reflections on Parenthood,* esp. Pt. II; Jeffrey Blustein, *Parents and Children: The Ethics of the Family;* Francis Shrag, "Children: Their Rights and Needs"; and Ferdinand Schoeman, "Rights of Children, Rights of Parents, and the Moral Basis of the Family". The objections raised in this chapter to rights-based approaches to children's issues are not objections to children's *positive* rights. On the contrary, one of the aims of the approach is to ground positive rights adequately (while accepting that there is much to be said against overemphasizing adversarial contexts in thinking about children's lives). However, we are ill placed to object to an overemphasis on *positive* rights unless and until we can offer an account of *fundamental* obligations to children. Given the dearth of obligation-based approaches, and in particular the lack of accounts of the grounds of fundamental imperfect obligations, in recent philosophical discussions of children's issues, I believe that the literary

Children can hardly learn to share or to show what Burke called "the unbought grace of life" if we are concerned only with their enforceable claims against others.

If imperfect obligations could be set aside, theories of obligations and of rights would have the same scope. They would offer two equivalent descriptions of a single set of ethical relationships. When we speak of (perfect) obligations we adopt the perspective of the *agent* and consider what must be done if there is to be no moral failure; when we speak of rights we adopt the perspective of the *recipient* (of perfect obligations) and consider what must be received or accorded if there is to be no moral failure. If imperfect obligations were set aside, we would be dealing with two perspectives rather than with distinct accounts of ethical relationships, and the only reason to prefer either idiom would be that the audience for a particular discussion was either in a position to act (so that discussion of its obligations would be relevant) or in a position to be affected by others' action (so that discussion of its rights would be relevant). Many audiences would be in a position both to act and to be affected; for them both perspectives would be important. However, if we think imperfect obligations important, we cannot see a choice between obligation-based and rights-based theories as mere choice of perspective, since the scope of a theory of fundamental rights is narrower. Nor, as we shall see, is a preference for rights-based perspectives vindicated by more theoretical considerations.

The construction of rights

It is an appealing feature of theories of rights and of obligations that both allow a *constructivist* account of ethical justification. *Foundationalist* attempts to provide an objective grounding for ethics have not borne fruit, and the subjective account of the good to which utilitarian consequentialists appeal is widely criticized because it assimilates the good and the desired. Proponents of constructivist theories of rights and of obligations have hopes of avoiding both difficulties. They seek to construct accounts of ethical requirements from minimal claims about human rationality and the human condition;[10] they eschew stronger but controversial views of the metaphysical foundations of ethics.

> illustrations are revealing and not redundant. Some recent discussions of "rights to do wrong" are, I believe, also a sign of the failure of modern liberal political theory to show what, apart from appeals to fundamental perfect obligations and their corollary rights, could ground judgments of wrongdoing. This failure is avoidable. We have only to look back to the structure of the Kantian enterprise, or to the tradition of civic humanism (see Quentin Skinner, "The Idea of Negative Liberty: Philosophical and Historical Perspectives"), to see that a serious account of imperfect obligations is compatible with taking perfect obligations, and so rights, seriously.
>
> 10 There are other ways of making rights the fundamental ethical category. Theories of natural rights typically rely on a theological framework; some optimists simply posit that rights are fundamental. I take it, but will not here argue the point, that only a constructivist approach could offer good reasons for thinking rights fundamental. Constructivist approaches to rights have been used both by libertarian writers and by those who seek to establish "welfare" as well as "liberty" rights. See the works referred to in footnote 1 above.

Constructions that lack foundations cannot be arbitrary accretions. They must be put together on principles that allow the place of each element of the construction to be determined by the position of other elements. We have a ready analogy in space architecture. Space satellites do not have "foundations" or identifiable "higher" or "lower" parts, but their parts must interlock: Their construction is not arbitrary. Constructivist accounts of ethical requirements also propose no single foundation, yet do not appeal to a mere plurality of moral intuitions without order. As with other constructions, the parts are to be put together with an eye to the coherence and functioning of the structure. The art is to use minimal and plausible assumptions about human rationality and agency to construct an account of ethical requirements that is rich and strong enough to guide action and reflection.

Constructions of rights generally aim to determine the largest set of rights that can be held by each of a plurality of (approximately) equal, distinct rational beings. The appeal of this idea is enormous: It proposes that we construct a rational account of ethical requirements that presupposes only that we are separate beings whose interaction is mediated neither by natural instinct nor by supernatural programming, but by processes of practical reasoning. If such beings are to act at all, each must have some "sphere" of action. If they are without deep inequalities (no natural masters or slaves), it is plausible to think that the "spheres" should be equal. If the equal "spheres" are to define rights, these rights, and the obligations that are their correlates, must be mutually compatible. Of the many possible ways of constructing equal "spheres" of copossible proposed rights the one that yields maximal "spheres" is preferred as affording the best possibility and protection for agency. (Submaximal "spheres", it may be thought, would in practice leave some with extra territory, and so would undercut the equality of rights.) Such constructions identify ethical requirements with the possession of "the greatest liberty compatible with like liberty for all". Each is to be accorded an equal and maximal "sphere of action", whose boundaries others may not cross, within which it is up to the right-holder alone to determine what shall be done.

Constructions of rights of this type depend heavily on the spatial, indeed territorial, metaphors in which they are standardly presented. If we interpret them as claims that each person has a right to determine what happens within a certain spatial and temporal region, we obtain a fully coherent model for the construction. Each right-holder has a space, whose boundaries are definite, and no part of one right-holder's space is included within the space of any other right-holders. The copossibility requirement is then readily met, since obligations reduce to the requirement to keep out of others' spaces. The spaces of right-holders are then made as large as they can be compatibly with the requirement that they be of equal size.

If the spaces of different right-holders exhausted the available territory, there could be no imperfect obligations. This might be the case if each right-holder had an open-ended right to liberty, so that anything done by a right-holder within his or her own territory would be permissible but not obligatory and anything done in another's territory would be forbidden. Such an open-ended right to liberty has seemed plausible to some libertarian writers; but we do not have to imagine that the equal, maximal spaces tesselate the available territory. If they do not, there can be spaces that are part of no right-holder's domain. Action in these spaces neither violates rights nor is protected by others' lack of rights to use the same space. Without such interstitial spaces – an ethical no-man's-land – all obligations must be perfect obligations to observe one's own territorial limits, the mirror image of rights that others not infringe those territorial limits or restrict what may be done within them. Interstitial spaces can *allow* for action that is a permissible use of common space. Constructions of rights offer no account of imperfect obligations, but need not rule them out.

Despite its coherence, a spatial interpretation of maximal liberties does not fit well with other aspects of theories of rights. One difficulty is metaphysical. A spatial interpretation of rights fits most happily with a physicalist account of act individuation,[11] but theories of rights are more at home with conceptions of human freedom that may be hard to fit into a physicalist picture. It is hard even to see the point of according rights to agents whose freedom of action goes no deeper than uncoerced determination by natural causes. This is a difficult and complex matter, and I shall set it aside to focus on a more immediate difficulty with the project of constructing rights by working out what it would be for all to have maximal, equal liberties.

As long as the spatial metaphors on which constructions of rights depend are taken literally, we have no difficulty in interpreting what is meant by *sphere, territory* or *space, boundary, maximal liberty* or *infraction* of others' rights. However, there are problems (quite apart from those alluded to in the last paragraph) with taking the metaphors literally if the point of constructing an account of fundamental rights is to show how we should coordinate uses of a world that we share rather than to partition that world into exclusive domains.

When the literal interpretation is dropped, the territorial metaphors lose sense and precision.[12] When rights (and obligations) are individuated in terms of act descriptions rather than spatial regions, we can still tell whether sets of proposed rights are equal and copossible, but we lose our grip on claims that one right is larger than another, or that some set of rights is maximal. Is, for example, an older child's right to freedom of association *larger* than his or her freedom of conscience? Is either *larger* than the child's right to adequate parental care and supervision? Might

11 The spatial metaphorics are closely associated with classical writing on rights – for example, in Hobbes and Locke. For the combination of libertarian constructivism with a physicalist theory of action see Hillel Steiner, "Individual Liberty".

12 For discussions of the limitations and difficulties of spatial interpretations of rights see Charles Taylor, "What's Wrong with Negative Liberty?", esp. pp. 218ff.; Onora O'Neill, "The Most Extensive Liberty"; and Dworkin, "What Rights Do We Have?", in his *Taking Rights Seriously*, pp. 270ff.

we give a different answer in the case of a younger child? By what metric are we to determine the "size" of a right or of the "territory" that is constrained by the counterpart obligations the right imposes? Which way of accommodating proposed rights to one another – of guaranteeing their copossibility – affords the greatest liberty? Can we show that there is a unique accommodation that permits us to identify maximal copossible equal rights? If we cannot, how can a constructivist approach determine what rights there are?

There is no unique way of accommodating different rights. There are indefinitely many ways of describing possible actions, and hence indefinitely many ways of picking out sets of copossible, equal rights. Without a metric for rights we could count a set of rights *maximal* only if it dominated all other sets of rights. Since we can always adjust the boundaries between any two proposed rights, we will find no set of rights that dominates all others. The principle of construction to which we gesture in speaking of "the greatest possible liberty compatible with like liberty for all" turns out to be radically indeterminate because there are multiple nondominated sets of copossible rights. (We can, of course, identify sets of copossible, equal rights as *submaximal,* when they are dominated by another such set; but this is not enough for identifying a unique maximal set of such rights.)

This problem does not depend on a particular interpretation of liberty. A negative interpretation of liberty yields a libertarian construction of rights as *liberty rights* not to be interfered with. Libertarian accounts of rights may seem peculiarly inappropriate to children, since only children whom we think of (oxymoronically) as "mature minors" have much use for liberty rights. Even if we were prepared to settle for a libertarian account of rights, we could not identify a maximal set of liberty rights. For any pair of proposed equal liberty rights – for example, the rights of assembly and of liberty of access to public places – can be variously accommodated, in ways that yield alternative sets of copossible rights neither of which dominates the other. Hence we cannot identify any set of proposed liberty rights as maximal.

Positive interpretations of liberty apparently allow for constructions of rights more widely relevant to children. They construe rights as entitlements to whatever goods or services, as well as forbearances, may be needed to nurture and sustain the possibility of agency. Unfortunately, once again we cannot tell which accommodation of various proposed *welfare* (or welfare and liberty) rights would be maximal. Is a child's right to, say, material well-being greater than its right to stay with its family of origin? Of the many ways in which these two rights could be adjusted, which would afford maximal (positive) liberty? Without a spatial metric it is not evident how to determine which of different copossible sets of equal *liberty* or *welfare* rights is maximal. Whichever view is taken of human liberty, the notion of maximal liberty, and so of the most extensive set of copossible equal rights, is indeterminate.

A tempting fallback position might be to look for some set of equal copossible rights that is avowedly not maximal but rather thought to be basic. Perhaps a "core" set of rights that would be included within any nondominated set of rights can be constructed. However, the requirements for individuating rights outside a physicalist framework show that no such core set of rights can be determined. Any candidates for inclusion in such a core set can be mutually adjusted to form a further, distinct set of equal copossible rights that neither dominates nor is dominated by the original set.

The scheme of constructing a theory of rights by determining which of the indefinitely numerous copossible sets of equal proposed rights is either maximal or basic turns out to be indeterminate in ways that flaw the entire project of construction. It is essential to the scheme that human rights be identified by their comembership in a unique set of rights that are not just equal and copossible but either *greater* than or *basic to* any other equal and copossible set. Either way, no right can be identified unless all are identified. Rights that are identified by comembership of a maximal or basic set of rights can no more stand alone than the poles of a wigwam: Their very identification depends on their role in the construction, and if the principles of construction are inadequate, the construction "materials" cannot be picked out.

Constructions of obligations

An analogous project for constructing obligations faces fewer difficulties, because it does not depend on maximizing nor therefore on there being a plausible metric for obligations. If a plurality of distinct rational beings is to have the same obligations, we can begin constructing the content of those obligations by identifying and rejecting any principles of action that *cannot* guide the action of all members of a plurality of approximately equal rational beings. If there are any such principles, their rejection will be obligatory for rational beings with equal obligations. (Such approaches are versions of Kantian universalizing.) Even if we cannot identify a complete set of principles of obligation, we may be able to identify some members of the set. The advantage of this principle of construction is that it allows obligations to be identified *successively,* rather then requiring the identification of all obligations in order to identify any.

An example of the construction of principles of obligation might be the following: We find that a principle of deceit *cannot* guide all communication among a plurality of rational beings, since its adoption is incompatible with maintaining conditions of trust, and so with the possibility of communication that deceit itself requires. A principle of untrammeled deception cannot be part of *any* set of equal and copossible principles of obligation. We may conclude that nondeceit (at least) is an obligatory fundamental principle of action among any plurality of rational beings who communicate, even if we cannot work out all the other obligations of rational beings. The content of individual obligations constructed by this method can be determined even if we cannot identify a full or maximal or basic set of principles of obligation.

Universalizing methods of constructing obligations are not without problems. They are inadequate unless linked with a theory of action that indicates which level and type of principle of action is to be tested by the method.[13] If principles were judged nonuniversalizable (and their rejection obligatory) merely because they mention spatiotemporal particulars, the construction of obligations by universalizing procedures would produce unsatisfactory results. If the identification of principles of action is too closely linked to agents' self-consciousness, other unsatisfactory results arise.[14] A constructivist account of obligations will be able to deliver what it promises only if it resolves these difficulties. Even if the difficulties are resolved, it may deliver a less complete account of perfect obligations than constructivist accounts of rights promise. For the method of construction does not guarantee that all obligations can be identified; equally it does not postpone the identification of any obligations until all have been identified. A construction made from the agent's perspective (rather than from the perspective of recipience) may deliver more, although it promises less, since it does not aim at an all-or-nothing construction of ethical requirements.[15]

There are other advantages in applying a constructivist approach to obligations rather than to rights. In particular, a constructivist account of obligations not merely allows for imperfect obligations, but can be extended in a quite natural way to ground some imperfect obligations that are particularly important for lives that are dependent and vulnerable, including children's lives.

Imperfect obligations are traditionally thought to comprise matters such as help, care or consideration, and the development of talents, to whose specific enactment others have no right, but which agents are obliged to provide for some others in some form. These can be incorporated within a universalizing construction by a simple extension of the basic construction. The basis of the universalizing construction is rejection of action that reflects principles that cannot be universally acted on by a plurality of distinct rational beings. Human beings are, however, not merely distinct rational beings; they are also *vulnerable* and *needy* beings in the sense that their rationality and their mutual independence – the very basis of their agency – is incomplete, mutually vulnerable and socially produced. Our agency is vulnerable to others' action in multiple ways, and particu-

---

13 These points are compressed here. I have worked through them in more detail in *Faces of Hunger: An Essay on Poverty, Development and Justice*, Chaps. 6–8.

14 This large topic embraces questions about the ideological context of ethical reasoning. The literature both on ethics and on ideology is immense, but little of it takes ideology as a practical problem. I have tried to do so in *Faces of Hunger*, and in "Ethical Reasoning and Ideological Pluralism".

15 This topic has been closely debated in discussions of Kant's concept of a maxim. Cf. Rüdiger Bittner, "Maximen"; Otfried Höffe, "Kants kategorischer Imperativ als Kriterium des Sittlichen"; and the essays in Part II of this volume.

larly vulnerable at certain stages of our lives. Unless children receive both physical care and adequate socialization, they will not survive; if they merely survive, they may not become competent agents; without education and instruction appropriate to their society they will lack capacities to act that they need to function in the specific contexts available to them. A plurality of distinct rational beings who are also needy cannot therefore universally act on principles of mutual indifference. If they did, agency would fail or diminish for some, who then could adopt no principles of action, so that the very possibility of action on principles that can be universally shared would be undermined. Rational and needy beings cannot universally act on principles of refusing all help to one another or of doing nothing to strengthen and develop abilities to act. However, it is impossible to help all others in all ways. Hence obligations to help and to develop others' capacities must be imperfect obligations; they do not mandate specific acts of helpfulness to specified others or any specific contribution to developing talents in specified others. The construction of imperfect obligations commits rational and needy beings only to avoiding *principled* refusal to help and *principled* neglect to develop human potentialities. The specific acts required by these commitments will vary in different lives. Those who live or work with children are likely to find that they must take an active part both in their care and in their education if inaction is not to amount to principled refusal of those commitments.[16]

Fundamental imperfect obligations cannot be identified with any counterpart set of fundamental rights. Unless and until they are institutionalized these obligations have no allocated right-holders. When we consider them in the abstract, nothing can be said from the perspective of recipience: No right-holders are specified; there is nobody to claim or waive performance. However, if a constructive argument shows that universal indifference to helping others and universal neglect to develop human capacities for action are matters of (imperfect) obligation, we will have reason to act to try to further these obligations. In particular we will have reason to construct and support institutions that realize and foster the discharge of these obligations.[17] For example, where we can foresee the incidence

16 The background to these points lies in Kant's treatment of the "contradiction in the will" version of the Formula of Universal Law. I have offered an interpretation of the argument that connects it to aspects of human needs and vulnerability in *Faces of Hunger*, Chaps. 7 and 8, as well as in Chapters 6 and 12 in this volume and in "Rights, Obligations and Needs".

17 It is a point of controversy whether imperfect obligations should ever be legally enforced. I shall take no stand on the matter. All that is claimed here is that institutionalizing such obligations we make them *enforceable;* modes of enforcement may use social or psychological sanctions rather than legal ones. It may be the case that certain sorts of sanction that are available ought not to be used to enforce certain types of obligation. If it is the case (it seems plausible, but I have not argued the point here) that the act descriptions in principles of imperfect obligation are less determinate than those in principles of perfect obligation, legal enforcement of certain imperfect obligations may have to be indirect — that is to say, it may work only by way of constituting certain institutions on whom specific interpretations of principles of imperfect obligation are laid as positive obligations.

of need in broad outline (as we can for children) and the incidence of opportunity to meet or deny needs (as we can for those who in a given society are charged with care of children), we may find strong reasons to establish a legal and social framework that secures certain positive obligations and so positive rights to care and education of a certain standard for children. The argument behind such a grounding of children's statutory and customary rights will appeal to a combination of perfect and imperfect obligations, and use these to work out how the actual practices of caring for and educating children of a particular society at a given time should be developed or modified. An argument for the same legal and social changes that appealed directly to children's fundamental rights would have the more daunting task of demonstrating in abstraction from particular institutions and practices that each child has a fundamental right to specific forms of care and education.

Politics: the rhetoric of children's rights

None of these arguments shows that it is always pointless to talk about children's fundamental rights. Whatever we say about fundamental perfect obligations can, after all, be stated just as accurately in terms of the counterpart fundamental rights. However, since children depend so much on others who perform their imperfect obligations, a shift to the idiom of rights in discussions of children risks excluding and neglecting things that matter for children. Yet we all know that the idiom of rights has become a common and respected way of approaching ethical issues to do with children. The success of this idiom, we have seen, cannot be attributed either to its being the only or obvious nonconsequentialist approach to fundamental principles that matter for the treatment of children, or to its preeminent theoretical coherence. What then accounts for its present prominence? Why does so much current discussion of fundamental ethical issues focus on children's rights and not on obligations to children?

I believe that a large part of the answer to this question is historical, and that a short consideration of that history suggests good reasons for caution in using the rhetoric of rights to think about ethical issues in children's lives.

The rhetoric of rights was separated from its parent theories of natural law and human obligations in the eighteenth century. The discourse of rights is an entirely legitimate descendant of older discussions of obligation and justice, of virtue and happiness, which have been ubiquitous both in popular and in philosophical discussion in ethics since antiquity. Rights can readily be derived from a theory of obligations, merely by considering perfect obligations from the perspective of recipience. However, the legitimacy of the discourse of rights becomes problematic when it aspires to become the sole or fundamental ethical category.

The shift to the perspective of recipience may sometimes have a liberating force. On the surface it may seem strange that a shift away from the perspective of agency to that of recipience could liberate or energize. Because rights will be unmet, indeed violated, unless those who hold the counterpart obligations do what they ought, it may seem puzzling that an idiom that addresses recipients rather than agents should be at all important. However, the rhetoric of rights had powerful uses in its original context of confrontation with absolute monarchies and other undemocratic and oppressive institutions. By adopting the perspective of the recipient of others' obligations, it insists that the recipient is no mere loyal *subject* who petitions for some boon or favor, but rather a *claimant* who demands what is owed, and is wronged if a rightful claim is denied. Of course, claims, like petitions, may go unheeded by the powerful; but, unlike petitioners, claimants construe such rejection as injustice. The rhetoric of rights disputes established powers and their categories and seeks to empower the powerless; it is the rhetoric of those who lack power but do not accept the status quo. Those who claim their rights deny that the powers that be may define who they are, what they may do or what they are entitled to. Although the rights of the powerless can only be met, as they can be thwarted, by the action of the powerful, the powerless in claiming their rights assert limits to others' power (which they may fail to establish). The charters and declarations of the human rights movement from the grand eighteenth-century documents to the UN Universal Declaration of Human Rights, as well as the activities of contemporary movements for civil rights, women's rights and minority rights, constantly appeal over the heads of the powers that be, urging those who are powerless to claim their rights and so to take the first step away from dependence.

If the powerless gain recognition for the rights they claim, those on whom the counterpart obligations fall must acknowledge and fulfill them. Sometimes these obligations will be fulfilled with little urging from those whose rights are acknowledged; sometimes enormous "pressure from below" is needed before there is change. The *political* point of the rhetoric of rights is therefore evident: Rhetoric has to be one of the main weapons of those who lack power. This also explains the easy and frequent *misuse* of that rhetoric to claim spurious "rights" even when no corresponding obligations can be justified. Many of the "rights" promulgated in international documents, including the International Declaration of the Rights of the Child, are perhaps not spurious, but they are patently no more than "manifesto" rights,[18] which cannot be claimed unless or until practices and institutions

---

18　The phrase is Joel Feinberg's in "The Nature and Value of Rights". Although manifesto rights cannot be claimed or enforced as they stand, they propose principles to be institutionalized. For example, The United Nations Declaration of the Rights of the Child includes the child's rights "to grow and develop in health" (Principle 4), "to an atmosphere of affection and of moral and material security" (Principle 6) and to "an education which will promote his general culture and enable him on a basis of equal opportunity to develop his abilities and his sense of moral and social responsibility" (Principle 7). None of these "rights" is well formed as an enforceable claim; but they can be seen as ideals that should inform the construction of institutions that secure enforceable claims.

are established that determine against whom claims on behalf of a particular child may be lodged. Mere insistence that certain ideals or goals are rights cannot make them into rights; but a proleptic rhetoric of rights may be politically useful in working to set up institutions that secure positive rights that constitute (one possible) realization of fundamental imperfect obligations.

We have already seen that a constructivist account of fundamental rights faces *theoretical* difficulties in dealing with ethical issues to do with children. A rights-based approach suffers not only from the *general* difficulty that its construction is indeterminate, but from the specific problem that it cannot ground the imperfect obligations whose fulfillment is so important in children's lives. Such theoretical difficulties might, however, not lead to political failure. The perspective of rights may be ideologically and politically important in spite of its theoretical difficulties because its rhetoric empowers the powerless. Can appeals to children's fundamental rights be politically significant, in the way that other appeals to rights have been? Do they or can they help empower children or their advocates to wring recognition and fulfillment of obligations from the powerful?

Appeals to children's rights might have political and rhetorical importance if children's dependence on others is like that of oppressed social groups whom the rhetoric of rights has served well. However, the analogy between children's dependence and that of oppressed groups is suspect. When colonial peoples, or the working classes or religious and racial minorities or women, have demanded their rights, they have sought recognition and respect for capacities for rational and independent life and action that are demonstrably there and thwarted by the denial of rights. No doubt oppression takes its toll, and those who have been treated as dependent all their adult lives often lack confidence and are more subservient and less independent than they may become; but the potential for empowerment is there, and activity and agitation to claim rights that are denied may itself build confidence and independence. But the dependence of children is very different from the dependence of oppressed social groups on those who exercise power over them.

Younger children are completely and unavoidably dependent on those who have power over their lives. Theirs is not a dependence that has been artificially produced (although it can be artificially prolonged); nor can it be ended merely by social or political changes; nor are others reciprocally dependent on children. The dependence of oppressed social groups, on the other hand, is often limited, artificially produced, reducible and frequently matched by the reciprocal dependence of the privileged on the oppressed, who provide servants, workers and soldiers. It is not surprising that oppressors often try to suggest that they stand in a paternal relation to those whom they oppress: In that way they suggest that the latter's dependence is natural and irremediable and their own exercise of power a burden that they bear with benevolent fortitude. The vocabulary and trappings of paternalism are often misused to mask the unacceptable faces of power. It is not mere metaphor, but highly political rhetoric, when oppressors describe what they do as "paternalistic".

Child-rearing and educational practices are often harsh and ill-judged. Yet they are fundamentally different from other exercises of power in that (with few exceptions) parents and educators seek to reduce (some or all of) children's incapacities and dependence. Even when they are reluctant to lose their power over children, they do not want specifically *childish* dependence to continue indefinitely. This is not because parents or educators are always high-minded, but because children's dependence is a burden for those on whom they depend. When power over children is systematically used to perpetuate forms of dependence or subservience that are *not* peculiar to childhood, we criticize not just those child-rearing and educational practices, but also whatever wider social relations keep those who have left childhood in positions of economic and social dependence. The rhetoric of rights may have relevance and resonance for the *adults* of such societies, who find themselves still dependent and powerless even when they lose the peculiar dependence of childhood. Yet an appeal to rights will have little chance of empowering those who are still children: If they are too young, they will be wholly unable to respond to the appeal; if they are old enough to respond, they will probably find themselves well on the way to majority, and to the ending of the forms of disability and dependence that are peculiar to children.

The crucial difference between (early) childhood dependence and the dependence of oppressed social groups is that childhood is a stage of life, from which children normally emerge and are helped and urged to emerge by those who have most power over them. Those with power over children's lives usually have some interest in ending childish dependence. Oppressors usually have an interest in maintaining the oppression of social groups. Children have both less need and less capacity to exert "pressure from below", and less potential for using the rhetoric of rights as a political instrument. Those who urge respect for children's rights must address not children but those whose action may affect children; they have reason to prefer the rhetoric of obligations to that of rights, both because its scope is wider and because it addresses the relevant audience more directly.

Since the ranks of childhood are continuously depleted by entry into adult life, no "children's movement" on the model of the women's movement or of civil rights movements can be envisaged. However, "mature minors" can find themselves in a position partly analogous to that of oppressed social groups.[19] Their minority may sometimes be prolonged unnecessarily by civil disabilities and modes of life that damage their social development and postpone competence. Mature and maturing minors who are restricted and damaged by civil liabilities and infantilizing social practices can use the rhetoric of rights to help secure

---

19 See O'Neill and Ruddick, *Having Children*, Pt. III, for discussions of the situation and predicaments of "mature minors".

greater recognition and independence. This rhetoric may galvanize and empower those who find themselves with many mature capacities but still with the burdens of minority; it may even hasten the maturing of capacities. Vicarious action to secure rights may be valuable for other minors, whose maturing has been delayed or undermined by infantilizing (even if well-meant) treatment. For the majority of children, however, the rhetoric of rights is merely one *indirect* way of reminding others of *some* of their obligations.

If we care about children's lives we will have a number of good reasons *not* to base our arguments on appeals to children's fundamental rights. Some of these reasons are the theoretical difficulties of theories of fundamental rights. To look at rights is to look at what is ethically required indirectly by looking at what should be received. Constructivist accounts of what should be received are radically indeterminate, and hence blurred. All rights-based approaches are incomplete in that they tell us nothing about what should be done when nobody has a right to its being done; they are silent about imperfect obligations. The view we get from the perspective of rights is not merely *indirect,* but *blurred* and *incomplete.*

Other reasons against invoking children's fundamental rights are political. The rhetoric of rights is mainly useful to agents who are largely powerless but able to exert at least rhetorical pressure from below. Children are more fundamentally but less permanently powerless; their main remedy is to grow up. Because this remedy cannot be achieved rapidly they are peculiarly vulnerable and must rely more than other powerless groups on social practices and institutions that secure the performance of others' obligations. The great disanalogies between children's dependence and that of members of oppressed social groups suggest that the rhetoric of rights can rarely empower children.

These conclusions will be uncongenial to some of those who have hoped to add the momentum of the human rights movement to activism on behalf of children. I think that hope is illusory because it exaggerates the analogies between children's dependence and the dependence of oppressed social groups. Nor do I think we should be surprised that rights-based approaches have not proved congenial or illuminating ways of handling the full range of fundamental ethical issues that face those who live with children. Theories of rights were born and developed in large part in repudiation of paternalistic models of just political and social relations. Their proponents have repudiated the justice of familial analogies that liken kings to fathers, see colonial powers as mother countries, women and underdeveloped peoples as childlike and just social relations as patriarchal. However, it is no mere analogy when we speak of mothers and fathers as parents, and children are not just metaphorically childlike. There are good reasons to think that paternalism may be much of what is ethically required in dealing with children, even if it is inadequate in dealings with mature and maturing minors. Nothing is lost in debates about the allocation of obligations to children between families and public institutions if we do not suppose that fundamental rights are the basis of those obligations. However, a fuller account of fundamental obligations to children and of their appropriate institutionalization in families and in public institutions is a further story. The task of this essay has been to show why that story needs telling.

Constructivisms in ethics

Somewhere in the space between realist and relativist accounts of ethics there is said to be a third, distinct possibility. One such position, allegedly both antirealist and antirelativist, is John Rawls's "Kantian constructivism", first formulated in *A Theory of Justice* and since elaborated in a series of papers.[1] Rawls's critics doubt whether he has found any stable third possibility. On closer inspection, they suspect, every elaboration of the theory depends either on unvindicated transcendent moral claims or on the actual ethical beliefs of some society.

If these suspicions are well founded, Rawls has not constructed a position that is neither realist nor relativist. Nor have his critics shown the constructivist project impossible. However, they may have shown a great deal about constraints on the wider project by concentrating on the specific difficulties of Rawls's constructivism. I shall discuss Rawls's responses to those critics as a route into an account of a variant constructivism that may be less likely to be absorbed either into moral realism or into relativism.

Designs for original positions

Rawls's responses to his critics can be traced in successive formulations of his position. *A Theory of Justice* outlined his well-known method of "reflective equilibrium" for determining principles of justice. The method seeks coherence between "our considered moral judgments" and the principles that would be chosen by rational beings whose specific identities and desires have been obscured by a controversially tailored veil of ignorance, which defines a canonical "original position". Since coherentist strategies may yield multiple solutions, Rawls offered only *a* theory of justice; there is no claim that reflective equilibrating yields a unique solution (*TJ,* 50).

His critics detect traces both of relativism and of transcendent moral ideals in

This chapter originally appeared in *Proceedings of the Aristotelian Society,* 89 (1988–9), 1–17 (Presidential Address).

1   Since this chapter makes frequent references to John Rawls's writings, parenthetical references will be given. The works referred to are as follows. *TJ* – *A Theory of Justice; BS* – "The Basic Structure as Subject"; *KC* – "Kantian Constructivism in Moral Theory"; and *JFPM* – "Justice as Fairness: Political Not Metaphysical". See also Rawls, "The Independence of Moral Theory", and "A Kantian Conception of Equality".

this approach. The reference to "our" considered moral judgment has prompted queries about who "we" are. Can an account of justice that depends even in part on "our considered moral judgments" avoid contamination by the tenets of corrupt moral traditions, or of traditions that privilege certain sorts of lives and perceptions? Fears that Rawls's thinking cannot escape the claims of entrenched privilege are particularly evident in some discussions of gender justice and of international justice.[2] Here it matters a great deal who "we" are taken to be. Other critics have thought that reference to judgments made by idealized agents in an original position uncritically endorses moral ideals that need the type of metaphysical vindication that Rawls eschews. In bracketing "knowledge of those contingencies which set men at odds" (TJ, 19) we deem ideal the principles of beings whose relevance to human affairs looks rather scanty. Although Rawls criticizes utilitarians for not taking the distinction between persons seriously (TJ, 27), some of his critics have thought that he does not himself take the connection between persons seriously. Rawls's responses to both sets of critics can be traced in his successive comments on the nature of constructivism and on its Kantian background.

In A Theory of Justice Rawls mainly uses the metaphor of contract rather than that of construction to characterize his enterprise. Justice as fairness "carries to a higher level of abstraction the familiar theory of the social contract as found, say, in Locke, Rousseau, and Kant" (TJ, 11, cf. 3). However, the method of generating principles of justice by reference to choices made in an original position is also said to be "constructive" because it is a procedure that can settle disputes. Intuitionism is not constructive, because it cannot adjudicate conflicts between intuitions. Rawls offers "constructive criteria" (TJ, 34, 39–40, 52) by which the considered moral judgments of the status quo may be challenged and revised (TJ, 49) without reference to a supposed moral reality. The particular constructive procedures are deemed "Kantian" because they rely on a more abstract and austere account of the agency and rationality of those who are to "construct" principles of justice than is used, for example, by utilitarians.

Without doubt important aspects of A Theory of Justice are Kantian. However, Rawls departs fundamentally from Kant by relying on a solely instrumental conception of rationality.[3] Justice constructed on this basis must seemingly consist of principles that Kant would have rejected as heteronomous. This danger is to be averted by shrouding the original position in a veil of ignorance (TJ, 252). Those who do not know what they want cannot choose self-serving principles. However, instrumental reasoning is wholly at sea unless oriented by some goals. Hence Rawls lifts the veil enough to allow knowledge that certain "primary"

2   Susan Moller Okin, "Gender and Justice"; Charles Beitz, Political Theory and International Relations; O'Neill, "Ethical Reasoning and Ideological Pluralism".
3   TJ, 14, 142. For perceptive and diverging views of Rawls's Kantianism see Robert Paul Wolff, Understanding Rawls; and Stephen Darwall, "Is There a Kantian Foundation for Rawlsian Justice?".

goods – rights and liberties, powers and opportunities, income and wealth (*TJ*, 62) – are universally desired. This filtered access to knowledge of desires is carefully limited to ensure that parties in the original position are mutually disinterested. Unless the theory veils the cross-referring structure of human desires – second-orderedness, reactive attitudes to others, altruism, malevolence and envy – an account of human motivation as well as a shortlist of primary goods will be needed to orient choice in the original position. Detailed motivational premises will introduce controversy and may disable the decision procedures of a revised original position. However, blanket ignorance of second-order desires in turn obscures too much, since it deprives choosers of reasons to care about a future beyond their own lives. Hence Rawls once more lifts the veil to let in a limited assumption about second-order desires: He thinks of parties to the original position as "representing continuing lines of claims, as being so to speak deputies for a kind of everlasting moral agent or institution" (*TJ*, 128). The agents in the original position, we discover, are to be thought of as heads or representatives of families who, although generally uninterested in others, care at least about their immediate descendants. Much depends on artful tailoring of the veil of ignorance.

Abstract agents and idealized persons

In *A Theory of Justice* Rawls describes his method as *abstracting* from features of actual human choosing. He aims to argue from "widely accepted but weak premises" (*TJ*, 18). The "veil of ignorance is arrived at in a natural way" (*TJ*, 19), because we only restrict and do not augment our knowledge of human choosing. We approach a theory of justice minimally by seeing it as part of a theory of rational choice (*TJ*, 16, 47); we hinge nothing on a metaphysically demanding account of the self. What we have is a "procedural interpretation of Kant's conception of autonomy and the categorical imperative" (*TJ*, 256) that does not depend on the dubious metaphysics of transcendental idealism (cf. *BS*, 165).

Like the social contract theorists in whose tradition he stands, Rawls has often been criticized for being too abstract. It is not easy to see just why this is a failing. Abstraction, taken strictly, is simply a matter of detaching certain claims from others. Abstract reasoning hinges nothing on the satisfaction or nonsatisfaction of predicates from which it abstracts. Rawls hinges nothing on the determinate desires and ideals of particular human beings. Why should this matter? All uses of language must abstract more or less: The most detailed describing cannot abolish the indeterminacy of language. There is no general reason to object to an account of justice that argues from abstract premises to abstract principles. Highly abstract ways of reasoning are often admired (mathematics, physics), even well paid (accountancy, law). Abstract principles are surely needed for reasoning that has broad scope. Of course, we will also need to apply abstract principles in specific contexts: but that is just as true in law as in ethics, just as true of less abstract and relativized as of the most abstract and supposedly nonrelativized ethical principles.

Why then is ethical reasoning so often criticized for being abstract? Is some other difficulty perhaps confused with abstraction? In particular, is there more than abstraction behind the construction of the original position? At first it may seem that Rawls does no more than abstract. The veil of ignorance merely obscures; it only limits claims about agents in the original position. They simply know less than actual human agents. Rawls does not add to their information or desires in any respect. However, the ways in which he abstracts are governed by a certain ideal. The artful tailoring of the veil of ignorance is determined by a highly selective abstraction from actual human choosing, which reflects a certain ideal of the human subject. This ideal is used not just to determine how "thick" or "thin" the veil of ignorance should be, but rather to tear some carefully placed holes in it.

Abstraction, taken strictly, is unavoidable and in itself innocuous. Idealization is another matter. Objections to supposedly "abstract" ethical principles and reasoning are often objections to idealization. The objection is not to reasoning that is detached from certain predicates that are true of the objects discussed, but to reasoning that assumes predicates that are false of them. Reasoning that abstracts from some predicate makes claims that do not depend on the predicate's either being satisfied or not being satisfied by the objects to which the reasoning applies. Reasoning that idealizes makes claims that apply only to objects that live up to a certain ideal.

The veil of ignorance described in *A Theory of Justice* was tailored to hide the interlocking structure of desires and attitudes that is typical of human agents. Once the social relations between agents were masked it could seem plausible to assign to each desires for a uniform shortlist of primary goods, and to build a determinate ideal of mutual independence into a conception of justice. This ideal is not met by any human agents. It is not only deficient and backward human agents whose choosing would be misrepresented by these ideal agents of construction. The construction assumes a mutual independence of persons and their desires that is false of all human beings. Such independence is as much an idealization of human social relations as an assumption of generalized altruism would be.[4]

Idealizations have no doubt many theoretical advantages: Above all they allow us to construct models that can readily be manipulated. However, they may fail to apply to any significant domain of human choosing. This failure is sometimes defended by construing ideals not as abstractions but as "simplifications". This

---

4   Cf. Arthur Ripstein, "Foundationalism in Political Theory". Ripstein argues that Hobbes's accounts both of instrumental rationality and of mutual indifference are not abstractions from a state of nature, but ungrounded idealizations.

too is strictly inaccurate. A theory simplifies if it either leaves things out (i.e., abstracts) or smooths out variations. If it incorporates predicates that are not even approximately true of the agents to whom the model is supposed to apply, it does not simplify. If idealizations do not "simplify" the descriptions that are true of actual agents, then they are not innocuous ways of extending the scope of reasoning. They covertly assume and endorse "enhanced" versions of specific human characteristics and capacities. Idealization masquerading as abstraction produces theories that may appear to apply widely, but in fact covertly exclude from their scope those who do not match a certain ideal. They privilege certain sorts of human agent and life by presenting their specific characteristics as universal ideals.

Toward Kantian constructivism

In the papers Rawls published during the seventies the role of a certain ideal of the person is fully acknowledged. In *A Theory of Justice* the principles of justice define, but are said not to presuppose, an ideal of the person (*TJ*, 260–1). Later papers take increasing account of the complex structure of human desires. Here Rawls argues that an ideal of the moral person plays an essential part in determining the principles of justice. The 1980 Dewey Lectures no longer see primary goods just as essential means to whatever ends human beings actually have. They are rather "generally necessary as social conditions and all-purpose means to enable human beings to realize and exercise their moral powers" (*KC*, 526). These "moral powers" are capacities to develop a sense of justice and a conception of the good; they are the motivational analogues, and antecedents, of Rawls's two principles of justice. These powers define a certain ideal of the moral person and thereby the highest-order interests of actual persons. This ideal is now built into the original position, whose agents of construction are "moved solely by the highest-order interests in their moral powers and by their concern to advance their determinate but unknown final ends" (*KC*, 528, cf. 547; 568). This revised account of the original position explicitly bases principles of justice not on a conception of the person that abstracts from the diversity of human agents, but on one that idealizes a certain sort of agent.

The ideal that Rawls elaborates is "the Kantian ideal of the person". By stressing that it is an *ideal* of the person that informs the original position Rawls avoids endorsing an account, let alone the suspect Kantian account, of the metaphysics of the self. Procedural Kantianism endorses only (a version of) the ideal of the independent and autonomous character that we associate with Kant. In this way obscure and panicky metaphysics are to be avoided.

Yet ideals too need vindication. How can Rawls provide such a vindication if he does not offer a metaphysics of the self or of the person? Some critics of Kantian constructivism believe that Rawls commits himself to a task that is impossible within the antirealist constraints that he sets on his moral theory.[5] Rawls's basic assumptions about agency and rationality set only weak feasibility constraints on ideals of the person. Differing ideals of the person could form part of other constructive procedures that would generate other conceptions of justice. Rawls indeed acknowledges the possibility of variant constructivisms (*KC*, 535; cf. *TJ*, 17). He therefore needs to vindicate a specific ideal of the person. Either he must show that the Kantian ideal is a "uniquely plausible ideal of the person"[6] or he must provide some other reason for singling it out.

"Justice as Fairness: Political Not Metaphysical" provides that other reason. Here Rawls still avoids "claims to universal truth or about the essential nature and identity of persons" (*JFPM*, 223). "Justice as fairness", he now argues, "is a political conception [of justice] because it starts from within a certain political tradition" (*JFPM*, 225). The ideal of the person on which his argument rests is not that of the abstract individual (as certain critics had supposed), but that of persons as citizens of a modern democratic polity, who (though they may disagree about the good) accept the original position as a "device of representation" (*JFPM*, 236) that accurately captures their ideal of a fair system of cooperation between citizens who so disagree. Far from deriving a justification of democratic citizenship from metaphysical foundations, Rawls invites us to read *A Theory of Justice* as a recursive vindication of those deep principles of justice "we" would discover in drawing on "our" underlying conceptions of free and equal citizenship. This vindication of justice does not address others who, unlike "us", do not start with such ideals of citizenship; it has nothing to say to those others. It is "our" ideal, and "our" justice. Worries about relativism come flooding back.

In a way these worries are intensified, for it is not just by way of equilibrating theory with "our considered moral judgments", but in the very formulation of the most abstract theoretical principles, that Rawls now appeals to the judgments of "our" tradition. Kantian constructivism, it seems, claims only to offer a coherent articulation of the outlook of modern liberal societies. The Kantian ideal of the person is socially embedded, and antirelativism is not attainable. We are offered a coherent articulation of the deep moral commitments of "our" society. With hindsight many of Rawls's earlier writings can be seen to acknowledge this derivation of justice.

Toward a more Kantian constructivism

Was there any other possibility? Could Rawls have avoided idealizing premises and relied on a genuinely abstract yet nonidealizing account of agency and rationality? If so, what would he have relied on?

---

5 David O. Brink, "Rawlsian Constructivism in Moral Theory", esp. p. 73; see also Gerald Doppelt, "Rawls' Kantian Ideal and the Viability of Modern Liberalism".
6 Brink, "Rawlsian Constructivism in Moral Theory", p. 90.

If we stand back from the entire project, we can see that many of the difficulties of formulating a "Kantian" theory of justice arose from uncertainty about the degree to which principles of construction should rely on and reflect desires. Once Rawls had committed himself to a merely instrumental conception of rationality, all desires would be reflected in the outcomes of construction, unless specifically bracketed. The veil of ignorance had to be spread to avoid heteronomy. The veil then had to be breached selectively to avoid complete indeterminacy. A specific ideal of the person had to be invoked to explain just how the veil should be tailored. Finally "our" tradition was invoked to vindicate this ideal without having to establish metaphysical claims about agency. In short, some of the *least* Kantian features of Rawls's constructivism produced a train of difficulties.

Could a more nearly Kantian constructivism do better? It could surely avoid the need to vindicate selective bracketing of desires, by detaching principles of justice from all claims about desires. However, a more Kantian constructivism would be pointless if it merely rehearsed the supposed empty formalism of Kant's ethics, and so fell foul of Mill's old charge of failing grotesquely to derive any actual principles of duty. Can a construction do any work if it draws neither on decontextualized and unvindicated accounts of ideal rationality and independence, nor on the moral ideals of a specific culture?

Rather than tackle the question in general form, I shall sketch the outlines of another construction. Constructivism might begin simply by abstracting from the circumstances of justice, meagerly construed. The problem of justice arises only for a plurality of at least potentially interacting agents. It does not arise where there is no plurality, or no genuine plurality of agents, and hence no potential for conflict. (The action of "agents" in such a degenerate plurality might be automatically coordinated, perhaps by instinct or by a preestablished harmony.) Nor does it arise among agents who cannot interact: Castaways, isolates, the men and women of Rousseau's earliest state of nature, are outside circumstances of justice.

Some assumptions about the agents of such a plurality are needed if any construction is to be possible. If idealization is to be avoided, these assumptions must only abstract. They must not smuggle in reference to unvindicated moral ideals. A more Kantian constructivism (perhaps not the one everybody would attribute to Kant)[7] must then start from the *least determinate* conceptions both of the rationality and of the mutual independence of agents.

A meager and indeterminate view of rationality might credit agents only with the capacity to understand and follow *some* form of social life, and with a commitment to seek *some* means to any ends (desired or otherwise) to which they are committed. (This weak view of instrumental rationality is noncommittal about

---

7   This would be a gross understatement if the starting point of Kant's moral philosophy were
    metaphysically exorbitant, as is usually feared. Here I rely on, but do not rehearse, the alternative
    accounts of Kant's views on reason and freedom discussed in Part I of this volume.

the efficient pursuit of ends; efficiency comes into play only if some metric of "costs" and "benefits" together with procedures for decomposing action into "options" is assumed. A construction premised on efficient pursuit of ends covertly privileges specific moral and social ideals.)

A meager and indeterminate view of the identity and of the mutual independence of agents can assume only that agents have capacities for varying sorts and degrees of dependence and interdependence. A complete erosion of capacities for independent action destroys plurality and with it the context of justice; a complete erosion of dependence privileges an ideal of the person whose relevance to human life is wholly unestablished. Natural persons are always artificial too, in many ways. Their beliefs and desires and their very identities can interlock in many ways, which only approximate to varying ideals of the person. Constructivism that does not privilege any one ideal of the person cannot be premised on a fixed account of the forms of rationality or the degree of mutual independence of agents. It must seek principles for agents who are numerous, not ideally rational and not ideally independent of one another.

As sketched this blueprint seems too indefinite to guide any construction. It surely cannot guide an answer to the *hypothetical* question "What principles *would* a plurality of agents, with minimal rationality and indeterminate capacities for independence, choose to live by?" Materials for answering hypothetical questions are lacking. However, the blueprint may permit a beginning of an answer to a *modal* question such as "What principles can a plurality of agents of minimal rationality and indeterminate capacities for mutual independence live by?" No plurality can choose to live by principles that aim to destroy, undercut or erode the agency (of whatever determinate shape) of some of its members.[8] Those who become victims of action on such principles not merely *do not* act on their oppressor's principles; they *cannot* do so. Victims cannot share the principles on which others destroy or limit their very capacities to act on principles.[9]

Entitlements and obligations

If we are to move from this very indeterminate claim about the principles that a plurality of agents, of whom we assume only minimal rationality and indeterminate mutual independence, could live by, we need to take some view of the task of

8   This statement throws a heavy weight on the question of membership. Who counts in universalizability tests? An adequate answer for present purposes is that we cannot exclude from membership those with whom we interact and on whose rationality we rely. Distant others on whose abilities to translate, negotiate and trade we presume cannot be excluded; extraterrestrials can be (for the time being). Nor can we anticipate the loss of capacities for agency by victims of violence in order to vindicate inflicting that loss.

9   Colluding victims are not a counterexample. If collusion itself is coerced, they are not truly willing; if it is not, they are not truly victims. Although the principle is clear, cases are often highly ambiguous; witness the Patty Hearst trial.

those principles. In *A Theory of Justice* Rawls notes that constructivism might undertake various tasks: "the contractarian idea can be extended to the choice of more or less an entire ethical system . . . including principles for all the virtues" (*TJ*, 17). His own more limited aim is to construct principles of justice that will determine the basic structure of a society, thereby constraining the actions both of institutions and of individuals. What he actually argues for are in part principles of *entitlement* rather than of *obligation*. His first principle of justice assigns to each "an equal right to the most extensive basic liberty compatible with like liberty for all" (*TJ*, 60). The second principle's main demand, as finally stated, is that social and economic inequalities be arranged to the greatest benefit of the least advantaged (*TJ*, 302). A battery of objections has been fired at these claims. In particular, the priority assigned to liberty has been diagnosed as privileging the very ideal of mutual independence that has already been queried. For present purposes the details of these debates do not matter. However, Rawls's focus on entitlement rather than on obligation is significant. Constructing a set of entitlements is not the same as constructing principles of obligation.

This is perhaps surprising. Within an account of justice it may seem unimportant whether we adopt the perspective of agents and their obligations, or of recipients and their entitlements. The set of obligations and the set of entitlements will presumably be reciprocally defined. (This would not be the case if we were considering a wider range of obligations, some of them "imperfect" obligations to whose performance nobody was entitled.) However, the perspective of recipience and entitlement has other difficulties that obstruct the project of construction.

A constructivist approach that stays with the perspective of entitlement that Rawls prefers, but asks the Kantian, modal question, has to look for a set of entitlements that can consistently be held by all. There are many copossible sets of entitlements, so a further move is needed to identify the just set. It is tempting to think that this move can be made simply by seeking the *maximal* set of entitlements that can consistently be held by all. This move would parallel the two moves Rawls makes to determine first which system of liberties and then which social and economic inequalities are just. Each of Rawls's principles purports to identify a *maximal* set of entitlements. We can find maxima only where there is some metric. Unfortunately, liberty has no metric, and social and economic arrangements have one only on utilitarian premises that Rawls skirts and that a more Kantian constructivism would reject. By detaching justice from the desires either of idealized or of actual agents we discard the framework needed to make sense of metric and maximizing notions. The notion of a maximal set of entitlements (whether liberties or social and economic arrangements, or the two taken together) is indeterminate.

However, principles of justice could be fixed by constructing principles of obligation rather than of entitlement. In the tradition of the social contract theory, but not in its contemporary descendants, principles of justice define obligations rather than entitlements. A return to this perspective is, I believe, required for a nonidealizing constructivism because obligations of justice, unlike entitlements, can be constructed without assuming a metric either for liberty or more generally for actions. At a later stage of the argument a constructivist approach to justice that successfully identifies principles of obligation by using modal arguments may also identify the entitlements that are the reciprocals of these obligations.

A construction of justice

Everything then hinges on constructing principles of justice without presupposing a determinate ideal of the person and without privileging the perspective of entitlements and rights. The core of any such construction is the thought that there are certain constraints on the principles of action that could be adopted by all of a plurality of potentially interacting agents of whom we assume only minimal rationality and indeterminate mutual independence. Principles that cannot be acted on by all must be rejected by any plurality for whom the problem of justice arises.

This may seem too meager a basis for justice. One classical objection to Kantian formalism has been that *any* internally coherent principle for individual action is universalizable: What is open to any arbitrarily chosen agent is open to all, apart from uninteresting exceptions that refer to unique performances, competitive successes and the like. This formalistic interpretation of universalizability ignores the constraint posed by the fact that we are considering the case of a plurality of *potentially interacting* beings, that is, of beings who share a world. Any principle of action that is adopted by all members of such pluralities affects the world that they share and becomes a background condition of their action. This is why certain principles of action that can coherently be adopted by some cannot coherently be adopted by all. Justice, taken in the traditional, minimal, formal sense of like requirements for like cases, will then require that those principles be rejected.

Examples of principles that cannot be universalized can illustrate the point. A principle of deception, which undermines trust, would, if universally adopted, destroy all trust and so make all projects of deception impossible. Selective deception is not improbable; universal deception is. A principle of coercion, whose enactment destroys or undercuts the agency and willing of at least some others for at least some time, cannot be universally followed. Those who are at a given time the victims of coercion cannot act, so cannot make coercion their own principle. Equally, action on a principle of violence damages the agency of some, so cannot be universally acted on. Put quite generally, principles of action that hinge on victimizing some, whether by destroying, paralyzing or undercutting their capacities for agency for at least some time and in some ways, can be adopted by some but cannot be universally adopted.

From principles to judgments

To keep matters under control let us assume only that justice demands (at least) that action and institutions not be based on principles of victimization (deception, coercion, violence).[10] Still, it may seem, we are far from showing what justice demands, since we do not know what rejecting principles of deceit or of coercion would demand of us in specific circumstances. These guidelines are highly indeterminate. Even if the most formalistic objection to "Kantian" formalism fails, have we not paid the classic price of abstraction, reaching highly abstract principles that do not tell us what to do in specific contexts?

Principles are always to some extent abstract; but they are not the whole of practical reasoning. They must always be applied in ways that take account of actual context; and they never determine their own applications. Even the culturally specific principles that relativists favor do not determine their own applications. So a fuller account of practical reasoning must say *something* about processes of judgment and deliberation; but it cannot say everything. Ethical principles are not algorithms.

How much should be said? Should we expect the most abstract principles of justice to entail a specific code, for example one to which legislators could appeal? Some people clearly expect principles alone to give very detailed guidance. For example, there is a luxuriant and sometimes fierce philosophical debate on coercion. This debate aims to distinguish threats (and possibly offers) that coerce from those that do not. If rejecting principles and policies of coercion is a requirement of justice, should we worry that this debate remains inconclusive? I would suggest that there is no reason to expect the issues to be resolved *unless we agree on a determinate conception or ideal of the person.* Coercion is a matter of force or threat, and what constitutes threat must vary with the vulnerabilities of those who are threatened. Vulnerability depends on many things, including the forms of rationality and of dependence and independence that particular agents have at particular times. Coercers know very well that sucessful threats take account of victims' specific vulnerabilities. It is unreasonable to look for a set of necessary and sufficient conditions of coercion that will apply quite generally unless we can

10 There may be other principles of justice; the constructive procedure sketched here does not determine a complete set of such principles. This is simply a corollary of detachment from metric assumptions. Because the parallel modal construction of entitlements presents just entitlements as the mutually limiting copossible components of a maximal set, it can identify all just entitlements if it identifies any. Equally, if it cannot identify all, it identifies none. A modal construction of obligations establishes each principle by showing why its rejection cannot be universally adopted. Hence obligations can be identified seriatim, and completeness is not guaranteed; indeed, it may not even make sense to speak of a *complete* set of principles of action.

vindicate a specific ideal of the independence of persons, which will provide a standard for distinguishing those who weakly succumb to mere gestures of threat from those who forgivably yield to overwhelming duress. Equally, we should not expect to be able to find a formula that shows which specific actions must be foresworn by those who do not rely on principles or policies of coercion. Parallel points can be made about the rejection of deception and of violence.

What then can be said about the move from an abstract principle to judgments about specific institutions or actions if we lack a determinate ideal of the person? Is there any way to operationalize the idea of rejecting unsharable principles, without subordinating it to the categories and views of the status quo? Even if we have found principles whose *vindication* does not depend on accepted moral views, we do not escape relativism if their *application* unavoidably endorses the categories and concerns of the powers that be, rather than subjecting them to scrutiny.

To avoid sliding back into relativism we must rely not merely on the abstract principles that could be accepted (or rejected) by any plurality of minimally rational agents of indeterminate mutual independence. We must rely on specific interpretations of these principles that can be accepted (or rejected) by those actually involved. Only action and policies that guarantee the refusability by actual agents of institutions, offers and involvements that others propose can ensure consent that is not merely nominal but legitimating.

The appeal to consent here is neither to the hypothetical consent of the ideally rational and independent nor to an actual consent that might reflect oppression. (Those routes lead back to realism and to relativism.) Rather, the appeal is to the *possible consent* of *actual agents.* The criterion for such consent is not that consent is ostensibly given (that might reflect false consciousness or duress) but that any arrangements or offers could have been refused or renegotiated. If we are to be sure that a principle could have been shared even by those on whom it bears hard, we need to be sure that they could (even if ignorant and weak) have refused or renegotiated the roles or tasks that action on that principle imposed on them. Neither the apparent consent of the vulnerable nor the hypothetical consent of the glitteringly self-sufficient legitimates. Equally, the absence of expressed consent in those who have opportunity and capacities to refuse does not signal injustice.

Thinking in this way about applying principles of justice we can see that *it demands more, not less, to be just to the vulnerable* and that *genuine, legitimating consent is undermined by the very institutions that most readily secure an appearance of consent.* The vulnerable are simply easier to deceive and to victimize than the strong. By contrast both idealized and relativized accounts of justice tend to conceal the fact that justice to the weak demands more than justice to the strong. Idealized accounts of justice tend to ignore actual vulnerabilities, and relativized accounts tend to legitimate them.

This line of thought can be applied to institutional as well as individual injustice. When relations between agents are ones of structured dependence, it is hard or impossible for agents to refuse an apparent consent to arrangements that structure their lives and identities. The weak risk too much by dissenting unless institutions are structured to secure the option of refusal; and when this option is secured they will no longer be so weak.

Put generally the point is that in applying abstract, nonidealizing principles we have to take account not indeed of the actual beliefs, ideals or categories of others, all of which may reflect unjust traditions, but of others' actual capacities and opportunities to act – and of their incapacities and lack of opportunities. This move does not lead back to relativism; no principle is endorsed simply because currently accepted. A more nearly Kantian constructivism would use modal notions to identify principles, but indicative ones to apply them. The principles of justice hold for any possible plurality; for they demand only the rejection of principles that cannot be shared by all members of a plurality. The determination of justice for actual situations is regulated but not entailed by these principles. The feature of actual situations that must be taken into account in judgments of justice is in the first place the security or vulnerability of agents that allows agents to dissent from the arrangements that affect their lives, and whose absence compromises any ostensible "consent".

Between realism and relativism

Rawlsian constructivism has ended up on an uncomfortable knife edge, and teeters between idealizing and relativized conceptions of ethics. The idealized readings demand proofs of a moral reality Rawls does not discern; the relativized readings can only offer an internal critique of the justice of modern liberal societies.

Several features distance the alternative contructivism sketched here from Rawls's pioneering project. First, idealized accounts of agents, their rationality and their mutual independence are explicitly rejected: There is no appeal, however oblique, to transcendent moral claims. Second, abstraction from the determinate desires of agents is complete: Hence no special ingenuity is needed to avoid either heteronomy or cruder forms of relativism. Third, and as a consequence, it is impossible to answer questions about the hypothetical choices of abstract agents. Fourth, the construction therefore has to fall back on modal questions about the possible choices of abstract agents, and construct an answer to the question "What principles must a plurality of abstractly characterized agents reject?" Finally, rejection of nonuniversalizable principles can guide action by requiring that we ensure that the agents actually affected, with their particular identities and vulnerabilities, can genuinely choose or refuse those principles. If this sketch can be filled out, there is at least some space between realism and relativism.

The great maxims of justice and charity

Near the beginning of his *Second Treatise of Government* Locke speaks approvingly of Hooker's derivation of two fundamental principles of human obligation, "the great maxims of justice and charity".[1] The Law of Nature obliges us not merely to deal justly with others but to preserve them.[2] Charity is concern for the needs of others;[3] it is not a marginal matter of discretionary philanthropy. Like justice, charity is a serious obligation, whose violation might in certain circumstances amount to murder.[4] The status of charity here is strikingly different from its status in recent liberal thinking. Modern liberals, who are agnostic about the good for man and uncertain about human needs, typically depict charity as institutionally and intellectually marginal.

Utilitarian liberals urge us to maximize subjective good. They demand action that satisfies human desires. Concern to meet claims of need is then submerged in generalized beneficence. This has two results. First, charity may be less urgent than fulfilling strong desires for unneeded items. Those whom need reduces to apathy register faint claims on consequentialist scales. Second, since any open-ended commitment to beneficence generates an alarming "overload" of obligations,[5] utilitarian liberals often compromise and settle for quite a limited conception of beneficence.

This chapter originally appeared in *Enlightenment, Rights and Revolution*, ed. Neil MacCormick and Zenon Bankowski, Aberdeen University Press, Aberdeen, 1989.

1   John Locke, *Two Treatises of Government*, II, para. 5.   2   Ibid., para. 6.
3   See John Dunn, *The Political Thought of John Locke: An Historical Account of the Argument of the "Two Treaties of Government"*; James Tully, *A Discourse on Property: John Locke and His Adversaries;* and J. B. Schneewind, "Ideas of Charity: Some Historical Reflections".
4   John Locke, *Venditio*, p. 86: "he that sells his corn in a town pressed with famine at the utmost rate he can get for it does no injustice against the common rule of traffic, yet if he carry it away unless they give him more than they are able, or extorts so much from their present necessity as not to leave them the means of subsistence afterwards he offends against the common rule of charity as a man and if they perish is no doubt guilty of murder". For confirmation that Locke thinks those in dire need have rights to charity, see also *Two Treatises of Government*, I, para. 42, where he writes: "As *Justice* gives every Man a Title to the produce of his honest Industry, and the fair Acquisitions of his Ancestors descended to him; so *Charity* gives every Man a Title to so much out of another's plenty as will keep him from extreme want."
5   James Fishkin, *The Limits of Obligation;* S. Kagan, "Does Consequentialism Demand Too Much? Recent Work on the Limits of Obligation".

Deontological liberals also marginalize charity.[6] Since they are agnostic about the good for man they have nothing to say about virtues, not even about the virtue of justice. They seek principles for building institutions rather than characters. Plato had hoped that good men would need no laws; deontological liberals hope that good laws will work without good men or women. They make few, sometimes unflattering, assumptions about human nature. Human beings are seen as bearers of intrinsically arbitrary but rationally ordered desires or preferences, which just institutions accommodate and arbitrate. Modern deontological liberals do not even argue that private vices may be public virtues, nor that greed can have fortunate economic consequences. They are not concerned whether preferences are greedy or generous, selfish or altruistic. Those are the debates of another age, which demanded an account of the good for man, took character as seriously as institutions and still looked for a doctrine of virtue. If liberalism is only about institutions that will justly mediate conflicting preferences, it will have nothing to say about character, about virtues and vices or about charity and greed.

Deontological liberals are then inclined to picture charity as no more than individual philanthropic activity, whose commitment to meeting needs or preserving mankind may without fault be not merely selective but even capricious, and which will certainly be insufficient to see needs met. They differ over how much activity that might formerly have been classified as charitable can properly be brought within the sphere of justice. They agree that charity, understood as philanthropy, is not obligatory, and most classify philanthropy as supererogatory. However, those who hold this position typically mean no more than that philanthropy is not a matter of obligation: They offer no account of the good for man to explain why we should take seriously principles that we have no obligation to follow.[7] If charity is supererogatory and supererogation reflects no more than personal preference, a principle of charity can hardly be a great maxim, on a level with the principle of justice.

There is little point in arguing whether the identification of charity either with a "great maxim" that binds us as strongly as the principle of justice or with optional private philanthropy is correct. Many differences of framework and method separate the protagonists of these two interpretations of charity. Neither group will be convinced by any merely conceptual claim that charity is essentially what the other asserts it is. I shall therefore try a more historical and speculative approach to the disagreement.

6 Countless works could be cited: evidently John Rawls, *A Theory of Justice,* and Robert Nozick, *Anarchy, State and Utopia;* also the writings of Alan Gewirth and Ronald Dworkin.

7 Cf. Alan Gewirth, "Private Philanthropy and Positive Rights", p. 56: "the philanthropic relation . . . is one of supererogation. In its simplest form one person A freely gives another to person B some good X . . . such that A has no strict moral duty to give X to B and B has, correlatively, no claim right to receive X from A. Thus, A's gift to B is an act of generosity or charity." See also John O'Connor, "Philanthropy and Selfishness", p. 113: "Philanthropic activities are similar to supererogatory acts in that they are beyond duty."

I begin by asking how and why charity, once a great maxim, was marginalized. I shall sketch one account of the matter, which is quite widely accepted, but which I shall query. I will go on to suggest that the modern reconstrual and marginalization of charity is less deeply grounded than this received view of its decline suggests. Finally I shall argue that there is no intrinsic reason for liberals to think of obligations to meet the needs of others as peripheral.

A conventional story?

A conventional account of the marginalization of charity might run like this. The Thomist synthesis always was a patch-up job. Despite the antiquity of the project,[8] the union of Stoic Natural Law and the new law of the Gospels remained programmatic. Justice was one of the cardinal virtues of antiquity; charity the greatest of the theological virtues. The reconciliation of the City of Man and the City of God may be impossible. Within Christianity the more pessimistic Augustinian tradition looked askance at it. So it should be no surprise that justice and charity met separate fates when the Christian synthesis fell apart. On this view all that we learn from an attentive reading of Locke, such as Dunn provides for us, is that he is less modern than interpreters such as MacPherson — let alone appropriators such as Nozick — suppose. Locke still thinks within a theological framework, and so still thinks that charity is obligatory. Modern liberals drop the theological framework, and in doing so lose the basis for any doctrine of virtue or specifically of charity.

This conventional liberal story can have a second, forward-looking chapter. Once we discard the theological framework we can revise Locke, extract the sound core of deontological liberalism and concentrate on principles for building institutions rather than characters. We can have a universal theory of justice and bracket a concern with virtues. Any further discussion of the virtues will have to be reoriented — for example, by locating them within a naturalistic account of human motives, which construes them as dispositions that are important in discussions of moral education or of psychology. The link between obligation and virtue may be severed, but a revised, reduced and relocated discourse of the virtues can still be available.

This story is accepted, in part if not in all its aspects, in many quarters. Members of the libertarian right are generally pleased to be agnostic about the good for man, although some of them regret having nothing to say about the good life — or at least nothing that goes beyond the consumer-preference vision of the Sunday color supplements — because this makes it hard to know what to say

---

8   Cf. *Decretum Gratiani:* "Natural law is that which is contained in the Scriptures and the Gospel" (quoted in A. P. d'Entrèves, *Natural Law,* p. 37).

about education. For libertarians charity (construed as philanthropy) remains an option, but is suspect because it may damage recipients' self-respect.[9]

Welfare liberals too think that the boundaries of obligation are the boundaries of justice; but they worry that too much may be left beyond the pale. They argue that justice untempered will not be cold and harsh because it includes welfare rights. On this view much that used to be thought charity is indeed a matter of obligation, not because charity is a matter of obligation but because at least part of what used to be thought charity is more correctly seen as a matter of justice. Justice demands more than libertarians suppose; it includes obligations to provide the means of life and to secure others' agency.[10] However, libertarians and welfare liberals agree that we can have only a theory of justice and no doctrine of virtue. Charity is not the only virtue that modern liberalism has revalued – or rather devalued. Modern liberalism marginalizes the entire tradition of the virtues.

Those who aim to revive that tradition also present justice and charity as alternatives. They typically reject and criticize liberalism and abstract ethical reasoning, and the very aspiration to give a universal account of justice; they prefer a relativist or historicist, or more recently "communitarian", framework.[11] Recent neo-Hegelian works depict abstract liberal accounts of justice and rights as expressive of a social order that eroded the communities that made sense of particular configurations of virtues. They insist that obligations can best be embodied in characters and traditions rather than in formal institutions. Justice need not be abandoned, but must be domesticated. Justice too is specific to actual communities. International justice and human rights cannot be vindicated – except within circles where these have become the prevailing outlook.

The diverging fates of justice and charity in the modern period are symptoms of deep social and intellectual changes. The liberal challenge leaves those who are still drawn to the virtues with profound dilemmas. On some accounts the virtuous person in modern times, at least in dark times, either may or must shun political involvement. Good characters can manage their lives, if at all, only on the margins of the institutions. In sunnier times those who pursue both social justice and personal integrity are still likely to be torn apart, not merely because of contingent factors but because universal justice and the virtues belong in different worlds.

The friends of virtue think we can have a contextualized doctrine of virtue but

---

9 Cf. Nozick, *Anarchy, State and Utopia;* and Ellen Frankel Paul et al., *Beneficence, Philanthropy and the Public Good.*

10 Cf. Rawls, *A Theory of Justice;* Ronald Dworkin, *Taking Rights Seriously;* Alan Gewirth, *Human Rights: Essays on Justification and Applications;* and Henry Shue, *Basic Rights: Subsistence, Affluence and U.S. Foreign Policy.*

11 These approaches may be Wittgensteinian, or more recently mainly quasi-Hegelian or revisionary Aristotelian. See, for example, Alasdair MacIntyre, *After Virtue: A Study in Moral Theory* and *Whose Justice? Which Rationality?;* Michael Sandel, *Liberalism and the Limits of Justice;* and Michael Walzer, *Spheres of Justice: A Defence of Pluralism and Equality.*

no universal theory of justice. Deontological liberals think we can have a universal theory of justice but no doctrine of virtue at all. Modern liberals and their critics apparently agree that we cannot have both a universal theory of justice and a doctrine of virtue. Both deny that justice and charity can be conceived as coordinate great maxims.

A hypothesis: Natural Law to natural rights

These conventional stories cannot, I believe, explain the marginalization of charity and other virtues in so much modern ethical thinking. I offer for the moment just two reasons.

First, the loss of theological foundations was a crisis not only for accounts of good character but for a theory of good institutions. Why was this *more* of a crisis for an account of good character? Why did the friends of virtue, but not those of justice, adopt historicist and relativist positions? Could not the friends of virtue too find ahistorical vindication? May not the friends of justice also need historicist vindications?[12] Unless we can understand what makes the case of justice and of charity so different, the loss of theological foundations cannot be the whole story.

Second, even where theological foundations are retained, charity and other virtues may be demoted. Many modern Christians, for example, take justice seriously, yet treat meeting the needs of others as a marginal matter; they do not see it as something that should make major inroads into their lives or pockets. Abstract theism, like abstract liberalism, is often inhospitable to a doctrine of virtue. If the loss of theological foundations is neither sufficient nor necessary to explain the diverging fates of the two great maxims, what can explain it? I shall propose a hypothesis.

The most striking theoretical difference between Lockean liberalism and contemporary deontological liberalism is not the loss of theological foundations. It is that for Locke the obligations of Natural Law are fundamental whereas for our contemporaries human rights are fundamental, and duties or obligations the corollaries of rights.

If rights and obligations were correlative, this would not be a fundamental difference. It would be rather a matter of looking at one set of ethical relationships from two perspectives. One perspective would take the agent's view of the bearers of obligations, and the other the recipient's view of the holders of rights who could claim the performance of obligations from others. But if the two perspec-

---

12 Various rapprochements have been tried. For example, John Rawls in "Justice as Fairness: Political Not Metaphysical" provides a quasi-communitarian underpinning for his liberal principles of justice; in the process he sheds claims to universal scope. Bernard Williams in *Ethics and the Limits of Philosophy* depicts liberal ideals, such as truthfulness and the meaning of individual lives, as emerging within determinate social orders.

tives are not equivalent, there may be some ethical relations that can be discerned and appreciated from one perspective only.

It is a matter of general agreement that there are no rights that lack correlative obligations. Such "rights" would be unclaimable, mere rhetorical gesture. However, the whole point about the obligations of charity, as traditionally conceived, is that these were meant to be obligations without correlative rights. Such obligations were traditionally said to be "imperfect". If we are to understand the diverging fates of justice and charity, it may then be important to reexamine the status of imperfect obligations and the implications of treating rights rather than obligations as fundamental.

Imperfect obligations

The term *imperfect obligation* means simply "incomplete obligation". Since there are many ways in which an obligation might be incomplete, it is not surprising that the notion of an imperfect obligation has received various interpretations. However, one of these interpretations is particularly significant.

Sometimes obligations are said to be incomplete or imperfect because the act descriptions that they incorporate specify incompletely what ought to be done. However, *all* act descriptions underdetermine action in this sense. Even obligations of justice are expressed in general principles, whose application and interpretation need judgment. That process of judgment is both a conceptual and an institutional necessity. It requires elaborate judicial and administrative procedures. The indeterminacy of act descriptions does not draw a line – certainly not a clear line – between obligations of justice and supposed imperfect obligations, such as those of charity. Indeterminacy cannot distinguish clearly between perfect and imperfect obligations.

Sometimes obligations are said to be imperfect on the grounds that they ought not to be enforced, or at least not enforced by legal sanctions. Perhaps obligations of justice ought to be enforced by law and other obligations ought not. However, it is not obvious that we should assume an exhaustive contrast between legal enforcement and nonenforcement: There are many modes of social regulation that can be effective and oppressive. At least at the start of ethical discussions it might be a good idea to be aware of the multiplicity of ways in which lives can be regulated and disciplined while legal sanctions are kept far in the background.[13] In any case, the claim that certain obligations ought not to be legally enforced can hardly be the *basis* for calling them imperfect. If obligations are dividable into those that ought and those that ought not to be enforced with legal sanctions, there must presumably be some other basis for so dividing them.

13 Foucault's work is here a great corrective; and may need correcting by consideration of the distinctive part state power can, perhaps in modern societies must, play in the revision and destruction of disciplinary regimes. Cf. Michael Walzer, "The Politics of Michel Foucault".

A third interpretation of the notion of an imperfect obligation is that it is an obligation whose performance is not, or not initially, allocated to specified right-holders. On this account obligations are imperfect if no right-holders have been defined and nobody can claim or waive a right. If the obligation is breached, nobody will have been wronged, although wrong will be done. From the perspective of recipience there is no ethical claim. From the perspective of agency, however, the claim is clear enough, although its allocation is undetermined. If there are obligations that are imperfect in this sense, a theory of rights can incorporate only part of a theory of obligations – the part that covers perfect obligations, those that are mirrored by rights. Perspective then makes a substantive difference.

If there are any obligations that are imperfect in this sense, it makes sense to think of them as embodied in characters and traditions rather than in formal institutions. Institutional relationships allocate agents to recipients, or provide procedures for determining allocations. They define roles and special relationships. Institutionalized claims can be grasped and pressed either by agents or by recipients. Claims that are appreciable only from the perspective of agents must be embodied in those agents and their ways of life rather than in the relationships between agents and recipients. This is what lies behind the traditional identification of imperfect obligations and the virtues: Both categories are not merely action-centered, but specifically agent-centered.

A proposal: Obligations are prior to rights

Modern liberalism may have wiped charity off its ethical map not because it has lost its theological underpinnings but simply because it privileges rights over obligations, and there are no rights to charity. If modern deontological liberals cannot allow for imperfect obligations, it is not surprising that they oscillate between classifying charity as mere personal preference and seeing it as supererogatory. Yet either account of charity is disquieting. If charity is no more than personal preference, then callous and kindly actions to others in need are equally permissible, provided justice is not breached. If charity is supererogatory then it seems that – ridiculously – mundane help to others in need will be in the same category as saintly or heroic action, of which deontological liberals in any case give no satisfactory account. It is not surprising that liberals who think they face this dilemma often try to show that much that used to be thought charity is really a matter of justice.

Perhaps liberals can avoid the dilemma. Why should liberalism not be seen as one part of a theory of obligations, rather than of rights?[14] By beginning with

---

14 Cf. Simone Weil, *The Need for Roots*, p. 3, where she writes: "The notion of obligations comes before that of rights, which is subordinate and relative to the former".

obligations one might at least discover whether any imperfect obligations can be established, rather than discounting them from the start by privileging a perspective that makes them invisible.

This revisionary approach would have to confront the central questions of deontological liberalism. If we do not appeal to Natural Law or Scripture, can we ground *any* obligations or rights? If we can, which are they? The interminable disagreements over the identification and interpretation of human rights are reminder enough that this problem is unsolved. Starting from the perspective of obligations, in which imperfect obligations too are possible, may worsen rather than resolve the disputes. However, since the debates that begin with human rights have not settled (cannot settle, I shall argue) the central issues, it is worth seeing what can be done by approaching matters from another angle.

Maximal equal liberty

A well-trodden path into modern deontological liberalism is to construct an account of rights by taking seriously the equality and liberty of agents. Human rights are construed as those equal liberties (construed negatively by libertarians, and positively by "welfare" liberals) that can consistently be assigned to all. Justice is a matter of securing the maximal or "best" set of liberties that can consistently be enjoyed by all.

This type of construction can be developed in a way that eliminates the very possibility of imperfect obligations. If the largest liberty is held to include an open-ended right to liberty that, so to speak, "mops up" any space that is not absorbed in meeting obligations to respect others' liberties, then there is no space for imperfect obligations. Such an open-ended right to liberty divides acts exhaustively into impermissible violations of another's rights and permissible uses of one's own. Obligations would be only what it took to refrain from violating other's rights; hence all obligations would be perfect obligations with correlative rights. Those who assume an open-ended right to liberty not merely give no account of imperfect obligations; they can allow for none. It is clear enough why such liberals must either construe charity as mere preference or (if that is too uncomfortable) assign it to the lofty but ungrounded sphere of the supererogatory.

Why should the largest set of equal liberties include an open-ended right to liberty? Some would object that any open-ended right to liberty will in practice make power, and so rights, most unequal. Others will object more generally that the priority given to liberty is unvindicated. Both objections can be bracketed, because another, more fundamental difficulty undermines the whole project of making rights ethically basic. It is this. Many distinct sets of equal liberties could consistently be assigned to all: Consequently the favorite deontological liberal construction is indeterminate.

The favored resolution of this problem is to try to identify the *largest* set of equal liberties that can consistently be held by all. Its difficulty is that liberty has no metric.[15] What makes one set of liberties larger than another, or any set maximal? Is liberty of access larger than freedom of speech? We do not know how to answer so specific a question. Still less do we know how to determine what rights and obligations are contained within the largest liberty compatible with like liberty for all. A sufficient reason for bracketing issues about the priority of liberty is that we can see that no attempt to construct the largest set of equal and consistent rights will work, since it must assume a metric where there is none.[16]

If the construction of rights is indeterminate, we have further reason to worry not merely about giving priority to liberty, but quite generally about giving priority to rights. We have already seen that privileging the perspective of rights marginalizes or even undercuts imperfect obligations and virtues. We also know that concern for virtue need not be ruled out by concern for rights and liberty. A stress on justice and even on negative liberty and rights can be linked with rather than insulated from an emphasis on the virtues. The link between justice and charity that Locke affirms runs through many Natural Law writers. Skinner's writings on the tradition of civic humanism remind us of a tradition that insists that the practice of civic virtue is the condition of maintaining liberties.[17] Rousseau and Kant both argue for justice *and* virtue. Modern deontological liberals surely ought to explain fully why they cannot or should not any longer be concerned with virtue. For it may be true that failure to cultivate and practice the virtues and to recognize those obligations that are not mirrored in rights will eventually undermine liberty and rights.

The arguments offered so far have only a limited objective. They suggest that liberals rule out the possibility of imperfect obligations only by taking a recent and unnecessarily constrained view of their task. However, it is one thing to argue that there may be imperfect obligations and another to show that there definitely are any. I have so far argued neither that there are imperfect obligations, nor that charity is one such. All I have claimed is that there are good reasons for constructing a liberal account of justice in ways that do not rule out imperfect obligations.

---

15 If rights were based on a physicalist account of act individuation, a metric would be available. Cf. Hillel Steiner, "Individual Liberty". However, this approach has difficulty in giving a "thick" enough account of liberty and its value to explain why either liberty itself or liberty rights should be taken as ethically fundamental.

16 One reason why deontological liberals are preoccupied with determining a maximal liberty is that they are constantly seduced by preference-based accounts of practical rationality, where the possibility of finding a metric of value seems tantalizingly close. The reason it is close is that this account of practical reason meets the demands of consequentialism. Deontological liberals deploy it at their peril: In adding assumptions that secure the desired metric properties for actions and options they risk undercutting their reasons for rejecting consequentialism. Why try to ground rights without reference to other values if those values have been already been accepted? Rawls's discussions of rationality and Nozick's of compensation for rights violations provide examples of this tendency.

17 Quentin Skinner, "The Idea of Negative Liberty: Philosophical and Historical Perspectives".

If liberals could construct principles of imperfect obligation, they might be able once again to offer an account of the virtues.

Prospect: the construction of obligations

How should such a construction proceed? What would it establish? Would it show anything about charity or about other virtues? Here I offer only a sketch.

The basic idea of the alternative construction is to focus in the first instance on obligations and not simply on rights. This allows for the possibility of imperfect as well as perfect obligations. Imperfect obligations, since they constrain agents rather than the relationships between agents and recipients, can be thought of as principles underlying and defining the virtues of agents, agencies or traditions.

The method of construction for imperfect as for perfect obligations is to consider what obligations can be had by all. This is parallel to the constructivist account of rights except in one respect. In constructing the set of human rights it was necessary to determine what the maximal set of equal copossible rights is. That turned out to be the weak link of the construction. In constructing an account of obligations it is unnecessary to maximize. The aim is only to determine whether any given principle (on which an act, a life or an institution might be built) can be acted on by all; if it cannot, its rejection is a matter of obligation. The operative idea in the construction is modal, not metric.

If we are looking to work out a set of universal obligations, principles of action that cannot be universally adopted must be rejected. One type of principle that can be adopted by one agent yet cannot be adopted by all is a principle whose enactment destroys or disables or undercuts agency in at least some others on at least some occasions and so renders those others at least temporarily unable to adopt that same principle. For example, principles of coercion or deception or violence undercut or destroy somebody's agency in some respect; so their rejection is part of any set of principles that can hold universally. What is going on here is a strict version of Kantian universalizing. It identifies as principles of obligation those principles that must be adopted if nonuniversalizable principles are rejected.

Matters that are usually identified as central to justice – rejecting violence, coercion and deceit – are components of the set of principles that must be adopted by rational agents *of any sort* who act on principles that can be adopted by all. The construction is just a way of identifying principles that must be adopted by any rational beings who do not organize their acts or lives or institutions on lines that cannot be shared by all of a plurality of agents.

This constitutes a method for constructing principles of perfect obligation, which can be universally adhered to in all interactions, and so can potentially be demanded by those who find themselves on the receiving end of action. Perfect obligations have corresponding rights. The discourse of rights, with its peculiarly powerful political impact, remains accessible to those who begin their systematic ethical thinking from the perspective of agency and obligation.

Although the approach can be used to identify rights as easily as to identify obligations, it does not propose any algorithm for just action. The construction determines only a set of principles: Their application is a matter for deliberation and judgment. There are no algorithms for applying principles to cases. It follows that the exact demands of justice must vary with circumstances. For example, what constitutes coercion will vary depending on the vulnerability of those who would be victimized.[18] Activity that might be normal bargaining or negotiating procedure in interaction with an equal may coerce the vulnerable.

The reason why metric notions can be avoided in this construction is that it does not aim to determine the total set of principles of obligation. It provides only a procedure for determining whether any proposed principle of action is one that could form the basis for action by all. If nobody were tempted to acts that violate a given principle of obligation, that principle would remain undiscovered: a theoretical but not a practical blemish. By contrast, standard constructivist accounts of rights must determine all rights if they are to determine any, since rights are individuated as mutually limiting components of the largest set of liberties compatible with like liberty for all.

This way of constructing an account of obligations allows that there may be an indefinite number of distinct principles of obligation. In many situations an act that violates none of them may be available; in others agents will find that there is no way to avoid all wrongdoing. Since no ethical algorithm is on offer, there is no guarantee that painful and tragic dilemmas are even in principle avoidable.

So far the construction has been sketched only for the general case of unspecified ("arbitrary") rational agents, without any reference to the peculiarities of human agents. There may, of course, be further principles that could be universally acted on among pluralities of some sorts of rational beings, but not among pluralities of other sorts of rational beings.

The point can best be made by a couple of examples. Imagine in the first instance agents of a slightly idealized sort who without fail have well-ordered preferences, unerring capacities to calculate, a high degree of self-sufficiency, excellent knowledge of options and outcomes and the capacities to enact their decisions. Could such beings universally act on the principle of refusing to help others in need? I take it that they could: Nothing in the account of these beings shows that their capacities to act are at risk. We have no reason to think that they have needs, or that leaving needs unmet would destroy or undercut their agency. Among such idealized agents a principle of self-centeredness could be universally adopted.

Among human agents things may be different. Here we are considering agents

18   Further details are in Onora O'Neill, "Which Are the Offers *You* Can't Refuse?".

who are embodied in vulnerable form, are subject to illness and death and need regular nourishment and at times in their lives the care and attention of others. They need these things not merely for some arbitrary purpose but as conditions of becoming and remaining agents. Among such rational and needy beings, a principle of self-centered indifference to others' needs could not be universally adopted. Its attempted adoption would erode or destroy the capacities for agency of some of their number, thereby guaranteeing that its adoption would be less than universal. If rational and needy beings are to act only on principles they all can act on, they must eschew principles of undercutting or destroying one another's capacities to adopt principles. They must make it a matter of principle not merely not to coerce or deceive, but to reject self-centered indifference to others' needs insofar as this indifference threatens the other's agency. This means that they must make it a matter of principle to help meet at least some of the needs of at least some others. Among rational and needy beings, charity, in the old sense of concern for the needs of others, is an obligation.

Welfare rights and imperfect obligations

This line of thought has a good deal in common with that advocated by certain "welfare" liberals who begin their argument from the perspective of rights.[19] It stresses the need to maintain the conditions of agency. Why then does it not lead to the same conclusion, namely that there is a right to have agency-threatening needs met? What shows that there is only an imperfect obligation to meet the needs of others? Why could we not come to the conclusion that rejecting coercion and deceit is a matter of perfect obligation among all possible sorts of rational beings, and that help to those in need is a matter of perfect obligation among rational and needy beings? What shows that we are not dealing with perfect obligations and their correlative rights in both cases?

The asymmetry between obligations not to coerce or deceive (and their like) and obligations to help those in agency-threatening need is in fact an obvious one (and incidentally one much stressed by libertarians). It is just this. We can refuse to coerce or deceive any others; but we could not meet a universal demand for help for those in agency-threatening need. Helping others needs time, presence, effort and resources. Nobody can offer more than selective help. Hence obligations to help those in agency-threatening need cannot be owed to all in need. Yet obligations to help are also not merely special obligations owed to specified others in virtue of certain special relationships or agreements. Obligations to help are not merely institutionalized, positive obligations. They are in the first instance *unallocated* obligations. That they are obligations is established by the very argument by which obligations of justice are determined, subject to the restriction

19　See, for example, the work of Alan Gewirth and Henry Shue.

that we are considering rational beings whose vulnerable embodiment creates needs. That they are only *imperfect* obligations follows from the fact that the argument fails to establish who owes whom which sorts of help. It does not follow that obligations to meet needs cannot be allocated: Indeed, they often must be allocated before needs can be met. Among human beings the paradigm of needing help that no special relationship can supply is not the much-discussed one of needing to be rescued by some present and competent stranger (the concern of so-called Good Samaritan laws), but that of needing support that could be supplied by others who are absent and numerous. It follows that the allocation of recipients to agents – a process of institutionalization – is indispensable; but it is a separate and further move, which can be made only when principles of obligation have been established. Obligations here are clearly prior to rights, since the identification of rights to be helped awaits the allocation of recipients to agents, which itself presupposes the identification of principles of obligation.

Charity and welfare

It may seem that we have strayed from standard paths of liberal debate to little purpose. For showing that charity – the duty to care for the needs of others – is an imperfect duty seems to do very little to secure help for the needy (even in the sense in which arguments may help in practical tasks). What is the use to the vulnerable and needy of an obligation to help that they cannot claim? Isn't the intuition that we should worry only about justice, about claimable obligations and their correlative rights, a sound one?

To be sure, justice and claimable rights are essential for everyone, including the needy and vulnerable. But it does not follow that we can afford to worry only about justice. In particular, if the welfare liberal's aim of showing that meeting needs is a matter of perfect obligation cannot be achieved, we have reason to think hard about imperfect obligations as well as about justice. How important can unallocated obligations, and in particular an obligation of charity, be for those in need? Several considerations are relevant.

First, I have not identified charity with familiar forms of private philanthropy, which clearly are unable to meet all needs,[20] and which may have built-in difficulties such as encouraging a "culture of dependency". An obligation to help meet the needs of others does not have to be discharged by means of private philanthropy. Its optimal enactment might demand that quite other sorts of institution be constructed. Second, I have not assumed or shown that it is part of the definition of imperfect obligations, or specifically of charity, that enforcement is wrong. It is clear that enforcement will require that recipients be allocated to agents (or that procedures of allocation be established). Once allocation is

20   Thomas Nagel, "Poverty and Food: Why Charity Is Not Enough".

achieved, enforcement is possible, and there may be reasons for thinking that it should take place. I have argued only that imperfect obligations, including charity, cannot be enforced until tasks are allocated. How legal sanctions should then be used, if at all, remains a matter for discussion.

Third, I have argued only that an initial constructivist vindication of the principle of charity fails to determine any allocation of needy recipients to obligation-bearers, and hence (since the obligation cannot be universally performed) that such a vindication establishes no rights. The next step would be to consider how obligations to meet the agency-threatening needs of others might best be institutionalized. Often adequate institutionalization would have to give the needy claims against specified others (perhaps both agents and agencies). The rights that would then be established would, however, be institutional rather than fundamental or human rights, although the obligations whose discharge these rights secured would be fundamental obligations and would provide a standard by which modes of institutionalization could be judged and vindicated. Adequate institutionalization presumably takes different forms in different times and societies. In mass societies it may be that the most appropriate institutionalization of an obligation of charity is some form of the welfare state. In saying this, I do not, of course, mean that nobody has rights to the services so established; but these rights are vindicated not merely by a fundamental argument that determines ethical principles but also by considerations for allocating and institutionalizing fundamental obligations. The missing element in the argument here is that nothing has been said about the legitimacy or otherwise of institutionalizing imperfect obligations in forms that rely in part on legal enforcement. Rather than offer such an argument I merely note again that there may be reasons to discard a supposedly exhaustive contrast between that which is enforced by law and that which is simply voluntary.

Conclusions

In trying to link an account of justice with an account of the virtues I have been trespassing across some now well-established boundaries. In the background lie various unexplored issues. Much of the point of attempting an account of justice along constructivist lines is that this is a way in which one can go when relying on conceptions of agency that do not hinge on preference, and on conceptions of moral reasoning that do not invoke a subjective conception of the good or rely on maximizing notions. The working parts of the construction I have sketched rely on modal notions, and specifically on the idea of determining what principles can and cannot be shared by all of a plurality of rational, or rational and needy, agents. The reappropriation of the notion of an imperfect obligation has relied not on any determinate account of the good for man, but simply on identifying some modes of finitude that bear on the conditions for producing and maintaining human agency. These starting points, however, are economical rather than alien. They are, I suggest, weaker than the more luxuriant models of rational choice that are generally preferred, and they are embedded in ordinary conceptions of action and reason.

The conclusions offered are also in some ways economical. In arguing for a reconsideration of imperfect obligations and of charity I am well aware that no general duty of beneficence, such as Utilitarianism may entail, has been established. Nothing has been said about obligations to please others or to make them happy, let alone to maximize happiness. In the sense in which the phrase is generally used there is here no "overload of obligations" problem. Charity as here constructed is a much narrower duty than beneficence; it is concerned only with meeting agency-threatening needs.

In spite of this atmosphere of economy I shall put my largest conclusions quite extravagantly. First, if the liberal tradition is to salvage an account of justice from the shipwreck of the Natural Law tradition, then it can also take charity and other virtues seriously. It can vindicate an obligation not to neglect the agency-threatening needs of vulnerable and needy beings. Second, if liberalism is taken to be primarily a theory of rights, then a constructivist approach does not yield determinate results, and if it did, it could justify only those obligations whose recipients are allocated, that is, the rights libertarians favor. Although that conclusion may be taken in ways that are less harsh than its usual libertarian interpretation, by working out what it takes to fulfill perfect obligations in the light of others' vulnerabilities, a successful rights-based construction would not establish obligations to act to end agency-threatening need. Third, although the obligation to meet agency-threatening needs that can be established is only an imperfect obligation, it provides grounds for thinking not that charity is marginal or optional, or that it could be wholly met by sporadic contribution to voluntary philanthropic organizations, but that it is urgent to see how such an obligation can be best embodied not only in characters and traditions, but also in social relations that put the needy in a position to direct claims to specified others.

References

Kant references (German)

All references are to *Kants gesammelte Schriften: herausgegeben von der Deutschen Akademie der Wissenschaften* (formerly *Königlichen Preussischen Akademie der Wissenschaften*), 29 vols., Berlin, Walter de Gruyter, 1902–. The works cited appear in the volumes indicated; the abbreviations used in the text for identifying purposes also appear.

Kritik der reinen Vernunft (1st ed., 1781; 2nd ed., 1787), vols. 3 and 4. *(CPR)*
Idee zu einer allgemeinen Geschichte in weltbürgerlicher Absicht (1784), vol. 8. *(IUH)*
Beantwortung der Frage: Was ist Aufklärung? (1784), vol. 8. *(WE)*
Grundlegung zur Metaphysik der Sitten (1785), vol. 4. *(G)*
Was heisst: Sich im Denken orientieren? (1786), vol. 8. *(WOT)*
Kritik der praktischen Vernunft (1788), vol. 5. *(CPrR)*
Kritik der Urteilskraft (1790), vol. 5 *(CJ)*
Die Religion innerhalb der blossen Vernunft (1793), vol. 6. *(R)*
Über den Gemeinspruch: Das mag in der Theorie richtig sein, taugt aber nicht für die Praxis (1793), vol. 8. *(TP)*
Zum ewigen Frieden (1795), vol. 8. *(PP)*
Die Metaphysik der Sitten (1797), vol. 6 *(MM)*, comprising:
  Erster Theil: *Metaphysische Anfangsgründe der Rechtslehre.* *(MEJ)*
  Zweiter Theil: *Metaphysische Anfangsgründe der Tugendlehre.* *(DV)*
Über ein vermeintes Recht aus Menschenliebe zu lügen (1797), vol. 8. *(SRL)*
Der Streit der Fakultäten (1798), vol. 7. *(CF)*
Anthropologie in pragmatischer Hinsicht (1798), vol. 7. *(A)*
Logik (1800), vol. 9. *(L)*
Erste Einleitung in die Kritik der Urteilskraft (written 1789/90; 1st publ. in entirety 1922 [in Cassirer ed.]), vol. 20. *(FI)*

English translations of Kant

An Answer to the Question: "What Is Enlightenment?", trans. H. B. Nisbet, in *Kant's Political Writings*, ed. Hans Reiss, Cambridge University Press, Cambridge, 1970. *(WE)*
Anthropology from a Pragmatic Point of View, trans. Mary J. Gregor, Martinus Nijhoff, The Hague, 1974. *(A)*
The Conflict of the Faculties, trans. Mary Gregor, Abaris Books, New York, 1979. *(CF)*
Critique of Judgment, trans. James Meredith, Clarendon Press, Oxford, 1978. *(CJ)*
Critique of Practicial Reason, trans L. W. Beck, Bobbs-Merrill, Indianapolis, 1977. *(CPrR)*
Critique of Pure Reason, trans. Norman Kemp Smith, Macmillan, London, 1933. *(CPR)*

The Doctrine of Virtue, trans. Mary Gregor, Harper and Row, New York, 1964. (*DV =* Metaphysic of Morals, Pt. II; includes the introduction [*MM*])

First Introduction to the Critique of Judgment, trans. James Haden, Bobbs-Merrill, Indianapolis, 1965. (*FI*)

Groundwork of the Metaphysic of Morals, trans. H. J. Paton, as *The Moral Law,* Hutchinson, London, 1953. (*G*)

Idea of a Universal History from a Cosmopolitan Point of View, trans. H. B. Nisbet, in *Kant's Political Writings,* ed. Hans Reiss, Cambridge University Press, Cambridge, 1970. (*IUH*)

Logic, trans. Robert Hartman and Wolfgang Schwartz, Bobbs-Merrill, Indianapolis, 1974. (*L*)

The Metaphysical Elements of Justice, trans. John Ladd, Bobbs-Merrill, Indianapolis, 1965. (*MEJ = Metaphysic of Morals,* Pt. I; includes the introduction [*MM*])

On a Supposed Right to Lie out of Benevolent Motives, trans. L. W. Beck, in *Kant's Critique of Practical Reason and Other Writings on Moral Philosophy,* University of Chicago Press, Chicago, 1949. (*SRL*)

On the Common Saying "This May Be True in Theory, but It Does Not Apply in Practice"; trans. H. B. Nisbet, in *Kant's Political Writings,* ed. Hans Reiss, Cambridge University Press, Cambridge, 1970. (*TP*)

Perpetual Peace, trans. H. B. Nisbet, in *Kant's Political Writings,* ed. Hans Reiss, Cambridge University Press, Cambridge, 1970. (*PP*)

Religion within the Limits of Reason Alone, trans. Theodore M. Greene and Hoyt H. Hudson, Harper and Row, New York, 1960. (*R*)

What Is Orientation in Thinking? trans. L. W. Beck, in *Kant's Critique of Practical Reason and Other Writings on Moral Philosophy,* University of Chicago Press, Chicago, 1949. (*WOT*)

Other references

Arendt, Hannah, *Lectures on Kant's Political Philosophy,* ed. Ronald Beiner, University of Chicago Press, Chicago, 1982.

Aristotle, *Nichomachean Ethics,* trans. W. D. Ross, in *Basic Works of Aristotle,* ed. Richard McKeon, Random House, New York, 1941.

Aune, Bruce, *Kant's Theory of Morals,* Princeton University Press, Princeton, 1979.

Auxter, Thomas, "Kant's Conception of the Private Sphere", *Philosophical Forum,* XII (1981), 295–310.

Bacon, Francis, *Instauratio Magna,* in *The Works of Francis Bacon,* ed. James Spedding, Robert Leslie Ellis and Douglas Denon Heath, Longman, London, 1858, vol. 1; facs. reprint Friedrich Fromann Verlag, Stuttgart, 1963.

Beardsmore, R., *Moral Reasoning,* Routledge and Kegan Paul, London, 1969.

Beardsworth, T., "The Place of Literature in Moral Education", *Moral Education,* 1 (1969), 52–62.

Beehler, Rodger, *Moral Life,* Blackwell, Oxford, 1978.

Beiner, Ronald, *Political Judgment,* Methuen, London, 1983.

REFERENCES

Beitz, Charles, *Political Theory and International Relations,* Princeton University Press, Princeton, 1979.

Bittner, Rüdiger "Maximen", *Akten des 4. Internationalen Kant-Kongresses,* Berlin, ed. G. Funke, II(2)(1975), 485–9.

Blustein, Jeffrey, *Parents and Children: The Ethics of the Family,* Oxford University Press, New York, 1982.

Brink, David O., "Rawlsian Constructivism in Moral Theory", *Canadian Journal of Philosophy,* 17 (1987), 71–90.

Broad, C. D., *Five Types of Ethical Theory,* Littlefield Adams and Co., Totowa, N.J., 1965.

Burgess, Anthony, *The Long Day Wanes: A Malayan Trilogy,* Penguin, Harmondsworth, 1972.

Butler, Christopher, "Literature and Moral Education", *Moral Education,* 1 (1969), 39–46.

Carnois, Bernard, *The Coherence of Kant's Doctrine of Freedom,* trans. David Booth, University of Chicago Press, Chicago, 1987.

Clarke, Barry, "Beyond the Banality of Evil", *British Journal of Political Science,* 10 (1980), 17–39.

Clark, Stephen, *The Moral Status of Animals,* Oxford University Press, Oxford, 1977.

Danford, John, *Wittgenstein and Political Philosophy,* University of Chicago Press, Chicago, 1978.

Darwall, Stephen, "Is There a Kantian Foundation for Rawlsian Justice?", in *Rawls' Theory of Social Justice,* ed. Gene Blocker and Elizabeth Smith, Ohio University Press, Athens, 1980, pp. 311–343.

d'Entrèves, A. P., *Natural Law,* Hutchinson, London, 1951.

Descartes, René, *Discourse on the Method of Rightly Conducting One's Reason and Seeking the Truth in the Sciences,* in *The Philosophical Writings of Descartes,* vol. I, trans. John Cottingham, Robert Stoothof and Dugald Murdoch, Cambridge University Press, Cambridge, 1985.

Diamond, Cora, "Anything but Argument?", *Philosophical Investigations,* 1 (1978), 23–41.

Doppelt, Gerald, "Rawls' Kantian Ideal and the Viability of Modern Liberalism", *Inquiry,* 31 (1988), 413–49.

Dunn, John, *The Political Thought of John Locke: An Historical Account of the Argument of the "Two Treatises of Government",* Cambridge University Press, Cambridge, 1969.

Dworkin, Ronald, *Taking Rights Seriously,* Duckworth, London, 1977.
  "Liberalism", in *Public and Private Morality,* ed. Stuart Hampshire, Cambridge University Press, Cambridge, 1978, pp. 113–43.

Elster, John, *Ulysses and the Sirens,* Cambridge University Press, Cambridge, 1979.

Feinberg, Joel, "The Nature and Value of Rights", in his *Rights, Justice and the Bounds of Liberty: Essays in Social Philosophy,* Princeton University Press, Princeton, 1980, pp. 143–55.

Fishkin, James, *The Limits of Obligation,* Yale University Press, New Haven, 1982.

Foot, Phillipa, "The Problem of Abortion and the Doctrine of Double Effect", in her *Virtues and Vices,* Oxford, Blackwell, 1978, pp. 19–32.

Frankena, William K., *Ethics,* Prentice-Hall, Englewood Cliffs, N.J., 1963.

Frankfurt, Harry, "Freedom of the Will and the Concept of a Person", *Journal of Philosophy,* 68 (1971), 5–20.

REFERENCES

Gewirth, Alan, *Human Rights: Essays on Justification and Applications,* Chicago University Press, Chicago, 1982.

"Private Philanthropy and Positive Rights", in Ellen Frankel Paul et al., *Beneficence, Philanthropy and the Public Good,* Blackwell, Oxford, 1987, pp. 57–78.

Gilligan, Carol, *In a Different Voice: Psychological Theory and Women's Dependence,* Harvard University Press, Cambridge, Mass., 1982.

Goldmann, Lucien, *Immanuel Kant,* trans. Robert Black, New Left Books, London, 1971.

Gosse, Edmund, *Father and Son,* Penguin, Harmondsworth, 1987.

Harman, Gilbert, *The Nature of Morality,* Oxford University Press, New York, 1977.

Harrison, Jonathan, "Kant's Examples of the First Formulation of the Categorical Imperative", in *Foundations of the Metaphysics of Morals: Text and Critical Essays,* ed. R. P. Wolff, Bobbs-Merrill, Indianapolis, 1969, pp. 208–29.

Hart, H. L. A., "Are There Any Natural Rights?", *Philosophical Review,* 64 (1955), 175–91.

Herman, Barbara, "Mutual Aid and Respect for Persons", *Ethics,* 94 (1984), 577–602.

"The Practice of Moral Judgement", *Journal of Philosophy,* 82 (1985), 414–36.

"Murder and Mayhem," unpublished manuscript.

Hill, Thomas E., Jr., "Humanity as an End in Itself", *Ethics,* 91 (1980/1), 84–99.

"Kant's Argument for the Rationality of Moral Conduct", *Pacific Philosophical Quarterly,* 66 (1985), 3–23.

Hirsch, F., *The Social Limits to Growth,* Harvard University Press, Cambridge, Mass., 1976.

Höffe, Otfried, "Kants kategorischer Imperativ als Kriterium des Sittlichen", *Zeitschrift für philosophische Forschung,* 31 (1977), 354–84.

Holland, R. F., *Against Empiricism,* Blackwell, Oxford, 1980.

Jones, Clive, "The Contribution of History and Literature to Moral Education", *Journal of Moral Education,* 5 (1976), 127–38.

Kagan, S., "Does Consequentialism Demand Too Much? Recent Work on the Limits of Obligation", *Philosophy and Public Affairs,* 13 (1984), 239–54.

Keane, Molly, *Good Behaviour,* Sphere Books, London, 1982.

Kemp, John, *The Philosophy of Kant,* Oxford University Press, Oxford, 1968.

"Kant's Examples of the Categorical Imperative", in *Foundations of the Metaphysics of Morals: Text and Critical Essays,* ed. R. P. Wolff, Bobbs-Merrill, Indianapolis, 1969, pp. 230–44.

Keneally, Thomas, *Schindler's Ark,* Hodder and Stoughton, London, 1982.

Kersting, Wolfgang, "Der kategorischer Imperativ, die vollkommenen und die unvollkommenen Pflichten", *Zeitschrift für philosophische Forschung,* 37 (1983), 404–12.

Kittay, Eva Feders, and Meyers, Diane, eds., *Women and Moral Theory,* Rowman and Littlefield, Totowa, N.J., 1987.

Korsgaard, Christine, "The Right to Lie: Kant on Dealing with Evil", *Philosophy and Public Affairs,* 15 (1986), 325–49.

Kosman, L. Aryeh, "The Naive Narrator: Meditation in Descartes' *Meditations*", in *Essays on Descartes' Meditations,* ed. Amelie Oksenberg Rorty, University of California Press, Berkeley, 1986, pp. 21–43.

REFERENCES

Levin, Michael, "The Universalizability of Moral Judgements Revisited", *Mind,* 88
  (1979), 115–19.
Lindley, Richard, *Autonomy,* J. M. Dent and Sons, London, 1986.
Locke, John, *Two Treatises of Government,* ed. P. Laslett, Cambridge University Press,
  Cambridge, 1963.
  Venditio, reprinted as appendix to John Dunn, "Justice and the Interpretation of Locke's
    Political Theory", *Political Studies,* 15 (1968), 68–87.
Louden, Robert, "Kant's Virtue Ethics", *Philosophy,* 61 (1986), 473–89.
Lucas, George R., "Agency after Virtue", *International Philosophical Quarterly,* 28 (1988),
  293–311.
MacIntyre, Alasdair, *After Virtue: A Study in Moral Theory,* Duckworth, London, 1981.
  Whose Justice? Which Rationality? Duckworth, London, 1988.
McKenzie, D. F., "The Sociology of a Text: Orality, Print and Literacy in Early New
  Zealand", *The Library,* 6 (1984), 333–65.
McMillan, Carol, *Women, Reason and Nature,* Princeton University Press, Princeton, 1982.
Mayor, F. M., *The Rector's Daughter,* Penguin, Harmondsworth, 1973.
Mill, J. S., *Utilitarianism,* in his *Utilitarianism, Liberty and Representative Government,* ed.
  Mary Warnock, J. M. Dent and Sons, London, 1968.
Montague, Roger, "Winch on Agents", *Analysis,* 34 (1973/4), 161–6.
Mulholland, Leslie A., "Kant: On Willing Maxims to Become Laws of Nature", *Dialogue,*
  18 (1978), 92–105.
Murdoch, Iris, *The Sovereignty of Good,* Routledge and Kegan Paul, London, 1970.
Nagel, Thomas, "Poverty and Food: Why Charity Is Not Enough", in *Food Policy: The
  Responsibility of the United States in Life and Death Choices,* ed. Peter Brown and Henry
  Shue, Free Press, New York, 1977, pp. 54–62.
Nell (O'Neill), Onora, *Acting on Principle,* Columbia University Press, New York, 1975.
Noddings, Nell, *Caring: A Feminine Approach to Ethics and Moral Education,* University of
  California Press, Berkeley, 1984.
Nozick, Robert, *Anarchy, State and Utopia,* Blackwell, Oxford, 1974.
O'Connor, John, "Philanthropy and Selfishness", in Ellen Frankel Paul et al., *Beneficence,
  Philanthropy and the Public Good,* Blackwell, Oxford, 1987, pp. 113–27.
Okin, Susan Moller, "Justice and Gender", *Philosophy and Public Affairs,* 16 (1987), 42–72.
O'Neill, Onora, "The Most Extensive Liberty", *Proceedings of the Aristotelian Society* 80
  (1979/80), 45–59.
  "Transcendental Synthesis and Developmental Psychology", *Kant-studien,* 75 (1984),
    149–67.
  "Rights, Obligations and Needs", *Logos,* 6 (1985), 29–47.
  Faces of Hunger; An Essay on Poverty, Development and Justice, George Allen and Unwin,
    London, 1986.
  "Ethical Reasoning and Ideological Pluralism", *Ethics,* 98 (1988), 705–22.
  "Agency and Anthropology in Kant's *Groundwork*", in *Kant's Practical Philosophy Reconsid-
    ered,* ed. Y. Yovel, Reidel, Dordrecht, 1989.
  "Enlightenment as Autonomy: Kant's Vindication of Reason", in *The Enlightenment
    and Its Shadows,* ed. Ludmila Jordanova and Peter Hulme, Routledge, London,
    forthcoming.

239

"Practices of Toleration", in *Democracy and the Mass Media,* ed. Judith Lichtenberg, Cambridge University Press, Cambridge, forthcoming.

"Which Are the Offers *You* Can't Refuse?", *Social Philosophy and Policy,* forthcoming.

O'Neill, O., and Ruddick, W., eds., *Having Children: Legal and Philosophical Reflections on Parenthood,* Oxford University Press, New York, 1979.

Pateman, Carole, "Women and Consent", *Political Theory,* 8 (1980), 149–68.

"Defending Prostitution: Charges against Ericsson", *Ethics,* 93 (1983), 561–5.

The Sexual Contract, Polity Press, Cambridge, 1988.

Paton, H. J., *The Categorical Imperative,* Hutchinson, London, 1947.

Paul, Ellen Frankel, Miller, Fred D., Jr., Paul, Jeffrey, and Ahrens, John, eds., *Beneficence, Philanthropy and the Public Good,* Blackwell, Oxford, 1987.

Petersen, A. D. C., "A Vanishing Tradition in Moral Education", *Moral Education,* 1 (1969), 47–51.

Phillips, D. Z., "In Search of the Moral 'Must': Mrs Foot's Fugitive Thought", *Philosophical Quarterly,* 27 (1977), 140–57.

Through a Darkening Glass, Blackwell, Oxford, 1982.

Phillips, D. Z., and Mounce, H. O., *Moral Practices,* Routledge and Kegan Paul, London, 1970.

Pitkin, Hannah, *Wittgenstein and Justice,* University of California Press, Berkeley, 1972.

Raphael, D. D., *Moral Philosophy,* Oxford University Press, Oxford, 1981.

Rawls, John, *A Theory of Justice,* Harvard University Press, Cambridge, Mass., 1971.

"The Independence of Moral Theory", *Proceedings and Addresses of the American Philosophical Association,* 48 (1974), 5–22.

"A Kantian Conception of Equality", *Cambridge Review* (1975).

"The Basic Structure as Subject", *American Philosophical Quarterly,* 14 (1977), 159–65.

"Kantian Constructivism in Moral Theory", *Journal of Philosophy,* 77 (1980), 515–72.

"Justice as Fairness: Political Not Metaphysical", *Philosophy and Public Affairs,* 14 (1985), 223–51.

Raz, Joseph, "Right-Based Moralities", in *Theories of Rights,* ed. Jeremy Waldron, Oxford University Press, Oxford, 1984, pp. 182–200.

Rée, Jonathan, *Philosophical Tales,* Methuen, London, 1987.

Rhees, Rush, "Some Developments in Wittgenstein's View of Ethics", *Philosophical Review,* 74 (1965), 17–26.

Without Answers, Routledge and Kegan Paul, London, 1969.

Ricoeur, Paul, *The Conflict of Interpretations,* esp. "Freedom in the Light of Hope", Northwestern University Press, Chicago, 1974.

Ripstein, Arthur, "Foundationalism in Political Theory", *Philosophy and Public Affairs,* 16 (1987), 115–37.

Rorty, Amelie Oksenberg, "The Structure of Descartes' *Meditations*", in *Essays on Descartes' Meditations,* ed. Amelie Oksenberg Rorty, University of California Press, Berkeley, 1986, pp. 1–20.

Rosen, Michael, "Kant's Anti-Determinism", *Proceedings of the Aristotelian Society,* 89 (1988/9), 125–41.

Rosenthal, David M., and Shehadi, Fadlou, *Applied Ethics and Ethical Theory,* University of Utah Press, Salt Lake City, 1988.

Ruddick, William, "Philosophy and Public Affairs", *Social Research,* 47 (1980), 734–48.

Sandel, Michael, *Liberalism and the Limits of Justice,* Cambridge University Press, Cambridge, 1982.

Saner, Hans, *Kant's Political Thought: Its Origins and Development,* trans. H. B. Ashton, University of Chicago Press, Chicago, 1983.

Sartre, J.-P., "Existentialism Is a Humanism", in *Existentialism from Dostoevsky to Sartre,* ed. W. Kaufmann, World Publishing, Cleveland, 1956, pp. 287–311.

Schneewind, J. B., "Moral Problems and Moral Philosophy in the Victorian Period", in *English Literature and British Philosophy,* ed. S. P. Rosenbaum, University of Chicago Press, Chicago, 1971, pp. 185–207.

"Ideas of Charity: Some Historical Reflections", unpublished manuscript.

Schoeman, Ferdinand, "Rights of Children, Rights of Parents, and the Moral Basis of the Family", *Ethics,* 91 (1980), 6–19.

Schopenhauer, F., *On the Basis of Morality,* trans. E. F. J. Payne, Bobbs-Merrill, Indianapolis, 1965.

Shrag, Francis, "Children: Their Rights and Needs", in *Whose Child? Children's Rights, Parental Authority and State Power,* ed. William Aiken and Hugh LaFollette, Rowman and Littlefield, Totowa, N.J., 1980, pp. 237–53.

Shue, Henry, *Basic Rights: Subsistence, Affluence and U.S. Foreign Policy,* Princeton University Press, Princeton, 1980.

Silber, John R., "The Ethical Significance of Kant's *Religion*", introductory essay in Immanuel Kant, *Religion within the Limits of Reason Alone,* trans. Theodore M. Greene and Hoyt H. Hudson, Harper and Row, New York, 1960, pp. lxxix–cxxxiv.

Singer, Marcus, *Generalization in Ethics,* Alfred Knopf, New York, 1961.

Skinner, Quentin, "The Idea of Negative Liberty: Philosophical and Historical Perspectives", in *Philosophy in History,* ed. R. Rorty, J. Schneewind and Q. Skinner, Cambridge University Press, Cambridge, 1984, pp. 193–221.

Smart, J. J. C., and Williams, Bernard, *Utilitarianism: For and Against,* Cambridge University Press, Cambridge, 1973.

Steiner, Hillel, "Individual Liberty", *Proceedings of the Aristotelian Society,* 75 (1974/5), 33–50.

Stephens, James, *Francis Bacon and the Style of Science,* University of Chicago Press, Chicago, 1975.

Straughan, Roger, "Hypothetical Moral Situations", *Journal of Moral Education,* 4 (1975), 183–9.

Taylor, Charles, "What's Wrong with Negative Liberty?", reprinted in his *Philosophy and the Human Sciences,* Cambridge University Press, Cambridge, 1985, vol. 2, pp. 211–29.

Thomson, Judith Jarvis, "Some Ruminations on Rights", in *Reading Nozick,* ed. Jeffrey Paul, Blackwell, Oxford, 1982, pp. 130–47.

Rights, Restitution, and Risk: Essays in Moral Theory, Harvard University Press, Cambridge, Mass., 1986, pp. 1–19.

"A Defense of Abortion", reprinted in her *Rights, Restitution, and Risk,* pp. 1–19.

Thurber, James, "The Macbeth Murder Mystery", in his *The Thurber Carnival,* Hamish Hamilton, London, 1945, pp. 60–3.

Tully, James, *A Discourse on Property: John Locke and His Adversaries,* Cambridge University Press, Cambridge, 1980.

United Nations Declaration of the Rights of the Child, in *Having Children: Legal and Philosophical Reflections on Parenthood,* ed. O. O'Neill and W. Ruddick, Oxford University Press, New York, 1979, pp. 111–14.

Walzer, Michael, *Spheres of Justice: A Defence of Pluralism and Equality,* Martin Robertson, Oxford, 1983.

"The Politics of Michel Foucault", in *Foucault: A Critical Reader,* ed. David Couzens Hoy, Blackwell, Oxford, 1986, pp. 51–68.

Ward, L. O., "History – Humanity's Teacher", *Journal of Moral Education,* 4 (1974/5), 101–4.

Weil, Simone, *The Need for Roots,* trans. A. F. Wills, Routledge and Kegan Paul, London, 1952.

"Attention and Will", in *Gravity and Grace,* trans. Emma Crauford, Routledge and Kegan Paul, London, 1972, pp. 105–11.

"Reflections on the Right Use of School Studies with a View to the Love of God", in *The Simone Weil Reader,* ed. G. Paniches, David MacKay, New York, 1977, pp. 44–52.

Wertheimer, Alan, "Is Ordinary Language Analysis Conservative?", *Political Theory,* 4 (1976), 405–22.

Wiggins, David, "Deliberation and Practical Reason", *Proceedings of the Aristotelian Society,* 76 (1975/6), 29–51.

Williams, Bernard, *Ethics and the Limits of Philosophy,* Fontana, London, 1985.

Winch, Peter, "Can a Good Man Be Harmed?", in his *Ethics and Action,* Routledge and Kegan Paul, London, 1972, pp. 193–209.

"Moral Integrity", in *Ethics and Action,* pp. 171–92.

"Nature and Convention", in *Ethics and Action,* pp. 50–72.

"The Universalizability of Moral Judgements", in *Ethics and Action,* pp. 151–70.

Wittgenstein, Ludwig, "Lecture on Ethics", *Philosophical Review,* 74 (1965), 3–12, 12–26.

Philosophical Investigations, Blackwell, Oxford, 1984.

Wolff, Robert Paul, *The Autonomy of Reason,* Harper and Row, New York, 1973.

Understanding Rawls, Princeton University Press, Princeton, 1979.

Wood, Allen W., "Kant's Compatibilism", in *Self and Nature in Kant's Philosophy,* ed. Allen W. Wood, Cornell University Press, Ithaca, N.Y., 1984, pp. 73–101.

Young, Robert, *Personal Autonomy: Beyond Negative and Positive Liberty,* Croom Helm, Beckenham, U.K., 1986.

Yovel, Yirmiahu, *Kant and the Philosophy of History,* Princeton University Press, Princeton, 1980.

Index